Practical Data Science with Jupyter

Explore Data Cleaning, Pre-processing,
Data Wrangling, Feature Engineering and
Machine Learning using Python and Jupyter

Prateek Gupta

www.bpbonline.com

FIRST EDITION 2019

SECOND EDITION 2021

Copyright © BPB Publications, India

ISBN: 978-93-89898-064

Distributors:

BPB PUBLICATIONS
20, Ansari Road, Darya Ganj
New Delhi-110002
Ph: 23254990/23254991

DECCAN AGENCIES
4-3-329, Bank Street,
Hyderabad-500195
Ph: 24756967/24756400

MICRO MEDIA
Shop No. 5, Mahendra Chambers,
150 DN Rd. Next to Capital Cinema,
V.T. (C.S.T.) Station, MUMBAI-400 001
Ph: 22078296/22078297

BPB BOOK CENTRE
376 Old Lajpat Rai Market,
Delhi-110006
Ph: 23861747

To View Complete
BPB Publications Catalogue
Scan the QR Code:

Published by Manish Jain for BPB Publications, 20 Ansari Road, Darya Ganj, New Delhi-110002 and Printed by him at Repro India Ltd, Mumbai

Dedicated to

All Aspiring Data Scientists
Who have chosen to solve this world's problem with data

About the Author

Prateek Gupta is a seasoned Data Science professional with nine years of experience in finding patterns, applying advanced statistical methods and algorithms to uncover hidden insights. His data-driven solutions maximize revenue, profitability, and ensure efficient operations management. He has worked with several multinational IT giants like HCL, Zensar, and Sapient.

He is a self-starter and committed data enthusiast with expertise in fishing, winery, and e-commerce domain. He has helped various clients with his machine learning expertise in automatic product categorization, sentiment analysis, customer segmentation, product recommendation engine, and object detection and recognition models. He is a firm believer in "Hard work triumphs talent when talent doesn't work hard".

His keen area of interest is in the areas of cutting-edge research papers on machine learning and applications of natural language processing with computer vision techniques. In his leisure time, he enjoys sharing knowledge through his blog and motivates young minds to enter the exciting world of Data Science.

His Blog: **http://dsbyprateekg.blogspot.com/**

His LinkedIn Profile: **www.linkedin.com/in/prateek-gupta-64203354**

Acknowledgement

I would like to thank some of the brilliant knowledge sharing minds - Jason Brownlee Ph.D., Adrian Rosebrock, Ph.D., and Andrew Ng, from whom I have learned and am still learning many concepts. I would also like to thank open data science community, Kaggle and various data science bloggers for making data science and machine learning knowledge available to everyone.

I would also like to express my gratitude to almighty God, my parents, my wife Pragya, and my brother Anubhav, for being incredibly supportive throughout my life and for the writing of this book.

Finally, I would like to thank the entire BPB publications team, who made this book possible. Many thanks to Manish Jain, Nrip Jain, and Varun Jain for giving me the opportunity to write my second book.

Preface

Today, Data Science has become an indispensable part of every organization, for which employers are willing to pay top dollars to hire skilled professionals. Due to the rapidly changing needs of industry, data continues to grow and evolve, thereby increasing the demand for data scientists. However, the questions that continuously haunt every company – are there enough highly-skilled individuals who can analyze how much data will be available, where it will come from, and what the advancement are in analytical techniques to serve them more significant insights? If you have picked up this book, you must have already come across these topics through talks or blogs from several experts and leaders in the industry.

To become an expert in any field, everyone must start from a point to learn. This book is designed with keeping such perspective in mind, to serve as your starting point in the field of data science. When I started my career in this field, I had little luck finding a compact guide that I could use to learn concepts of data science, practice examples, and revise them when faced with similar problems at hand. I soon realized Data Science is a very vast domain, and having all the knowledge in a small version of a book is highly impossible. Therefore, I decided I accumulate my experience in the form of this book, where you'll gain essential knowledge and skill set required to become a data scientist, without wasting your valuable time finding material scattered across the internet.

I planned the chapters of this book in a chained form. In the first chapter, you will be made familiar with the data and the new data science skills set. The second chapter is all about setting up tools for the trade with the help of which you can practice the examples discussed in the book. In chapters three to six , you will learn all types of data structures in Python, which you will use in your day-to-day data science projects. In 7th chapter you will lean how to interact with different databases with Python. The eighth-chapter of this book will teach you the most used statistical concepts in data analysis. By the ninth chapter, you will be all set to start your journey of becoming a data scientist by learning how to read, load, and understand different types of data in Jupyter notebook for analysis. The tenth and eleventh chapters will guide you through different data cleaning and visualizing techniques.

From the twelfth chapter onwards, you will have to combine knowledge acquired from previous chapters to do data pre-processing of real-world use-cases. In chapters thirteen and fourteen, you will learn supervised and unsupervised machine learning problems and how to solve them. Chapters fifteen and sixteen will cover time series data and will teach you how to handle them. After covering the key concepts, I have included four different case studies, where you will apply all the knowledge acquired and practice solving real-world problems. The last three chapters of this book will make you industry-ready data scientists. Using best practices while structuring your project and use of GitHub repository along with your Data Science concepts will not make you feel naïve, while working with other software engineering team.

The book you are holding is my humble effort to not only cover fundamentals of Data Science using Python, but also save your time by focusing on minimum theory + more practical examples. These practical examples include real-world datasets and real problems, which will make you confident in tackling similar or related data problems. I hope you find this book valuable, and that it enables you to extend your data science knowledge as a practitioner in a short time.

Downloading the coloured images:

Please follow the link to download the
Coloured Images of the book:

https://rebrand.ly/75823

Errata

We take immense pride in our work at BPB Publications and follow best practices to ensure the accuracy of our content to provide with an indulging reading experience to our subscribers. Our readers are our mirrors, and we use their inputs to reflect and improve upon human errors, if any, that may have occurred during the publishing processes involved. To let us maintain the quality and help us reach out to any readers who might be having difficulties due to any unforeseen errors, please write to us at :

errata@bpbonline.com

Your support, suggestions and feedbacks are highly appreciated by the BPB Publications' Family.

Did you know that BPB offers eBook versions of every book published, with PDF and ePub files available? You can upgrade to the eBook version at www.bpbonline.com and as a print book customer, you are entitled to a discount on the eBook copy. Get in touch with us at :

business@bpbonline.com for more details.

At **www.bpbonline.com**, you can also read a collection of free technical articles, sign up for a range of free newsletters, and receive exclusive discounts and offers on BPB books and eBooks.

BPB is searching for authors like you

If you're interested in becoming an author for BPB, please visit **www.bpbonline.com** and apply today. We have worked with thousands of developers and tech professionals, just like you, to help them share their insight with the global tech community. You can make a general application, apply for a specific hot topic that we are recruiting an author for, or submit your own idea.

The code bundle for the book is also hosted on GitHub at **https://github.com/bpbpublications/Practical-Data-Science-with-Jupyter**. In case there's an update to the code, it will be updated on the existing GitHub repository.

We also have other code bundles from our rich catalog of books and videos available at **https://github.com/bpbpublications**. Check them out!

PIRACY

If you come across any illegal copies of our works in any form on the internet, we would be grateful if you would provide us with the location address or website name. Please contact us at **business@bpbonline.com** with a link to the material.

If you are interested in becoming an author

If there is a topic that you have expertise in, and you are interested in either writing or contributing to a book, please visit **www.bpbonline.com**.

REVIEWS

Please leave a review. Once you have read and used this book, why not leave a review on the site that you purchased it from? Potential readers can then see and use your unbiased opinion to make purchase decisions, we at BPB can understand what you think about our products, and our authors can see your feedback on their book. Thank you!

For more information about BPB, please visit **www.bpbonline.com**.

Table of Contents

CHAPTER 1
Data Science Fundamentals

> **"Learning from data is virtually universally useful. Master it and you will be welcomed anywhere."**
>
> *— John Elder, founder of the Elder Research*

*E*lder Research is America's largest and most experienced analytics consultancy. With his vision about data, John started his company in 1995, yet the importance of finding information from the data is a niche and the most demanding skill of the 21st century. Today data science is everywhere.

The explosive growth of the digital world requires professionals with not just strong skills, but also adaptability and a passion for staying on the forefront of technology. A recent study shows that demand for data scientists and analysts is projected to grow by 28 percent by 2021. This is on top of the current market need. According to the U.S. Bureau of Labor Statistics, growth for data science jobs skills will grow about 28% through 2026. Unless something changes, these skill-gaps will continue to widen. In this first chapter, you will learn how to be familiar with data, your role as an aspiring data scientist, and the importance of Python programming language in data science.

Structure

- What is data?
- What is data science?
- What does a data scientist do?
- Real-world use cases of data science
- Why Python for data science?

Objective

After studying this chapter, you should be able to understand the data types, the amount of the data generated daily, and the need for data scientists with currently available real-world use cases.

What is data?

The best way to describe data is to understand the types of data. Data is divided into the following three categories.

Structured data

A well-organized data in the form of tables that can be easily be operated is known as structured data. Searching and accessing information from such type of data is very easy. For example, data stored in the relational database, i.e., SQL in the form of tables having multiple rows and columns. The spreadsheet is another good example of structured data. Structured data represent only 5% to 10% of all data present in the world. The following *figure 1.1* is an example of SQL data, where an SQL table is holding the merchant related data:

merchant_id	merchant_name	subtitle	status	publish_date
83	Texas Chicken		1	2018-03-22 00:00:00
84	ZALORA		1	2018-03-29 00:00:00
85	Caltex		1	2018-04-02 00:00:00
86	COURTS		1	2018-04-09 00:00:00
87	Agoda		1	2018-04-07 00:00:00
88	Lerk Thai		1	2018-03-02 00:00:00
89	Peach Garden @ Gardens Bv the Bav		1	2018-02-16 00:00:00

Figure 1.1: Sample SQL Data

Unstructured data

Unstructured data requires advanced tools and software's to access information. For example, images and graphics, PDF files, word document, audio, video, emails, PowerPoint presentations, webpages and web contents, wikis, streaming data, location coordinates, etc., fall under the unstructured data category. Unstructured data represent around 80% of the data. The following *figure 1.2* shows various unstructured data types:

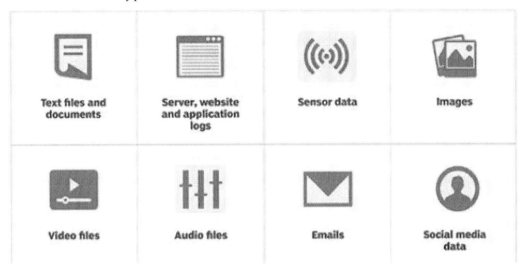

Figure 1.2: *Unstructured data types*

Semi-structured data

Semi-structured data is structured data that is unorganized. Web data such as **JSON (JavaScript Object Notation)** files, BibTex files, CSV files, tab-delimited text files, XML, and other markup languages are examples of semi-structured data found on the web. Semi-structured data represent only 5% to 10% of all data present in the world. The following *figure 1.3* shows an example of JSON data:

```json
{
    "custkey": "450002",
    "useragent": {
        "devicetype": "pc",
        "experience": "browser",
        "platform": "windows"
    },
    "pagetype": "home",
    "productline": "television",
    "customerprofile": {
        "age": 20,
        "gender": "male",
        "customerinterests": [
            "movies",
            "fashion",
            "music"
        ]
    }
}
```

Figure 1.3: JSON data

What is data science?

It's become a universal truth that modern businesses are awash with data. Last year, McKinsey estimated that Big Data initiatives in the US healthcare system *could account for $300 billion to $450 billion in reduced healthcare spending or 12-17 percent of the $2.6 trillion baselines in US healthcare costs.* On the other hand though, bad or unstructured data is estimated to be costing the US roughly $3.1 trillion a year.

Data-driven decision making is increasing in popularity. Accessing and finding information from the unstructured data is complex and cannot be done easily with some BI tools; here data science comes into the picture.

Data science is a field that extracts the knowledge and insights from the raw data. To do so, it uses mathematics, statistics, computer science, and programming language knowledge. A person who has all these skills is known as a data scientist. A data scientist is all about being curious, self-driven, and passionate about finding answers. The following *figure 1.4* shows the skills that a modern data scientist should have:

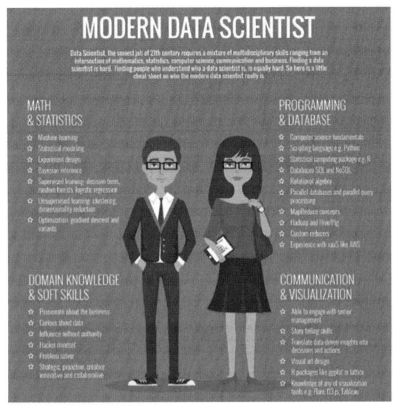

Figure 1.4: *Skills of a modern data scientist*

What does a data scientist do?

Most data scientists in the industry have advanced training in statistics, math, and computer science. Their experience is a vast horizon that also extends to data visualization, data mining, and information management. The primary job of a data scientist is to ask the right question. It's about surfacing hidden insight that can help enable companies to make smarter business decisions.

The job of a data scientist is not bound to a particular domain. Apart from scientific research, they are working in various domains including shipping, healthcare, e-commerce, aviation, finance, education, etc. They start their work by understanding the business problem and then they proceed with data collection, reading the data, transforming the data in the required format, visualizing, modeling, and evaluating the model and then deployment. You can imagine their work cycle as mentioned in the following *figure 1.5:*

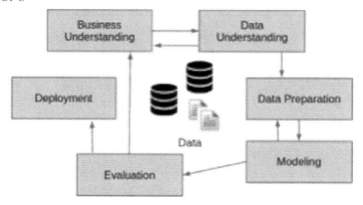

Figure 1.5: Work cycle of a data scientist

Eighty percent of a data scientist's time is spent in simply finding, cleansing, and organizing data, leaving only 20 percent to perform analysis. These processes can be time-consuming and tedious. But it's crucial to get them right since a model is only as good as the data that is used to build it. And because models generally improve as they are exposed to increasing amounts of data, it's in the data scientists' interests to include as much data as they can in their analysis.

In the later chapters of this book, you will learn all the above-required skills to be a data scientist.

Real-world use cases of data science

Information is the oil of the 21st century, and analytics is the combustion engine. Whether you are uploading a picture on Facebook, posting a tweet, emailing anybody, or shopping in an e-commerce site, the role of data science is everywhere. In the modern workplace, data science is applied to many problems to predict and calculate outcomes that would have taken several times more human hours to process. Following are some list of real-world examples where data scientists are playing a key role:

- Google's AI research arm is taking the help of data scientists to build the best performing algorithm for automatically detecting objects.

- *Amazon* has built a product recommendation system to personalize their product.

- *Santander Group of Bank* has built a model with the help of data scientists to identify the value of transactions for each potential customer.

- *Airbus* in the maritime industry is taking the help of data scientists to build a model that detects all ships in satellite images as quickly as possible to increase knowledge, anticipate threats, trigger alerts, and improve efficiency at sea.

- *YouTube* is using an automated video classification model in limited memory.

- Data scientists at the Chinese internet giant *Baidu Inc.* released details of a new deep learning algorithm that they claim can help pathologists identify tumors more accurately.

- The *Radiological Society of North America (RSNA®)* is using an algorithm to detect a visual signal for pneumonia in medical images which automatically locate lung opacities on chest radiographs.

- The *Inter-American Development Bank* is using an algorithm that considers a family's observable household attributes like the material of their walls and ceiling, or the assets found in the home to classify them and predict their level of need.

- *Netflix* data uses data science skills on the movie viewing patterns to understand what drives user interest and uses that to make decisions on which Netflix original series to produce.

Why Python for data science?

Python is very beginner friendly. The syntax (words and structure) is extremely simple to read and follow, most of which can be understood even if you do not know any programming. Python is a multi-paradigm programming language – a sort of Swiss Army knife for the coding world. It supports object-oriented programming, structured programming, and functional programming patterns, among others. There's a joke in the Python community that *Python is generally the second-best language for everything*.

Python is a free, open-source software, and consequently, anyone can write a library package to extend its functionality. Data science has been an early beneficiary of these extensions, particularly Pandas, the big daddy of them all.

Python's inherent readability and simplicity makes it relatively easy to pick up, and the number of dedicated analytical libraries available today means that data scientists in almost every sector will find packages already tailored to their needs, freely available for download.

The following survey (*figure 1.6*) was done by KDnuggets – a leading site on business analytics, Big Data, data mining, data science, and machine learning – clearly shows that Python is a preferable choice for data science/machine learning:

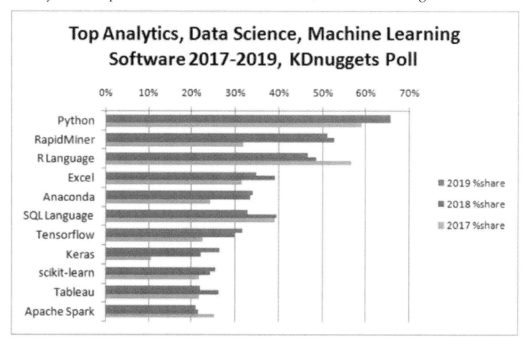

Figure 1.6: Survey by KDnuggets

Conclusion

Most of the people think that it is very difficult to become a data scientist. But, let me be clear, it is not tough!

If you love making discoveries about the world, and if you are fascinated by machine learning, then you can break into the data science industry no matter what your situation is. This book will push you to learn, improve, and master the data science skill on your own. There is only one thing you need to keep on, that is, LEARN-APPLY-REPEAT. In the next chapter, we will set up our machine, and be ready for our data science journey.

## CHAPTER 2

Installing Software and System Setup

In the last chapter, we covered the data science fundamentals, and now we are ready to move ahead and prepare our system for data science. In this chapter, we will learn about the most popular Python data science platform – Anaconda. With this platform, you don't need to install Python explicitly – just one installation in your system (Windows, macOS, or Linux) and you are ready to use the industry-standard platform for developing, testing, and training.

Structure

- System requirements
- Downloading the Anaconda
- Installing the Anaconda in Windows
- Installing the Anaconda in Linux
- How to install a new Python library in Anaconda
- Open your notebook – Jupyter
- Know your notebook

Objective

After studying this chapter, you should be able to install Anaconda in your system successfully and use the Jupyter notebook. You will also run your first Python program in your notebook.

System requirements

- **System architecture:** 64-bit x86, 32-bit x86 with Windows or Linux, Power8, or Power9
- **Operating system:** Windows Vista or newer, 64-bit macOS 10.10+, or Linux, including Ubuntu, RedHat, CentOS 6+
- Minimum 3 GB disk space to download and install

Downloading Anaconda

You can download the Anaconda Distribution from the following link:

https://www.anaconda.com/download/

Once you click on the preceding link, you will see the following screen (as shown in *figure 2.1*):

Individual Edition

Your data science toolkit

With over 20 million users worldwide, the open-source Individual Edition (Distribution) is the easiest way to perform Python/R data science and machine learning on a single machine. Developed for solo practitioners, it is the toolkit that equips you to work with thousands of open-source packages and libraries.

Figure 2.1: Anaconda Distribution download page

Anaconda Distribution shows different OS options – Windows, macOS, and Linux. According to your OS, select the appropriate option . For this example, I have selected the Windows OS's 64-Bit Graphical Installer (457 MB) option as shown in the following *figure 2.2* :

Anaconda Installers

Windows ▦	MacOS	Linux △
Python 3.8	Python 3.8	Python 3.8
64-Bit Graphical Installer (457 MB)	64-Bit Graphical Installer (435 MB)	64-Bit (x86) Installer (529 MB)
32-Bit Graphical Installer (403 MB)	64-Bit Command Line Installer (428 MB)	64-Bit (Power8 and Power9) Installer (279 MB)

Figure 2.2: Anaconda Distribution installer versions for Windows OS

Python community has stopped its support for Python 2.x and the prior version, so it is highly recommended that you should use Python 3.x. We are going to use Python 3.8 version throughout this book, so I will recommend downloading this version only. For downloading the distribution, see the two links just below the **Download** button; they are showing the Graphical Installer for each system architecture type-64-bit or 32-bit. Click on the appropriate link, and the downloading will start. This downloading process is the same for macOS and Linux.

Installing the Anaconda on Windows

1. Once the downloading is complete, double click on the installer to launch (the recommended way is to run the installer with admin privileges).

2. Click **Next**, accept the terms, select the users – **Just Me** or **All Users** and click **Next**.

3. Select the default destination folder or add a custom location to install the Anaconda, copy this path for later use and click **Next**.

> **Install Anaconda to a directory path that does not contain spaces or Unicode characters.**

4. Deselect (uncheck) the first following option (if checked already) – add Anaconda to my PATH environment variable, then click Install, wait till the installation is completed.

5. Click **Next**, click **Skip**, and then click **Finish**.

6. Now open the **Advanced system** settings in your machine and add the following two values in your **PATH** environment variable:

   - `C:\Users\prateek\Anaconda3`
   - `C:\Users\prateek\Anaconda3\Scripts`

   Here, replace the **C:\Users\prateek\Anaconda3** with the actual path of your Anaconda installation folder that you copied earlier.

7. Save the settings and restart your system.

8. Verify your installation by clicking on the Windows icon in the taskbar or simply type Anaconda in the search bar – you will see Anaconda Navigator option, click on this option, and the following screen will appear (as shown in *figure 2.3*):

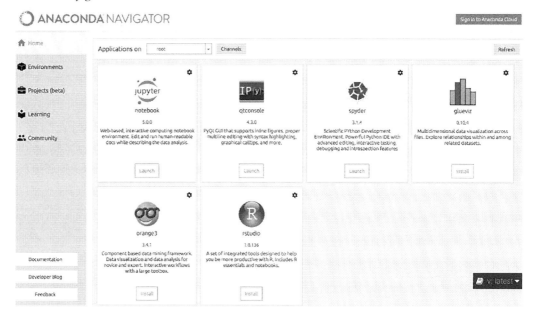

Figure 2.3: Anaconda Navigator

Installing the Anaconda with Graphical Installer in macOS is the same as we did above for Windows.

Installing the Anaconda in Linux

After downloading the 64bit(x86) installer, run the following two commands to check the data integrity:

- `Md5sum /path/filename`

- `Sha256sum /path/filename`

Replace `/path/filename` with the actual path and filename of the file you downloaded.

Enter the following to install Anaconda for Python 3.8, just replace ~/Downloads/ with the path to the file you downloaded:

```
bash ~/Downloads/Anaconda3-5.2.0-Linux-x86_64.sh
```

Figure 2.4: Installing Anaconda in Linux

Choose **Install Anaconda as a user** unless root privileges are required. The installer prompts – **In order to continue the installation process, please review the license agreement**. Click **Enter** to view license terms.

Scroll to the bottom of the license terms and enter **Yes** to agree. The installer prompts you to click Enter to accept the default install location, *CTRL + C* to cancel the installation, or specify an alternate installation directory. If you accept the default install location, the installer displays `PREFIX=/home/<user>/anaconda<3>` and continues the installation. It may take a few minutes to complete.

The installer prompts – **Do you wish the installer to prepend the Anaconda<3> install location to PATH in your /home/<user>/.bashrc?** Enter **Yes.**

> **If you enter No, you must manually add the path to Anaconda or conda will not work.**

The installer describes Microsoft VS Code and asks if you would like to install the VS Code. Enter yes or no. If you select yes, follow the instructions on the screen to complete the VS Code installation.

> **Installing VS Code with the Anaconda installer requires an internet connection. Offline users may be able to find an offline VS Code installer from Microsoft.**

The installer finishes and displays – **Thank you for installing Anaconda<3>!** Close and open your terminal window for the installation to take effect, or you can enter the command source `~/.bashrc`.

After your installation is complete, verify it by opening Anaconda Navigator, a program that is included with Anaconda – open a Terminal window and type anaconda-navigator. If Navigator opens, you have successfully installed Anaconda.

> You can find some known issues while installing Anaconda and their solutions in the following link: **https://docs.anaconda.com/anaconda/user-guide/troubleshooting/**

How to install a new Python library in Anaconda?

Most of the Python libraries/packages are preinstalled with the Anaconda Distribution, which you can verify by typing the following command in an Anaconda Prompt:

```
conda list
```

```
▨ Anaconda Prompt

C:\Users\prateek1.gupta>set "KERAS_BACKEND=theano"

(base) C:\Users\prateek1.gupta>conda list
# packages in environment at C:\Users\prateek1.gupta\AppData\Local\Continuum\anaconda3:
#
# Name                    Version                   Build  Channel
_ipyw_jlab_nb_ext_conf    0.1.0                 py36he6757f0_0
absl-py                   0.1.10                        py_0    conda-forge
agate                     1.6.1                        <pip>
agate-dbf                 0.2.0                        <pip>
agate-excel               0.2.2                        <pip>
agate-sql                 0.5.3                        <pip>
alabaster                 0.7.10                py36hcd07829_0
anaconda                  custom                py36h363777c_0
anaconda-client           1.6.5                 py36hd36550c_0
anaconda-project          0.8.0                 py36h8b3bf89_0
aniso8601                 3.0.0                         py36_0    conda-forge
argparse                  1.4.0                        <pip>
asn1crypto                0.22.0                py36h8e79faa_1
astroid                   1.6.4                         py36_0    anaconda
astropy                   2.0.2                 py36h06391c4_4
```

Figure 2.5: Anaconda Prompt

Now if you need to install any Python package which is not in the preceding list and is required for your task, then follow these steps. In the same Anaconda Prompt terminal, type `conda install <package-name>`.

For example, if you want to install `scipy` package, just type `conda install scipy`, then press enter and then enter `y` to continue.

A second recommended approach to install any new package in Anaconda is to search the same (`conda install <package-name>`) in Google first and then go to the first search result, which is shown as follows:

1. In Google search, I am searching a package for example `imageio` i.e. `conda install imageio`.

2. Go to the first search result; this will open the Anaconda official site showing the installers of the searched package. In our example, it is like **https://anaconda.org/menpo/imageio**

3. Now copy the text under– **To install this package with conda run:** and paste in the Anaconda Prompt. In our case, text is: `conda install -c menpoimageio`

Open your notebook – Jupyter

After installing Anaconda, the next step is to open the notebook – an open-source web application that allows you to create and share documents that contain live code, equations, visualizations, and narrative text. For the notebook, open Anaconda **Navigator** and click on **Launch** button under the Jupyter Notebook icon or just type Jupyter Notebook in the search bar in Windows and then select it as shown in the following *figure 2.6*:

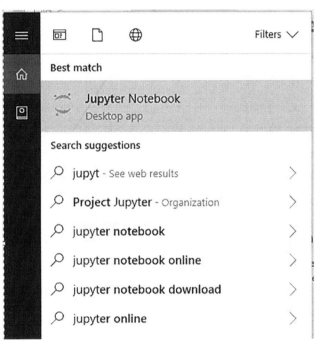

Figure 2.6: Windows search bar

Once you select it, a browser window (default is IE) will be opened showing the notebook as showing in the following *figure 2.7:*

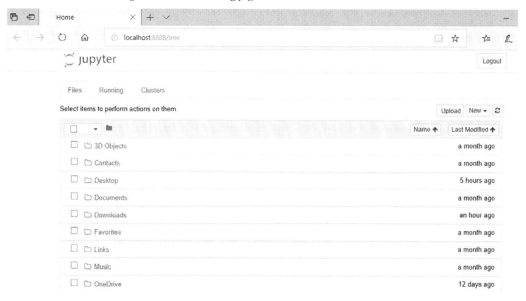

Figure 2.7: Browser window

Know your notebook

Once your notebook is opened in the browser, click on the **New** dropdown and select the default first option – Python 3 as shown in the following *figure 2.8:*

Figure 2.8: Dropdown menu

After clicking on Python 3 option, a new tab will be opened containing the new untitled notebook, as shown in the following *figure 2.9*:

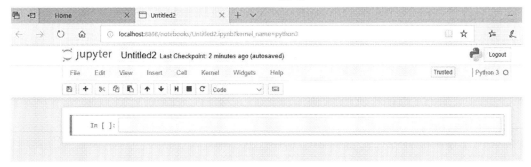

Figure 2.9: New tab

Rename your notebook with a proper name by double-clicking on the Untitled text and then enter any new name (I have named it MyFirstNotebook) and click **Rename** (refer to the following *figure 2.10*):

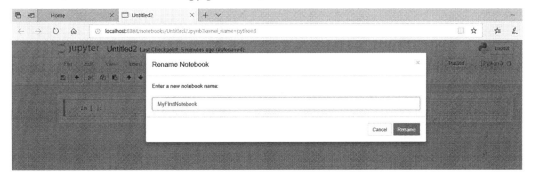

Figure 2.10: Rename

The preceding step will rename your notebook. Now it's time to run your first Python program in your first notebook. We will print a greeting message in Python for this purpose. In the cell (text bar) just type any welcome message inside the print block as shown in the following *figure 2.11*:

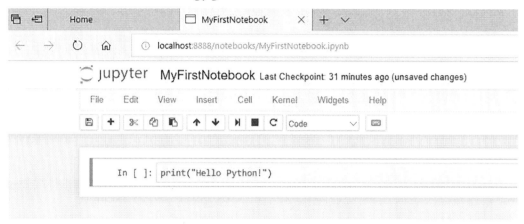

Figure 2.11: Welcome message

In the above cell, we are printing a string in Python 3.6. Now to run this program, you can simply press *Shift + Enter* keys together or click on the **Play** button just below the cell column (refer to the following *figure 2.12*):

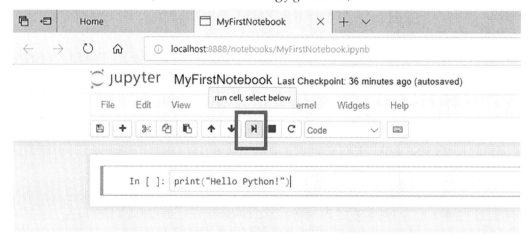

Figure 2.12: Play button

Once you run the cell, your program will run and give you the output, as shown just below the cell in the following *figure 2.13:*

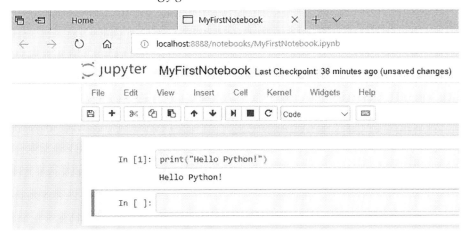

Figure 2.13: Output

Congrats! You have successfully run your first program in Python 3.7. This is just a one-line code using simple plain English text. Let's explore some more, the simplicity of the Python by doing some mathematical calculations.

Let's add two numbers by entering the `FirstNumber + SecondNumber` and then run it as shown in the following *figure 2.14:*

```
In [2]: 29+56
Out[2]: 85
```

Figure 2.14: Simple calculation

Quite interesting, right! Let's move ahead and ask the user to input numbers and let Python do the homework. In the following example, you need to enter the first number, press enter, then enter the second number and press enter. The calculation will be done, and output will be displayed within a millisecond (as shown in the following *figure 2.15*):

```
a = int(input())
b = int(input())
print("adding of two numbers: ", a+b)
print("difference in numbers: ", a-b)
print("multiplicaton of numbers: ", a*b)

4
2
adding of two numbers:    6
difference in numbers:    2
multiplicaton of numbers:  8
```

Figure 2.15: Mathematical calculation

Now, suppose you have done your given task and want to share the same with your project lead or manager. You can do it easily by going to the **File** option and hover on the **Download as** option, as shown in the following *figure 2.16*:

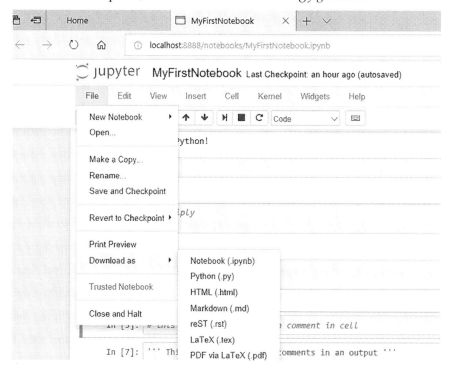

Figure 2.16: *Download as option*

You can save your current work in different formats – notebook, PDF, Python, or HTML. Once you select the required option, it will be saved in that format with the same name as you have given while renaming the notebook in the default location of your system. By saving in the various formats, you can carry and share your analysis with anyone.

Conclusion

Anaconda Distribution is the fastest and easiest way to do Python and Machine Learning work. You can load the data, pre-process it, visualize it, train your model, and evaluate the performance in a single notebook and then share your work with anyone easily. For a complete walk-around of your Jupyter notebook, I have added a cheat sheet section just after this chapter. I suggest you read that cheat sheet and play with your notebook. In the next chapter, you will learn about the data structures specific to data science, and also how to use them in your analysis task.

CHAPTER 3
Lists and Dictionaries

Data structures are a way of organizing and storing data in a programming language so that they can be accessed and worked on efficiently. They define the relationship between data and operations that can be performed on the data. As an aspiring data scientist, you will use various data structures in your daily job so learning data type is a must-have skill. In this chapter, we will learn the two most widely used Python data structures specific to data science when working with huge data – lists and dictionaries. We will also compare both with the other data structures that look the same but have fundamental differences.

Structure

- What is a list?
- How to create a list?
- Different list manipulating operations
- Difference between list and tuples
- What is a dictionary?
- How to create a dictionary?
- Some operations with the dictionary

Objective

After studying this chapter, you will have a strong knowledge on using list and dictionary.

What is a list?

A list is a non-primitive type of data structure in Python, which means it stores a collection of values in various formats rather than storing only a single value. Lists are mutable – we can change the content of a list. In simple words, list is a collection that is ordered, mutable, and may contain duplicate values. Here, ordered means the order in which you entered the elements in a list; the same order will be shown, once you print/get that list.

In Python, we can store a single value in the following primitive data types:

- `float` represents the rational number for examples 1.23 or 3.2
- `int` represents numeric data like 1,2 or -3
- `str` represents the string or text
- `bool` represents True/False

Consider a scenario where your family doctor needs heights and weights of every family member to calculate the body mass index. Now creating a separate variable to store each person's height and weight is very inconvenient. Here, Python list comes in the picture.

How to create a list?

In Python, a list is an object which is treated like any other data type (e.g., integers, strings, Boolean, etc.). This means that you can assign your list to a variable, so you can store and make it easier to access. We can create a list using the square brackets and separating the elements by a comma.

In your notebook, you can create an empty list, store it in a variable, and then check the type of the variable, as shown in the following *figure 3.1:*

```
In [2]:  # creating an empty list in Python
         height = []
         type(height)

Out[2]:  list
```

Figure 3.1: Creating an empty list in Python

Let's create a list containing the heights of family members in meters, as shown in the following *figure 3.2*:

```
In [3]:  # a list containing heights
         height_list = [1.76,1.64,1.79,1,57]
         print(height_list)

         [1.76, 1.64, 1.79, 1, 57]
```

Figure 3.2: A list containing heights

One advantage of the list is that we can store different types (`str`, `int`, `float`, etc.) of values in a list and even a list of a list itself. Interesting right? For example, we can add names of the family members, which is the string data type and its values is in float data type in our previously created list, as shown in the following *figure 3.3*:

```
In [4]:  # a list containing str and float
         name_height_list = ["Tom",1.76,"Harry",1.64,"Lisa",1.79,"Mona",1.57]
         print(name_height_list)

         ['Tom', 1.76, 'Harry', 1.64, 'Lisa', 1.79, 'Mona', 1.57]
```

Figure 3.3: A list containing str and float

Different list manipulation operations

After creating a list, you will often find a situation where you want to update that list. This list manipulation is the exact step you are going to learn in this section:

1. Let's create a list and print its element by its index one by one. In this example, we are storing the values python, c, and java in a list and then printing each of these values using their position (in other words we are accessing a list by index number) in the list.

    Here, the starting point of a list begins with number zero (0), not from one (1). To access the first element of a list, you need to use zero indexes, not the first index as shown in the following *figure 3.4*:

```
In [6]:  lang = ['python','c','java']

         print (lang[0] + ' is very easy to learn for Data Science')
         print (lang[1] + ' is the first language I have learnt')
         print (lang[2]+ ' is difficult to learn for Data Science')

         python is very easy to learn for Data Science
         c is the first language I have learnt
         java is difficult to learn for Data Science
```

Figure 3.4: Begin with number zero (0)

2. Since the list is mutable, we can change the existing value of any element; let's do this by changing the java language with `cobol` language as shown in the following *figure 3.5:*

```
In [1]:  lang = ['python','c','java']
         print("old list:", lang)
         lang[2] = 'cobol'
         print("new list:", lang)

         old list: ['python', 'c', 'java']
         new list: ['python', 'c', 'cobol']
```

Figure 3.5: Changing java with cobol language

3. Now you want to print all elements in the list one by one; you can do this by using for loop as shown in the following *figure 3.6:*

```
In [2]:  language_list = ['python','c','cobol']
         for language in language_list:
             print("language is: ", language)

         language is:  python
         language is:  c
         language is:  cobol
```

Figure 3.6: Using 'for' loop

4. Let's check how many elements there are in our language list using the list's `len()` method (refer to the following *figure 3.7*):

```
In [3]:  language_list = ['python','c','cobol']
         print("elements in the list: ", len(language_list))

         elements in the list:  3
```

Figure 3.7: Using list's len() method

5. Now you want to add a new language or item in your list; let's do this using list's `append()` method (refer to the following *figure 3.8*):

```
In [4]:  language_list = ['python','c','cobol']
         language_list.append('java')
         print("updated list is:", language_list)

         updated list is: ['python', 'c', 'cobol', 'java']
```

Figure 3.8: Using list's append() method

6. What if you want to add a new element in a specific position? You have guessed it right; we can use the index herewith `insert()` method. In the following *figure 3.9*, I am adding a new language .net in 3rd position or after the c language:

```
In [5]:  language_list = ['python','c','cobol','java']
         language_list.insert(2, '.net')
         print("modified list is:", language_list)

         modified list is: ['python', 'c', '.net', 'cobol', 'java']
```

Figure 3.9: Adding a new language .net

7. Sometimes you want to remove some element from your list. This can be done in three ways – either to remove the element by its name using `remove()` method or by its index using pop() method or by `del()` method. In the following *figure 3.10*, first I am removing the `cobol` language from my list and then from the updated list I am removing `java` language by its index:

```
In [8]:  language_list = ['python','c','.net','cobol','java']
         # remove element by name
         language_list.remove('cobol')
         print("updated list:", language_list)
         # remove element by index
         language_list.pop(3)
         print("latest list:", language_list)

         updated list: ['python', 'c', '.net', 'java']
         latest list: ['python', 'c', '.net']
```

Figure 3.10: Removing some element from the list

The `del()` method use case is different from the other ones. It also removes the element on the specified index but its syntax is different from `pop()` or `remove()` methods. Let's create a new list with duplicate elements to understand the difference between `remove()`, `del()`, and `pop()` methods.

In the following *figure 3.11*, digit 1 is repeated two times. When we apply to `remove()` method, it's removing the element 4 from the list. The `pop()` method is removing the 4th index of the list, which is a digit at last position, whereas `del()` method is removing the 4th index element with a different syntax structure:

```
In [11]: number_list = [1,2,3,4,1]
         number_list.remove(4)
         print("list after remove() example:", number_list)

         number_list = [1,2,3,4,1]
         number_list.pop(4)
         print("list after pop() example:", number_list)

         number_list = [1,2,3,4,1]
         del(number_list[4])
         print("list after del() example:", number_list)

         list after remove() example: [1, 2, 3, 1]
         list after pop() example: [1, 2, 3, 4]
         list after del() example: [1, 2, 3, 4]
```

Figure 3.11: *Applying different methods to remove an element*

8. Now you want to sort your list in ascending or descending order. This can be done by `sort()` method of the list as shown in the following *figure 3.12:*

```
In [18]: language_list = ['python','c','.net','cobol','java']
         language_list.sort()
         print("sort in ascending order:", language_list)
         languages_list = ['python','c','.net','cobol','java','c#']
         language_list.sort(reverse=True)
         print("sort in descending order:", language_list)

         sort in ascending order: ['.net', 'c', 'cobol', 'java', 'python']
         sort in descending order: ['python', 'java', 'cobol', 'c', '.net']
```

Figure 3.12: *Sorting list in ascending or descending order*

Difference between Lists and Tuples

In Python, there is a data type – Tuples, which is similar to lists, and it often confuses me as to which one to use in which condition. There are two main qualities of a tuple which distinguishes it from the list – first is the structure of a tuple, which means tuples are initialized with small brackets () rather than square brackets [] in lists, and the second major difference is that tuples are immutable, which means neither can we change or delete its value, nor can we add any new item after the declaration of a tuple. It means there is no `append()`, `remove()`, or `pop()` methods in tuples.

A tuple looks like how it's shown in the following *figure 3.13:*

```
tuple_example = ('CS','IT','EC','ME')
print("tuple example: ", tuple_example)
print("data type of the example is", type(tuple_example))

tuple example:  ('CS', 'IT', 'EC', 'ME')
data type of the example is <class 'tuple'>
```

Figure 3.13: *Tuples*

What is a Dictionary?

In Python, dictionaries are made up of key-value pairs. A key is used to identify the item and the value holds the value of the item. The main concept of dictionaries is that for every value, you have a unique key. A dictionary is initialized by defining key-value in the curly {} brackets, where they are separated by a colon : sign. Unlike the list, a dictionary is a collection that is unordered, which means the order of its element is not guaranteed when you get or print the dictionary.

How to create a dictionary?

Let's create a dictionary to store the information of a car, where in the key of that dictionary we store the car's property name and in the value, we will store its name or value,   as shown in the following *figure 3.14:*

```
In [19]: dict_example = {
             'brand':'Hyundai',
             'model':'Creta',
             'type':'SUV',
             'year':'2017'
         }
         print("dictionary example: ", dict_example)

         dictionary example:  {'brand': 'Hyundai', 'model': 'Creta', 'type': 'SUV', 'year': '2017'}
```

Figure 3.14: *Creating a dictionary*

Some operations with dictionary

1. Once you create a dictionary, you may want to access any item in that dictionary. This can be done in the following two ways – one is to use key

and second is to use `get()` method. Let's do both in our newly created car information dictionary (refer to the following *figure 3.15*):

```
In [22]: # access the brand value by key
         car_brand_by_key = dict_example['brand']
         print("car brand by key:", car_brand_by_key)
         # access the brand value by get()
         print("car brand by method:", dict_example.get('brand'))

car brand by key: Hyundai
car brand by method: Hyundai
```

Figure 3.15: Using key and get() methods

2. There may be a situation where you want to change any value in your dictionary; this can be done by referring to the key name as shown in the following *figure 3.16*, where we are changing the car manufacture year from 2017 to 2018:

```
In [24]: dict_example['year'] = '2018'
         print("updated dict: ", dict_example)

updated dict:  {'brand': 'Hyundai', 'model': 'Creta', 'type': 'SUV', 'year': '2018'}
```

Figure 3.16: Changing value in the dictionary

3. Sometimes you need the keys or values from a dictionary. You can print all key names or values with the for loop as shown in the following *figure 3.17*:

```
In [26]: # printing all keys
         for car_property in dict_example:
             print("key in dict:", car_property)

         # printing all values
         for car_property_value in dict_example.values():
             print("value in dict:", car_property_value)

key in dict: brand
key in dict: model
key in dict: type
key in dict: year
value in dict: Hyundai
value in dict: Creta
value in dict: SUV
value in dict: 2018
```

Figure 3.17: For loop

4. What if a business owner wants you to display car details in a key-value pair? No issue, we can do that in the following way (refer to *figure 3.18*):

```
In [27]:  for car_property, car_property_value in dict_example.items():
              print(car_property, car_property_value)

brand Hyundai
model Creta
type SUV
year 2018
```

Figure 3.18: *Displaying car details in a key-value pair*

The other methods in the dictionary are the same as we used in the list earlier; instead of the index, we need to use key here.

Conclusion

List and Dictionary are the two most used data types which are used to efficiently work with huge amounts of data. In your daily data clean-up process, you will need to store some information in variables, where learning this chapter will come in handy. After practicing notebook examples in your notebook, you will gain confidence and will not confuse which data structure to use in which condition. In the next chapter, we will learn about Python functions and packages.

## CHAPTER 4

Package, Function, and Loop

Package, function, and loop provide better modularity for your application and a high degree of code reusing. For your daily data science work, you don't need to reinvent the wheel or write some code from scratch. Remember, in the previous chapters, we have already used `print()` and `type()` functions. Python developers have written mostly used functionalities, which you can leverage easily in terms of functions. In this chapter, we will learn some other built-in Python functions, and how to use them to organize, and make our code reusable.

Structure

- The `help()` function in Python
- How to import a Python package?
- How to create and call a function?
- Passing parameter in a function
- Default parameter in a function
- How to use unknown parameters in a function?
- A global and local variable in a function
- What is a Lambda function?
- Understanding main in Python
- The `while` and `for` loop in Python

Objective

After studying the chapter, you will be able to use inbuilt Python functions and packages and write your function.

The help() function in Python

You must have already used and know the name of Python inbuilt functions, but sometimes you still have to figure out how to use it. To know more about a function, Python provides us another function, known as `help()`. In your Jupyter notebook, you can simply type `help(<function_name>)` and once you run this, it will give you all the information about that function.

For example, if I want to know about the inbuilt `len()` function, I will use `help()` function as shown in the following *figure 4.1*:

```
help(len)

Help on built-in function len in module builtins:

len(obj, /)
    Return the number of items in a container.
```

Figure 4.1: Using help() function

How to import a Python package?

To use some inbuilt functionalities, first you need to import such a package and for that, you just need to use import keyword. For example, you are working as a junior data scientist in an agriculture firm and you need to calculate the area of a circular land. You know it well that area of a circle can be calculated from the formula `pi*r^2` where r is the radius of the circle, but you don't remember the value of the `pi`. No need to worry, Python provides a math package to help you in this scenario as shown in the following *figure 4.2*:

```
import math

# define area as variable area
area = 0
# define radius as variable r
r = 5.89
# calculate area
area = math.pi * r**2
print("area of the land is: ", area)

area of the land is:  108.98844649760245
```

Figure 4.2: Math package provided by Python

Here we have imported the `math` package, but if we know the specific package, then we can also import only that sub-package from its package. For our example we don't need to import math package completely; in fact, we can import only the `pi` from the `math` package, as shown in the following *figure 4.3*:

```
from math import pi
# define radius as variable r
r = 5.89
# calculate area
area = math.pi * r**2
print("area of the land is: ", area)
```

```
area of the land is:  108.98844649760245
```

Figure 4.3: Importing pi package from math package

How to create and call a function?

In Python, we define a function using the `def` keyword followed by function name and colon. For example, if you want to print "hello world" in a function, we first need to define the function and then write the `print()` inside that function, then we will see how to call that function. In the following *figure 4.4*, notice the space before the `print()`, it's called Python's indentation and is required to ensure that this code is a part of the function. You don't need to explicitly give space; your notebook already knows it and once you press the Enter key after the colon sign, it will automatically add a space:

```
# defining my own function
def my_function():
    print("Hello World")
```

```
# calling my function
my_function()
```

```
Hello World
```

Figure 4.4: Create and call a function

Passing parameter in a function

We have written a simple function; sometimes you also need to pass some information in your function, which we can do in the form of parameters or arguments. For example, you want to get the sum of the two numbers with the help of a function, so we will write a function which will take two parameters – a and b considering both are integers, and we will give the sum of both numbers by using return statement as shown in the following *figure 4.5:*

```
# defining a function to return sum of two numbers
def add_two_numbers(a,b):
    return a + b
# call the function
add_two_numbers(9,8)
```

17

Figure 4.5: Defining a function to return sum of two numbers

Default parameter in a function

Sometimes you need to pass a default value to a parameter in your function. For example, you want to return the sum of two numbers where the second numerical value is pre-defined, as it is 6 here. You can do this in the following way (*figure 4.6*):

```
# defining a function with default parameter
def add_function(a,b = 6):
    return a + b
# call `add_function()` with only `a` parameter
add_function(a=1)
```

7

Figure 4.6: Default parameter in a function

In the `MyFirstNotebook`, I have shared an example to help you understand how to pass parameters to a function in runtime and determine the output value based on condition.

How to use unknown parameters in a function?

In previous examples you know there are only two parameters passed, but sometimes you don't know the number of arguments to pass in a function. In such a situation, you can pass *args parameter in your function as shown in the following *figure 4.7*. Here we are adding three numbers with the help of inbuilt sum() function:

```
# Define `add_function()` function to accept any no.of parameters
def add_function(*args):
    return sum(args)
# Calculate the sum of the numbers
add_function(9,4,8)
```

21

Figure 4.7: Sum() function to add three numbers

In the preceding example, instead of **args** you can give any name but ***** sign is important to place before any name. Try replacing ***args** with another name that includes the asterisk. You'll see that the preceding code keeps working!

A global and local variable in a function

We use variables to store some values before using them in function. But the use of declared variables in Python has some limits. We can define them as global or as a local variable. The main difference between both of them is that the local variables are defined within a function block and can only be accessed inside that function, while global variables can be accessed by all functions that might be in your script. In the next example we have created a global scoped variable my_text – outside of the functions and accessing the same in both two functions (refer to the following *figure 4.8*):

```
# define a Global scope variable
my_text = "I am learning Python for Data Science"

def first_function():
    """ This function uses global scope variable"""
    print(my_text)
first_function()

def second_function():
    """ This function alse uses global scope variable"""
    print(my_text)
second_function()
```

```
I am learning Python for Data Science
I am learning Python for Data Science
```

Figure 4.8: Global variable in a function

Now let us first try to print the value of globally scoped variable just after the function declaration as shown in the following *figure 4.9*. The point to notice here is that `my_text` variable is defined outside of the function. If we run the program, it will show `UnboundLocalError` because it is treating `my_text` as a local variable:

```
def my_function():
    print(my_text)
    my_text = "I am also learning"
    print(my_text)

# define a Global scope variable
my_text = "I am learning Python for Data Science"
my_function()
print(my_text)
```

```
UnboundLocalError                         Traceback (most recent call last)
<ipython-input-14-45a9008ed554> in <module>()
      6 # define a Global scope variable
      7 my_text = "I am learning Python for Data Science"
----> 8 my_function()
      9 print(my_text)

<ipython-input-14-45a9008ed554> in my_function()
      1 def my_function():
----> 2     print(my_text)
      3     my_text = "I am also learning"
      4     print(my_text)
      5

UnboundLocalError: local variable 'my_text' referenced before assignment
```

Figure 4.9: Printing value of globally scoped variable

Now, let us comment the first print line just after the function declaration; our program will run without any error giving you the desired output as shown in the following *figure 4.10*:

```
def my_function():
    #print(my_text)
    my_text = "I am also learning"
    print(my_text)

# define a Global scope variable
my_text = "I am learning Python for Data Science"
my_function()
print(my_text)
```

```
I am also learning
I am learning Python for Data Science
```

Figure 4.10: Commenting the first print line after function declaration

What is a Lambda function?

Lambda function is also known as anonyms function in Python. For declaring a lambda function, we don't use a def keyword, instead we use the lambda keyword in a different way. In the following *figure 4.11*, I am going to write a normal function to multiply by 5 and then we will write the same functionality with lambda function:

```
def multiply(x):
    return x*5
multiply(2)
```

```
10
```

```
#same functionality with lambda function
multiply = lambda x: x*5
multiply(2)
```

```
10
```

Figure 4.11: Normal function and lambda function

Following is another example of adding two numbers with the help of inbuilt sum() function (refer to *figure 4.12*):

```
def sum(x, y):
    return x+y
sum(9,8)
```

```
17
```

```
# same example with lambda function
sum = lambda x, y: x + y;
sum(9,8)
```

```
17
```

Figure 4.12: Adding two numbers using sum() function with lambda function

It's quite clear now that we use lambda functions when we require a nameless function for a short period of time, which is created at runtime.

Understanding main in Python

Python doesn't have a defined entry point like the main() method in other languages, i.e., Java. Rather Python executes a source file line by line. Before executing the code, it will define a few special variables. For example, if the Python interpreter is running that module (the source file) as the main program, it sets the special __ name__ variable to have a value __main__. If this file is being imported from another module, __name__ will be set to the module's name.

Sometimes you write a module (a Python file with .py extension) where it can be executed directly. Alternatively, it can also be imported and used in another module. Here you can put the main check (if __name__ == "__main__":), so that you can have that code only be executed when you want to run the module as a program and not have it executed when someone just wants to import your module and call your functions themselves.

Let's understand the preceding concept with an example. We will use a Python IDE to create Python files. You can download and install this IDE using the following link: **https://www.jetbrains.com/help/pycharm/install-and-set-up-pycharm.html**

After installing the PyCharm, open the IDE, and create a new project as shown in the following *figure 4.13*:

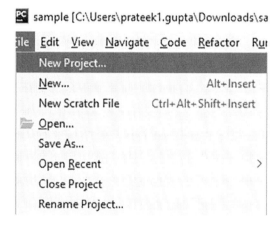

Figure 4.13: Creating new project

After creating the project, create a Python file with name my_module.py and put the following line of code there (refer to *figure 4.14*):

```
def hello():
    print("This is from my_module.py file!")

if __name__ == "__main__":
    print("Executing as main program")
    print("Value of __name__ is: ", __name__)
    hello()
```

Figure 4.14: Creating a Python file

You can run the previously created module by right-clicking on the file and clicking on **Run** `my_module` as shown in the following *figure 4.15:*

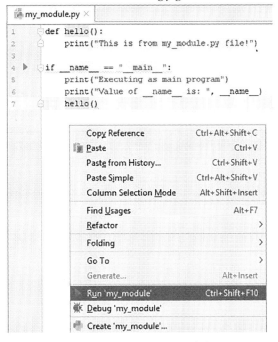

Figure 4.15: *Run 'my_module'*

This will generate the following result in the console:

```
Run:   my_module
  ▶   ↑   C:\Users\prateekl.gupta\Downloads\sample\venv\Scripts\python.exe C:/Users/prateekl.gupta/Downloads/sample/my_module.py
          Executing as main program
  ■   ↓   Value of __name__ is: __main__
  ‖   ⇄   This is from my_module.py file!
  ▣  ▣    Process finished with exit code 0
```

Figure 4.16: *'my_module' window*

As you can see in the result, we have created a new module and executed it as the main program, so the value of __name__ is set to __main__. As a result, if condition is satisfied and hello() function gets called. Now create a new file called `using_module.py` and import `my_module` thereby writing the following code (refer to *figure 4.17*):

```
 my_module.py      using_module.py

1      import my_module
2
3      my_module.hello()
4         💡
5      print(my_module.__name__)
```

Figure 4.17: *Code to import 'my_module'*

Now run this file and you will see the following outcome:

```
Run:    using_module
 ▶   ↑    C:\Users\prateek1.gupta\Downloads\sample\venv\Scripts\python.exe C:/Users/prateek1.gupta/Downloads/sample/using_module.py
 ■   ↓    This is from my_module.py file!
           my_module
 ‖   ⊠
           Process finished with exit code 0
```

Figure 4.18: Outcome of running the file

As you can see now, the statement in my_module fails to execute because the value of __name__ is set to my_module. From this small program, you can understand that every module in Python has a special attribute called __name__. The value of the __name__ attribute is set to __main__ when the module runs as the main program. Otherwise, the value of __name__ is set to contain the name of the module.

while and for loop in Python

A loop is a block of code that gets repeated over and over again, either a specified number of times or until some condition is met. There are two kinds of loops in Python, while loops and for loops. The while loop repeats a section of code while some condition is true. The while statement starts with the while keyword, followed by a test condition, and ends with a colon (:). The loop body contains the code that gets repeated at each step of the loop. Each line is indented with four spaces. When a while loop is executed, Python evaluates the test condition and determines if it is true or false. If the test condition is true, then the code in the loop body is executed. Otherwise, the code in the body is skipped and the rest of the program is executed.

For example, see the following line of the code snippet (*figure 4.19*):

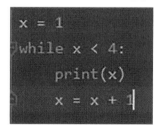

```
x = 1
while x < 4:
    print(x)
    x = x + 1
```

Figure 4.19: While loop code snippet

In the preceding code snippet, integer 1 is assigned to variable x. Then a while loop is created with the test condition x < 4, which checks whether or not the value of x is less than 4. If x is less than 4, the body of the loop is executed. Next, the value of x is printed on screen, and then x is incremented by 1.

A for loop executes a section of code once for each item in a collection of items. The number of times that the code is executed is determined by the number of items in the collection. The `for` statement begins with the for keyword, followed by a membership expression, and ends in a colon (:). The loop body contains the code to be executed at each step of the loop, and is indented with four spaces. For example, see following code snippet (*figure 4.20*):

```
for letter in "Science":
    print(letter)
```

Figure 4.20: For loop code snippet

In the preceding code snippet, at each step of the loop, the variable letter is assigned the next letter in the string `Science`, and then the value of the letter is printed. The loops run once for each character in the string `Science`, so the loop body executes seven times. Please note, a loop inside of another loop is called a nested loop, and they come up more often than you might expect. You can nest while loops inside of `for` loops, and vice versa.

Conclusion

As an aspiring data scientist, you'll constantly need to write your functions to solve problems that your data poses to you. In your daily work, you will import various packages, you will write your functions for different tasks, i.e., a function for data cleaning, another function for modeling, and another for evaluating your model, etc. In the next chapter, we will learn about the first fundamental package of Python used for scientific computing – NumPy.

CHAPTER 5
NumPy Foundation

NumPy is the fundamental package for scientific computing with Python. Most of the other packages such as `pandas`, `statsmodels` are built on top of it. NumPy is the short name for *Numeric Python* or *Numerical Python*. This package contains a powerful N-dimensional array object and useful linear algebra capabilities. In this chapter, we will learn about this N-dimensional array – a more powerful alternative to the list, and we will see how to use this in data manipulation.

Structure

- Importing a NumPy package
- Why use NumPy array over list?
- NumPy array attributes
- Creating NumPy arrays
- Accessing an element of a NumPy array
- Slicing in NumPy array

Objective

After studying the chapter, you will be able to use the NumPy array effectively.

Importing a NumPy package

The NumPy package comes preinstalled in Anaconda distribution, so we don't need to install this package; in fact for using it we just need to import it. We can import this package in the following way, as shown in *figure 5.1*:

```
# importing numpy package
import numpy as np
```

Figure 5.1: *Importing a NumPy package*

> In the preceding import statement, np is an alias pointing to NumPy. We can use this alias with any import to shorten the package name in further uses.

Why use NumPy array over list?

Say for example, you have the weather data telling about the distance and the wind speed. Now you are supposed to calculate and generate a new feature from the data – the time. Ideally, we would go ahead with using the list and calculate by applying the formula to the list of distance and speed as shown in the following *figure 5.2*:

```
distance = [55,60,45]
speed = [6,10,7]
time = distance/speed
print("time:", time)
```

Figure 5.2: *Calculating speed and distance*

But once you run your code, you see the unexpected result:

```
- - - - - - - - - - - - - - - - - - - - - - - - - - - - - - - - - - - - - - - - - - - - - - - - - -
TypeError                                Traceback (most recent call last)
<ipython-input-2-3554454633bc> in <module>()
      1 distance = [55,60,45]
      2 speed = [6,10,7]
----> 3 time = distance/speed
      4 print("time:", time)

TypeError: unsupported operand type(s) for /: 'list' and 'list'
```

Figure 5.3: *Result of running the code*

You must be confused and thinking, what I have done wrong with the list operations, but you have no clue!

The list has some limitations. You cannot perform some mathematical operations directly on the list and that's why Python has a NumPy array to solve such a problem. To solve this issue, we need to import the NumPy package first, then we need to convert our list into NumPy array, and then we need to perform our operation, as shown in the following *figure 5.4*:

```
import numpy as np
distance = [55,60,45]
speed = [6,10,7]
dist = np.array(distance)
spd = np.array(speed)
time= dist/spd
print(time)
```

```
[9.16666667 6.          6.42857143]
```

Figure 5.4: Using NumPy Array

In the preceding example, `distance` and `speed` variables are of type NumPy array and since time variable is associated with `dist` and speed NumPy arrays, its type is automatically assigned as NumPy array.

NumPy array attributes

NumPy array has its attributes like dimension, size, and shape. We can know these attributes by using it's `ndim`, `shape`, and `size` attributes as shown in our wind speed example (*figure 5.5*):

```
# data type
print("data type of array:", time.dtype)
# no. of dimensions
print("no. of dimensions:", time.ndim)
# size of each dimension
print("size of each dimension:", time.shape)
# total size of array
print("total size of array:", time.size)
```

```
data type of array: float64
no. of dimensions: 1
size of each dimension: (3,)
total size of array: 3
```

Figure 5.5: NumPy attributes

Creating NumPy arrays

An array can be one, two, or three dimensions. Based on the problem you are solving, you need to create any dimension array; so let's create an array using random numbers. For generating random numbers, in our case integer numbers, we will use NumPy's random function and then we will check individual array attributes as shown in the following *figure 5.6*:

```
# creating arrays with random values
np.random.seed(0)  # seed for reproducibility

x1 = np.random.randint(10, size=6)  # One-dimensional array
x2 = np.random.randint(10, size=(3, 4))  # Two-dimensional array
x3 = np.random.randint(10, size=(3, 4, 5))  # Three-dimensional array

print("x1 ndim: ", x1.ndim)
print("x1 shape:", x1.shape)
print("x1 size: ", x1.size)

print("x2 ndim: ", x2.ndim)
print("x2 shape:", x2.shape)
print("x2 size: ", x2.size)

print("x3 ndim: ", x3.ndim)
print("x3 shape:", x3.shape)
print("x3 size: ", x3.size)
```

```
x1 ndim:  1
x1 shape: (6,)
x1 size:  6
x2 ndim:  2
x2 shape: (3, 4)
x2 size:  12
x3 ndim:  3
x3 shape: (3, 4, 5)
x3 size:  60
```

Figure 5.6: Creating arrays with random values

As noted, `np.random.seed(0)` sets the random seed to 0, so the pseudo-random numbers you get from random will start from the same point, and `np.random.randint()` function return random integers from the *discrete uniform* distribution of the specified `dtype` in the *half-open* interval (low, high). If high is `None` (the default), then results are from (`0, low`).

Let's create another array using NumPy `arange()` function which returns evenly spaced values within a given interval. In the following *figure 5.7*, we are creating a sequence of integers from 0 to 20 with steps of 5:

```
f = np.arange(0, 20, 5)
print ("sequential array with steps of 5:\n", f)
```

```
sequential array with steps of 5:
 [ 0  5 10 15]
```

Figure 5.7: Using arange() function

Accessing an element of a NumPy array

For analyzing and manipulating an array, you need to access the elements. We will use indexes of every element in an array as we did in the list. In a one-dimensional array, the ith value (counting from zero) can be accessed by specifying the desired index in square brackets, just as with Python lists. As shown in the following *figure 5.8*, we are accessing the elements of the arrays we have created above using `np.random()` earlier:

```
print("1-d array:", x1)
print("second element of first array:", x1[1])
print("last element of first array:", x1[-1])
print("first element of first array:", x1[0])
```

```
1-d array: [5 0 3 3 7 9]
second element of first array: 0
last element of first array: 9
first element of first array: 5
```

Figure 5.8: Accessing elements of the arrays

What about other dimension's array? It's quite simple. We just need to use a comma-separated tuple of indices as shown in the following *figure 5.9*, where we are accessing the first elements of 2D and 3D arrays:

```
print("2-d array:\n", x2)
print("first elements of 2-d array:\n", x2[0,0])
print("3-d array:\n", x3)
print("first element of 3-d array:\n", x3[0,0,0])
```

```
2-d array:
 [[3 5 2 4]
 [7 6 8 8]
 [1 6 7 7]]
first elements of 2-d array:
 3
3-d array:
 [[[8 1 5 9 8]
  [9 4 3 0 3]
  [5 0 2 3 8]
  [1 3 3 3 7]]

 [[0 1 9 9 0]
  [4 7 3 2 7]
  [2 0 0 4 5]
  [5 6 8 4 1]]

 [[4 9 8 1 1]
  [7 9 9 3 6]
  [7 2 0 3 5]
  [9 4 4 6 4]]]
first element of 3-d array:
 8
```

Figure 5.9: Accessing first elements of 2D and 3D arrays

The multi-dimensional array has its importance while handling data. For example, let's take a look at how one might store a movie-related data. A movie is nothing more than a time-varying sequence of images – i.e., an array of images. Each image is a two-dimensional array, with each element of the array representing a color. Color has three components – Red, Green, Blue. So, a movie can be modeled as a multidimensional array.

Slicing in NumPy array

As we used square brackets to access individual array elements, we can also use them to access subarrays with the slice notation, marked by the colon (:) character. Slicing is an important concept to access the element of an array or list. But unlike the list in array slicing, they return views rather than copies of the array data. It means if we create a subarray for an array and then modify any element, then the original array will also be modified. In the following *figure 5.10*, we created a 1D array, and then we will access its elements using slicing:

```
# create an array
x = np.arange(10)
print("our array:", x)
print("first five elements:", x[:5])
print("elements after index 5:", x[5:])
print("middle sub-array:", x[4:7])
print("every other element:", x[::2])
print("every other element, starting at index 1:", x[1::2])
print("elements in reversed order:", x[::-1])
```

```
our array: [0 1 2 3 4 5 6 7 8 9]
first five elements: [0 1 2 3 4]
elements after index 5: [5 6 7 8 9]
middle sub-array: [4 5 6]
every other element: [0 2 4 6 8]
every other element, starting at index 1: [1 3 5 7 9]
elements in reversed order: [9 8 7 6 5 4 3 2 1 0]
```

Figure 5.10: Creating 1D array

Again, for the multi-dimensional array, we need to use multiple slices with comma as shown in the following *figure 5.11*:

```
print("2-d array:\n", x2)
print("two rows, three columns:\n", x2[:2, :3])
```

```
2-d array:
 [[3 5 2 4]
 [7 6 8 8]
 [1 6 7 7]]
two rows, three columns:
 [[3 5 2]
 [7 6 8]]
```

Figure 5.11: Using multiple slices with comma for multidimensional array

As I mentioned previously, if we create a subarray, form an array, and make any changes in the subarray, then it will also change the original array. So, how can we be sure about the data integrity of an array? In such cases, make a copy of the original array using `copy()` and then modify without affecting the original array as shown in the following *figures 5.12* and *5.13*:

```python
# original array
print("original 2-d array:\n", x2)
# creating a 2X2 subarray from the original array
x2_sub = x2[:2, :2]
print("sub-array:\n", x2_sub)
# modifying sub-array
x2_sub[0, 0] = 88
print("modified sub array:\n", x2_sub)
# original array after sub-array changes
print("original array after changes in sub-array:\n", x2)
print("making a copy of the original array")
x2_sub_copy = x2[:2, :2].copy()
print("copy of the orinal array:\n", x2_sub_copy)
# modifying copied array
x2_sub_copy[0, 0] = 42
print("copied array after changes:\n", x2_sub_copy)
print("original array:\n", x2)
```

Figure 5.12: Using copy() function

```
original 2-d array:
 [[3 5 2 4]
 [7 6 8 8]
 [1 6 7 7]]
sub-array:
 [[3 5]
 [7 6]]
modified sub array:
 [[88  5]
 [ 7  6]]
original array after changes in sub-array:
 [[88  5  2  4]
 [ 7  6  8  8]
 [ 1  6  7  7]]
making a copy of the original array
copy of the orinal array:
 [[88  5]
 [ 7  6]]
copied array after changes:
 [[42  5]
 [ 7  6]]
original array:
 [[88  5  2  4]
 [ 7  6  8  8]
 [ 1  6  7  7]]
```

Figure 5.13: Modifying the array

Array concatenation

In some scenarios, you may need to combine two arrays into a single one. For this situation, NumPy has different methods – np.concatenate(), np.vstack(), and np.hstack().

The np.concatenate() method is useful for combining arrays of the same dimensions while np.vstack() and np.hstack() are good when you are working with arrays of mixed dimensions. For understanding each uses, we will first see how to combine two same dimension arrays and then we will see how to add different dimension arrays into one, as shown in the following *figures 5.14* and *5.15*:

```
# creating two sample arrays
x = np.array([1, 2, 3])
y = np.array([3, 2, 1])
# combining both arrays using concatenate
np.concatenate([x, y])
```

```
array([1, 2, 3, 3, 2, 1])
```

Figure 5.14: Combining same dimension arrays

```
# creating a sample array
x = np.array([1, 2, 3])
# creating a 2-d array
grid = np.array([[9, 8, 7],
                 [6, 5, 4]])

# vertically stack the arrays
np.vstack([x, grid])
```

```
array([[1, 2, 3],
       [9, 8, 7],
       [6, 5, 4]])
```

```
# horizontally stack the arrays
y = np.array([[99],
              [99]])
np.hstack([grid, y])
```

```
array([[ 9,  8,  7, 99],
       [ 6,  5,  4, 99]])
```

Figure 5.15: Adding different dimension arrays into one

For seeing different NumPy inbuilt features in your notebook, just press the tab key after the dot sign of NumPy alias (np).

Conclusion

In this chapter, we learnt how to perform standard mathematical operations on individual elements or complete array using NumPy. The range of functions covered linear algebra, statistical operations, and other specialized mathematical operations. For our purpose, we just need to know about the N-dimensional array or ndarray and the range of mathematical functions that are relevant to our research purpose. Till then, go chase your dreams, have an awesome day, make every second count. See you in the next chapter where we will learn about the second most important Python package – Pandas.

CHAPTER 6
Pandas and DataFrame

Pandas is a popular Python package for data science. It offers powerful, expressive, and flexible data structures that make data manipulation and analysis easy, among many other things. Pandas `DataFrame` is one of the very powerful and useful data structure among these. The Pandas library is one of the most preferred tools for data scientists to do data manipulation and analysis, next to `matplotlib` for data visualization and NumPy, the fundamental library for scientific computing in Python on which `pandas` was built.

Structure

- Importing Pandas
- Pandas data structures
- .loc[] and .iloc[]
- Some useful DataFrame Functions
- Handling missing values in DataFrame

Objective

After studying this chapter, you will be able to create, manipulate, and access the information you need from your data with the help of `pandas` data structures.

Importing Pandas

Importing `pandas` in your notebook is quite simple. Pandas is preinstalled with Anaconda distribution, so you don't need to install it. In any case, if it is not installed, you can install it by typing the following command in Anaconda Prompt (*figure 6.1*):

```
Anaconda Prompt

C:\Users\prateek1.gupta>set "KERAS_BACKEND=theano"

(base) C:\Users\prateek1.gupta>conda install -c anaconda pandas
```

Figure 6.1: *Installing Pandas*

Once you installed the `pandas`, you can import it as below:

```
# importing Pandas package using alias
import pandas as pd
```

Figure 6.2: *Importing Pandas*

Pandas data structures

Pandas have two main data structures widely used in data science, which are as follows:

- Series
- DataFrame

Series

Pandas is a one-dimensional labeled array capable of holding any data type such as integers, floats, and strings. It is similar to a NumPy 1-dimensional array. In addition to the values that are specified by the programmer, `pandas` assigns a label to each of the values. If the labels are not provided by the programmer, then `pandas` assigns labels (0 for the first element, 1 for the second element, and so on). A benefit of assigning labels to data values is that it becomes easier to perform manipulations on the dataset as the whole dataset becomes more of a dictionary where each value is associated with a label.

A pandas Series can be constructed using pd.Series() as shown in the following *figure 6.3*:

```
# creating an empty Series
x = pd.Series()
print("empty series example: ", x)
```

empty series example: Series([], dtype: float64)

Figure 6.3: Constructing pandas Series

In the output cell, you can see that it is showing the default data type of the Series as the float. Let's create another example of Series from the list of numbers (*figure 6.4*):

```
# series example
series1 = pd.Series([10,20,30,50])
print(series1)
```

```
0    10
1    20
2    30
3    50
dtype: int64
```

Figure 6.4: Another example of Series

In the preceding code example, you can see that the output is in tabular form with two columns – the first one is showing indexes starting from zero and the second one is showing the elements. This index column is generated by Series and if you want to re-index this with your index name, then you can do it in using index parameter as shown in the following *figure 6.5*:

```
# re-indexing the default index column
series2 = pd.Series([10,20,30,50], index=['a','b','c','d'])
print(series2)
```

```
a    10
b    20
c    30
d    50
dtype: int64
```

Figure 6.5: Re-indexing the default index column

The ways of accessing elements in a `Series` object are similar to what we have seen in NumPy. You can perform NumPy operations on `Series` data arrays as shown in the following *figure 6.6*:

```
# accessing a Series element
series2['b']
```

```
20
```

Figure 6.6: *Accessing a Series element*

Data manipulation with `Series` is also an easy task. We can apply mathematical calculations as we did in NumPy, as shown in the following *figure 6.7*:

```
# data manipulation with Series
print("adding 5 to a Series:\n", series2 + 5)
print("filtering series with greater than 30:\n", series2[series2>30])
print("square root of Series elements:\n", np.sqrt(series2))
```

```
adding 5 to a Series:
 a    15
 b    25
 c    35
 d    55
dtype: int64
filtering series with greater than 30:
 d    50
dtype: int64
square root of Series elements:
 a    3.162278
 b    4.472136
 c    5.477226
 d    7.071068
dtype: float64
```

Figure 6.7: *Data manipulation with Series*

Remember the dictionary data structure we have seen in an earlier chapter? We can convert this data structure to a `Series` so that dictionary's key and value can be transformed into a tabular form, as shown in the following *figure 6.8*:

```
# a sample dictionary
data = {'abc': 1, 'def': 2, 'ghi': 3}
print("dictionary example:\n", data)
# converting dictionary to series
pd.Series(data)
```

```
dictionary example:
 {'abc': 1, 'def': 2, 'ghi': 3}

abc    1
def    2
ghi    3
dtype: int64
```

Figure 6.8: A sample dictionary

DataFrame

Pandas is a two-dimensional labeled data structure with columns of potentially different types. You can imagine a `DataFrame` containing three components – index, rows, and columns. A `DataFrame` is a tabular data structure in which data is laid out in rows and column format (similar to a CSV and SQL file), but it can also be used for higher-dimensional data sets. The `DataFrame` object can contain homogenous and heterogeneous values and can be thought of as a logical extension of Series data structures.

In contrast to `Series`, where there is one index, a `DataFrame` object has one index for columns and one index for rows. This allows flexibility in accessing and manipulating data. We can create a `DataFrame` using `pd.DataFrame()` as shown in the following *figure 6.9*:

```
# creating an empty dataframe
df = pd.DataFrame()
print("dataframe example:\n", df)
```

```
dataframe example:
 Empty DataFrame
Columns: []
Index: []
```

Figure 6.9: Creating an empty DataFrame

Let's create a `DataFrame` from a list where the list contains the name and age of a person. We will also rename the column names of our `DataFrame` using columns parameter as shown in the following *figure 6.10*:

```
# a sample list containing name and age
data = [['Tom',10],['Harry',12],['Jim',13]]
# creating a dataframe form given list with column names
df = pd.DataFrame(data,columns=['Name','Age'])
df
```

	Name	Age
0	Tom	10
1	Harry	12
2	Jim	13

Figure 6.10: A sample list containing name and age

Selecting a column in a `DataFrame` is same as what we have seen earlier with other data structures. For example, if you want to know all names under the `Name` column from the preceding `DataFrame`, then you can access them in two ways as shown in the following *figure 6.11*.

```
# accessing a dataframe column- first way
df['Name']
```

```
0        Tom
1      Harry
2        Jim
Name: Name, dtype: object
```

```
# accessing a dataframe column- second way
df.Name
```

```
0        Tom
1      Harry
2        Jim
Name: Name, dtype: object
```

Figure 6.11: Accessing a DataFrame column

Let us suppose you want to add a new column to your `DataFrame` which will store the birth year of a person. You can do it easily as shown in the following *figure 6.12*:

```
# adding a column in existing dataframe
df['Year'] = 2008
df
```

	Name	Age	Year
0	Tom	10	2008
1	Harry	12	2008
2	Jim	13	2008

Figure 6.12: Adding a column in existing DataFrame

Next, the deleting of a column is also an easy task. You can use `.pop()` to delete a column. Look at the following *figure 6.13*:

```
print("original dataframe:\n", df)
del df['Year']
print("dataframe after del:\n", df)
df.pop('Age')
print("dataframe after pop:\n", df)
```

```
original dataframe:
      Name  Age  Year
0      Tom   10  2008
1    Harry   12  2008
2      Jim   13  2008
dataframe after del:
      Name  Age
0      Tom   10
1    Harry   12
2      Jim   13
dataframe after pop:
      Name
0      Tom
1    Harry
2      Jim
```

Figure 6.13: Deleting a column in existing DataFrame

.loc[] and .iloc[]

Selecting a row or an index in a `DataFrame` is quite different but very easy if you know how to use the `.loc[]` and `.iloc[]` functions. For understanding both, let's first create a `DataFrame` to store the company stock price, as shown in the following *figure 6.14*:

```
# a sample dataframe containing compaany stock data
data = pd.DataFrame({'price':[95, 25, 85, 41],
                     'ticker':['AXP', 'CSCO', 'DIS', 'MSFT'],
                     'company':['American Express', 'Cisco', 'Walt Disney','Microsoft']})
data
```

	company	price	ticker
0	American Express	95	AXP
1	Cisco	25	CSCO
2	Walt Disney	85	DIS
3	Microsoft	41	MSFT

Figure 6.14: A sample DataFrame containing company stock data

To access the value that is at index 0, in column `company`, you can do it either using the label or by indicating the position. For label based indexing, you can use `.loc[]` and for position based indexing you can use `.iloc[]` as shown in the following *figure 6.15*:

```
# access the value that is at index 0, in column 'company' using loc
print(data.loc[0]['company'])
# access the value that is at index 0, in column 'company' using iloc
print(data.loc[0][0])
```

```
American Express
American Express
```

Figure 6.15: Accessing value that is at index 0

From the preceding example, it is quite clear that `.loc[]` works on labels of your index. This means that if you give in `loc[3]`, you look for the values of your `DataFrame` that have an index labeled 3.

On the other hand, `.iloc[]` works on the positions in your index. This means that if you give in `iloc[3]`, you look for the values of your `DataFrame` that are at index '3'.

Some Useful DataFrame Functions

DataFrame is a very useful data structure that you will use often in your daily task. Storing data in a DataFrame has various benefits and it's quite simple for data analysis. Let's see some quite useful functions of a DataFrame:

```
# inspecting top 5 rows of a dataframe
print("top five data:\n", data.head())
# inspecting below 5 rows of a dataframe
print("below 5 data:\n", data.tail())
```

```
top five data:
              company  price ticker
0   American Express     95    AXP
1              Cisco     25   CSCO
2        Walt Disney     85    DIS
3          Microsoft     41   MSFT
below 5 data:
              company  price ticker
0   American Express     95    AXP
1              Cisco     25   CSCO
2        Walt Disney     85    DIS
3          Microsoft     41   MSFT
```

Figure 6.16: Useful DataFrame functions

The .head() and .tail() are useful when you have thousands of rows and columns in your data and you want to inspect it in a quick view, as shown in the preceding *figure 6.16*.

Next, if you want to check data type of each column in your data, you can do so by using .dtypes, shown in the following *figure 6.17*:

```
# check data type of columns
data.dtypes
```

```
company       object
price          int64
ticker        object
dtype: object
```

Figure 6.17: Checking data type of columns

Pandas `DataFrame` has also one unique method which can give you descriptive statistics (mean, median, count, etc.) of your dataset. For knowing these statistics you can use `.describe()` as shown in the following *figure 6.18*. From this description, we can easily say the highest stock price is 95 and the minimum stock price is 25 and the total no. of stocks is 4. Imagine if this data contains records of millions of companies! Without `pandas` it will be much more difficult to know the statistics of the data.

```
# descriptive statistics of the data
data.describe()
```

	price
count	4.000000
mean	61.500000
std	33.798422
min	25.000000
25%	37.000000
50%	63.000000
75%	87.500000
max	95.000000

Figure 6.18: Using describe() function to know statistics

If you have non-numeric data, then applying to the describe function would produce statistics such as count, unique, frequency. In addition to this, you can also calculate skewness (skew), kurtosis (kurt), percent changes, difference, and other statistics.

Next, the important function of a Pandas `DataFrame` is to check the information of your data including column data type, non-null values, and memory usage. This can be achieved using `.info()` as shown in the following *figure 6.19*:

```
# information of the dataframe
data.info()

<class 'pandas.core.frame.DataFrame'>
RangeIndex: 4 entries, 0 to 3
Data columns (total 3 columns):
company    4 non-null object
price      4 non-null int64
ticker     4 non-null object
dtypes: int64(1), object(2)
memory usage: 176.0+ bytes
```

Figure 6.19: Checking information of the DataFrame

Similarly, there is `shape`, `columns`, `corr()`, `cov()` functions which you will see in the later chapters of this book. Try these functions in your notebook and explore what information you get from them.

Handling missing values in DataFrame

As a data scientist, you will come across uncleaned data with missing values most of the time. Here missing means data is not available (NA) for any reason. You cannot simply ignore those missing data. In fact, before applying any machine learning algorithm, you need to handle such values. Pandas provides a flexible way to handle missing data. Pandas uses NaN (Not a number) or sometimes NaTas, the default missing value marker; with the help of it you can detect it easily using `isnull()` function. Let's understand this function by first creating a DataFrame with missing values as shown in the following *figure 6.20*:

```
# a sample dataframe
df = pd.DataFrame(np.random.randn(5, 3), index=['a', 'c', 'e', 'f', 'h'],
                  columns=['one', 'two', 'three'])
# creating a data with missing values by reindexing
df2 = df.reindex(['a', 'b', 'c', 'd', 'e', 'f', 'g', 'h'])
df2
```

	one	two	three
a	-1.282674	1.081757	-0.559330
b	NaN	NaN	NaN
c	1.009585	0.876217	0.830863
d	NaN	NaN	NaN
e	1.308541	-0.434903	-1.224001
f	1.995670	1.199008	-0.671072
g	NaN	NaN	NaN
h	0.032248	-1.083125	-0.679454

Figure 6.20: A sample DataFrame

You can see missing values as NaN. Now we can check the missing values using isnull() function and then count the sum of the missing values using sum() function as shown in the following *figure 6.21*. The isnull() function returns a Boolean same-sized object indicating if the values are missing and sum() function counts the True values of the Boolean:

```
# checking missing values using isnull()
print(df2.isnull())
missing_values_count = df2.isnull().sum()
print("count of missing values:\n", missing_values_count)
```

```
     one    two  three
a  False  False  False
b   True   True   True
c  False  False  False
d   True   True   True
e  False  False  False
f  False  False  False
g   True   True   True
h  False  False  False
count of missing values:
 one      3
two      3
three    3
dtype: int64
```

Figure 6.21: Checking missing values

Once you know the total count of missing values, you can think about how to handle those. If you don't have any clue about why there are missing values, one simple way of dealing with them is by simply dropping them using .dropna() function as shown in the following *figure 6.22*:

```
# remove all the rows that contain a missing value
df2 = df2.dropna()
print(df2)
```

```
        one       two     three
a -1.282674  1.081757 -0.559330
c  1.009585  0.876217  0.830863
e  1.308541 -0.434903 -1.224001
f  1.995670  1.199008 -0.671072
h  0.032248 -1.083125 -0.679454
```

Figure 6.22: Removing all rows containing missing value

The `dropna()` function can also be applied on the basis of a column. You can remove all columns with at least one missing value using `axis=1` parameter in `dropna()` function. For example, let's apply this approach to the original `df2` DataFrame. You need to rerun the DataFrame `df2` creation cell before running the following cell, otherwise you will get the wrong output:

```
# remove all columns with at least one missing value
columns_with_na_dropped = df2.dropna(axis=1)
columns_with_na_dropped.head()
```

a

b

c

d

e

Figure 6.23: Removing all columns with missing values

Using column-based removal of NaN values could be risky, as you may risk losing all the columns if every column has NaN values. Instead, `dropna()` with rows approach is useful in this case.

The second approach to handle missing values is to fill them either with zero or with the mean/median or with the occurrence of a word. Let's see how we can fill missing values (refer to the following *figures 6.24* and *6.25*):

```
# filling NaN with zeros
df3 = df2.fillna(0)
df3
```

	one	two	three
a	2.000749	-0.256641	-0.041130
b	0.000000	0.000000	0.000000
c	-0.074203	-1.090353	-0.066285
d	0.000000	0.000000	0.000000
e	1.088535	-1.029808	0.553896
f	1.316821	0.125611	-0.627532
g	0.000000	0.000000	0.000000
h	-0.623504	-1.266855	1.043820

Figure 6.24: Filling missing values

```
# replace all NA's the value that comes directly after it in the same column
# then replace all the reamining na's with 0
df4 = df2.fillna(method = 'bfill', axis=0).fillna(0)
df4
```

	one	two	three
a	2.000749	-0.256641	-0.041130
b	-0.074203	-1.090353	-0.066285
c	-0.074203	-1.090353	-0.066285
d	1.088535	-1.029808	0.553896
e	1.088535	-1.029808	0.553896
f	1.316821	0.125611	-0.627532
g	-0.623504	-1.266855	1.043820
h	-0.623504	-1.266855	1.043820

Figure 6.25: Filling missing values

In the preceding code cell, we are filling the missing values using the backward filling method of Pandas DataFrame. Similarly, you can use forward filling using the ffil() method.

Conclusion

The fast, flexible, and expressive pandas data structures are designed to make real-world data analysis significantly easier; but this might not be immediately the case for those who are just getting started with it. There is so much functionality built into this package that learning the options in just one go could be overwhelming. It is highly recommended to practice the functionalities with suitable case-studies. So, open your notebook, apply the learnings of this chapter, and explore more. In the next chapter, we will learn how to interact with different databases in Python.

CHAPTER 7

Interacting with Databases

As a data scientist, you will interact with the databases constantly. For this purpose, you need to know how to query, build, and write to different databases. Knowledge of **SQL** (**Structured Query Language**) is a perfect fit for this. SQL is all about data. SQL is used for three things. It used to Read/Retrieve data – so data is often stored in a database. It is also used to Write data in a database, and to update and insert new data. Python has its toolkit – SQLAlchemy which provides an accessible and intuitive way to query, build, and write to SQLite, MySQL, and PostgreSQL databases (among many others). We will cover all required database details specific to data science here.

Structure

- What is SQLAlchemy?
- Installing SQLAlchemy package
- How to use SQLAlchemy?
- SQLAlchemy engine configuration
- Creating a table in a database
- Inserting data in the table
- Update a record

- How to join two tables

Objective

After studying this chapter, you will become familiar with the fundamentals of relational databases and relational model. You will learn how to connect to a database and interact with it by writing basic SQL queries, both in raw SQL as well as with SQLAlchemy.

What is SQLAlchemy?

SQLAlchemy is the Python SQL toolkit and Object Relational Mapper that gives you the full power and flexibility of SQL. It provides a nice *Pythonic* way of interacting with databases. Rather than dealing with the differences between specific dialects of traditional SQL such as MySQL or PostgreSQL or Oracle, you can leverage the Pythonic framework of SQLAlchemy to streamline your workflow and more efficiently query your data.

Installing SQLAlchemy package

Let's start our journey by first installing the SQLAlchemy package in our notebook. You can install this package from the Anaconda Distribution using the command (`conda install -c anaconda sqlalchemy`) in Anaconda Prompt as shown in the following *figure 7.1*:

```
Anaconda Prompt

C:\Users\prateek1.gupta>set "KERAS_BACKEND=theano"

(base) C:\Users\prateek1.gupta>conda install -c anaconda sqlalchemy
```

Figure 7.1: Installing SQLAlchemy package

Once this package is installed, you can import it in your notebook as shown in the following *figure 7.2*:

```
In [1]:   import sqlalchemy as db
```

Figure 7.2: Importing package in the notebook

How to use SQLAlchemy?

Before using our toolkit, there should be a database to whom you want to connect first. We can use SQLAlchemy to connect with PostgreSQL, MySQL, Oracle, Microsoft SQL, SQLite, and many others. For our learning purpose, we will use MySQL db. You can download and install the MYSQL database from their official website:

https://dev.mysql.com/downloads/installer/

And for creating the database, tables, etc., you can install workbench using the following link:

https://dev.mysql.com/downloads/workbench/

After installing the MySQL workbench, you need to first create a connection there. For this, open the workbench and click on the **+** icon as highlighted in the following *figure 7.3*:

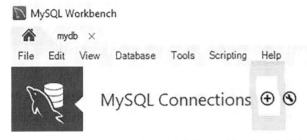

Figure 7.3: *Open MySQL workbench and click on the + icon*

Once you click on + icon, a pop-up screen will open. Here you need to give a connection name, username, and password for creating the connection. Note down the connection name, hostname, port, and password because we will need this information later. Once you complete this step, your connection is ready to be used:

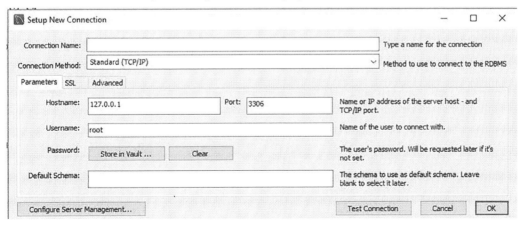

Figure 7.4: *Setting up new connection*

After the successful creation of a connection, the next step is to create a schema. For this right-click in the **SCHEMAS** menu and select option `Create Schema`:

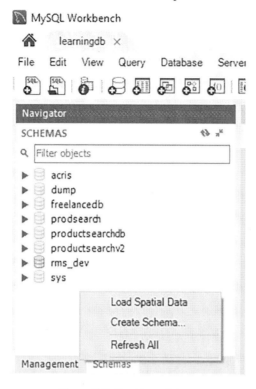

Figure 7.5: Creating a Schema

In the preceding *figure 7.5*, it is showing many schemas that I created earlier. Once you click on `Create Schema` option, follow the screen by entering the schema name and then selecting default options. In the preceding example, I have saved the schema with the name `rms_dev`.

SQLAlchemy engine configuration

Once you know your database information, the next step is to interact with the database. For this purpose, SQLAlchemy uses Engine. Creating an Engine with SQLAlchemy is quite simple. You need to use its `create_engine` api. You can import this API with the following import – `from sqlalchemy import create_engine`. This `create_engine()` API uses the following syntax to store the database information as parameters:

```
dialect+driver://username:password@host:port/database
```

Figure 7.6: SQLAlchemy create_engine() syntax

Here, dialect names include the identifying name of the SQLAlchemy dialect, a name such as `sqlite`, `mysql`, `postgresql`, `oracle`, or `mssql`. The `drivername` is the name of the DBAPI to be used to connect to the database using all lowercase letters. If not specified, a `default` DBAPI will be imported if available – this default is typically the most widely known driver available for that backend. You can check the name of the DBAPI by clicking on the following link:

https://docs.sqlalchemy.org/en/latest/core/engines.html#mysql

In the following *figure 7.7*, I am going to use my MySQL db connection details in the Jupyter notebook for creating an engine:

```
engine = db.create_engine('mysql://root:admin@127.0.0.1:3306/rms_dev')
```

```
connection = engine.connect()
```

Figure 7.7: Creating an engine

Here I am passing my db details (with username as root and password as admin) in the required format of `create_engine()` API, then I am connecting with the database using engine's `connect()`. Since we have created a new schema, there is no table. So, let's create a new table/data there first.

> If you face **No module named 'MySQLdb'** error, it means you need to install mysqlclient that you can install from the anaconda prompt using 'pip install mysqlclient' command.

Creating a table in a database

Since we have connected to our engine, let's create a table by using the `execute()` method of Engine. In this example, I am creating a table to hold customer-specific data-name and address. SQL syntax for creating a table is shown in the following *figure 7.8*:

```
CREATE  TABLE [IF NOT EXISTS] `TableName` (`fieldname` dataType [optional parameters]) ENGINE = sto
rage Engine;
```

Figure 7.8: Creating a table

In our case, we have already connected to our engine, so no need to use the `ENGINE` parameter. First I am storing my create table SQL query in a variable named `query`, then I am passing this query to Engine's `execute()` method. To check if my table is created or not, I am printing the table name and in the end, I am closing my database connection:

```
query = "CREATE TABLE customers (name VARCHAR(255), address VARCHAR(255))"
```

```
connection.execute(query)
print("Table Name:", engine.table_names())
connection.close()
```

```
Table Name: ['customers']
```

Figure 7.9: Printing the table name

Always remember to close the database connection after any operation, just like we did with `connection.close()`.

Inserting data in a table

Once you have created a table, it's time to insert some data into it. For adding new data to an existing table, we will use SQL insert query which syntax is as shown in the following *figure 7.10*:

```
INSERT INTO table_name ( field1, field2,...fieldN )
    VALUES
    ( value1, value2,...valueN );
```

Figure 7.10: Inserting data in a table

In our customers' table, let us add a customer name and address as shown in the following *figure 7.11*:

```
engine = db.create_engine('mysql://root:admin@127.0.0.1:3306/schemaexample')
connection = engine.connect()
sql = "INSERT INTO customers (name, address) VALUES ('Prateek', 'India')"
connection.execute(sql)
connection.close()
```

Figure 7.11: Inserting data in a table

Now, to check the existing records of the table, we can use the `select` query of SQL, and then we can fetch all rows using `fetchall()` of sqlalchemyapi as shown in the following *figure 7.12*:

```
engine = db.create_engine('mysql://root:admin@127.0.0.1:3306/schemaexample')
connection = engine.connect()
sql = "SELECT * from customers"
result = connection.execute(sql)
print("table data:", result.fetchall())
connection.close()
```

```
table data: [('Prateek', 'India')]
```

Figure 7.12: Checking existing records

In this way, you are now able to read the data from a database easily. You will be writing similar codes which will help you fetch thousands of data from a database for your analysis.

Update a record

Updating an existing record is a daily task and you must know how to run updates on your records in case a record was wrongly inserted into the db. In the following *figure 7.13*, we are going to update our existing customer's address using update SQL query:

```
engine = db.create_engine('mysql://root:admin@127.0.0.1:3306/schemaexample')
connection = engine.connect()
sql = "UPDATE customers SET address = 'Singapore' WHERE address = 'India'"
connection.execute(sql)
print("record(s) is updated")
q = "SELECT * from customers"
result = connection.execute(q)
print("table data:", result.fetchall())
connection.close()
```

```
record(s) is updated
table data: [('Prateek', 'Singapore')]
```

Figure 7.13: Updating a record

For deleting a record, you can use WHERE clause to delete a record based on a column as shown in the following *figure 7.14*:

```
engine = db.create_engine('mysql://root:admin@127.0.0.1:3306/schemaexample')
connection = engine.connect()
sql = "DELETE FROM customers WHERE address = 'Singapore'"
connection.execute(sql)
print("record is deleted!")
connection.close()
```

```
record is deleted!
```

Figure 7.14: Deleting a record

How to join two tables

In the relational database, there may be many tables, and in those tables, there may be a relationship between their columns. In such a condition you need to join tables. A real-world example of this scenario is from the e-commerce domain where product-related data is in one table, user-specific data is in another table, and inventory is in another one; here you need to fetch product details based on user or inventory. Joining the table can be done in three ways – inner join, left join, and right join. Let's understand each of these joining.

Inner join

We can join or combine rows from two or more tables based on a related column by using a JOIN statement. Let's create two tables – users and products in our db to understand this type of joining first. Don't forget to create and then connect your db connection before running the following code:

```
query = "CREATE TABLE IF NOT EXISTS users (id INT, name VARCHAR(255), prod_id INT)"
connection.execute(query)
sql = "INSERT INTO users (id, name, prod_id) VALUES (1, 'Prateek', 11),(2,'John',12),(3,'Tom',13)"
connection.execute(sql)
query2 = "CREATE TABLE IF NOT EXISTS products (id INT, name VARCHAR(255))"
connection.execute(query2)
sql2 = "INSERT INTO products (id, name) VALUES (11, 'Apple'),(12,'Samsung'),(15,'Vivo')"
connection.execute(sql2)
connection.close()
```

Figure 7.15: Inner join

Once you run the preceding code, you can also verify the outcome in your workbench. Go to your workbench and select the schema you created in the beginning, and then expand that schema. You will see a new table, which you have just created from the above cell, as shown in the following *figure 7.16*:

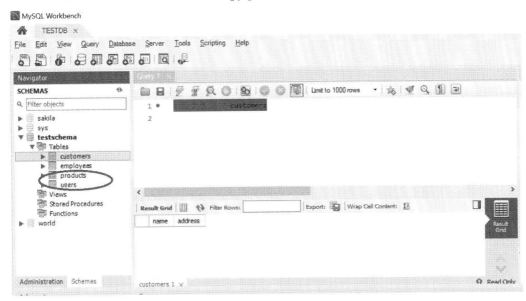

Figure 7.16: *A new table is created*

Since in our example, users and products tables have product ID as a common column, we can join users and products tables based on the product ID to see which user has bought which product, as shown in the following *figure 7.17*:

```
engine = db.create_engine('mysql://root:admin@127.0.0.1:3306/schemaexample')
connection = engine.connect()
join_query = "SELECT \
  users.name AS user, \
  products.name AS favorite \
  FROM users \
  INNER JOIN products ON users.prod_id = products.id"
result = connection.execute(join_query)
myresult = result.fetchall()
for bought_product in myresult:
    print(bought_product)

('Prateek', 'Apple')
('John', 'Samsung')
```

Figure 7.17: *Joining tables based on product ID*

INNER JOIN only shows the records where there is a match.

Left join

The left join returns all the rows from the table on the left even if no matching rows have been found in the table on the right. Where no matches have been found in the table on the right, none is returned as shown in the following *figure 7.18*:

```
left_join = "SELECT \
   users.name AS user, \
   products.name AS favorite \
   FROM users \
   LEFT JOIN products ON users.prod_id = products.id"
result = connection.execute(left_join)
myresult = result.fetchall()
for bought_product in myresult:
      print(bought_product)
```

```
('Prateek', 'Apple')
('John', 'Samsung')
('Tom', None)
```

Figure 7.18: Left join

Don't forget to create and connect the `dbconnection` before executing any query, as we have done in the earlier normal join example.

Right join

The right join is the opposite of the left join. The right join returns all the columns from the table on the right, even if no matching rows have been found in the table on the left. Where no matches have been found in the table on the left, none is returned, as shown in the following *figure 7.19*:

```
right_join = "SELECT \
   users.name AS user, \
   products.name AS favorite \
   FROM users \
   RIGHT JOIN products ON users.prod_id = products.id"
result = connection.execute(right_join)
myresult = result.fetchall()
for bought_product in myresult:
      print(bought_product)
```

```
('Prateek', 'Apple')
('John', 'Samsung')
(None, 'Vivo')
```

Figure 7.19: Right join

Don't forget to create and connect the db connection before executing any query, as we have done in the earlier normal join example.

Conclusion

SQL proficiency is a basic requirement for many data science jobs, including data analyst, business intelligence developer, programmer analyst, database administrator, and database developer. You'll need SQL to communicate with the database and work with the data. Learning SQL will give you a good understanding of relational databases, which are the bread and butter of data science. It will also boost your professional profile, especially compared to those with limited database experience. So, keep practicing the Python skills of interfacing with sql shared in this chapter by creating your databases/schemas. In the next chapter, we will learn about the core concepts of statistics that are often used in data science.

CHAPTER 8
Thinking Statistically in Data Science

Statistics play an important role in data science. If it is used wisely, you can extract knowledge from the vague, complex, and difficult real world. A clear understanding of statistics and the meanings of various statistical measures is important to distinguish between truth and misdirection. In this chapter, you will learn about the important statistical concepts and Python-based statistics tools that will help you understand the data focused on data science.

Structure

- Statistics in data science
- Types of statistical data/variables
- Mean, median, and mode
- Basics of probability
- Statistical distributions
- Pearson correlation coefficient
- Probability density function
- Real-world example
- Statistical inference and hypothesis testing

Objective

After studying the chapter, you will be able to apply statistics in a Pythonic way to analyze the data.

Statistics in data science

Statistics is the discipline of analyzing data. In data science, you will use two types of statistics – Descriptive and Inference statistics. Descriptive statistics include exploratory data analysis, unsupervised learning, clustering, and basic data summaries. Descriptive statistics have many uses, most notably helping us get familiar with a data set. Descriptive statistics usually are the starting point for any analysis; therefore, it enables us to present the data in a more meaningful way, which allows a simpler interpretation of the data.

The inference is the process of making conclusions about populations from samples. Inference includes most of the activities traditionally associated with statistics such as estimation, confidence intervals, hypothesis tests, and variability. Inference forces us to formally define targets of estimations or hypotheses. It forces us to think about the population that we're trying to generalize from our sample. In statistics, population refers to the total set of observations that can be made. For example, if we are studying the weight of adult women, the population is the set of weights of all the women in the world. If we are studying the **grade point average** (**GPA**) of students at Harvard, the population is the set of GPAs of all the students at Harvard.

Types of statistical data/variables

When working with statistics, it's important to recognize the different types of data. Most data fall into one of two groups – numerical or categorical. Example of numerical or quantitative data is a measurement, such as a person's height, weight, IQ, or blood pressure; or they're a count, such as the number of stocks shares a person owns, how many teeth a dog has, or how many pages you can read of your favorite book before you fall asleep. Categorical or qualitative data represent characteristics such as a person's gender, marital status, hometown, or the types of movies they like. Categorical data can take on numerical values (such as "1" indicating male and "2" indicating female), but those numbers don't have mathematical meaning. You couldn't add them together, for example. (Other names for categorical data are qualitative data, or Yes/No data).

These two types of variables in statistics can be divided further, as shown in the following *figure 8.1*:

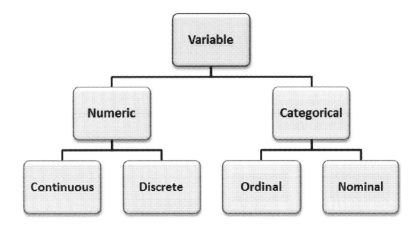

Figure 8.1: *Variables in statistics*

Let's understand these categorizations:

- **Discrete variables:** Discrete variables are countable in a finite amount of time. For example, you can count the change in your pocket. You can count the money in your bank account. You could also count the amount of money in everyone's bank accounts.

- **Continuous variables:** Continuous variables would take forever to count. You would never finish counting them. For example, take the example of a person's age. You can't count *age* because it could be – 25 years, 10 months, 2 days, 5 hours, 4 seconds, 4 milliseconds, 8 microseconds, 9 nanoseconds, and so on. You could turn age into a discrete variable and then you could count it; for example, a person's age in years.

- **Nominal variables:** Nominal variables are variables that have two or more categories, but which do not have an intrinsic order. For example, a real estate agent could classify their types of property into distinct categories such as houses, condos, co-ops, or bungalows. So, the *type of property* is a nominal variable with 4 categories called houses, condos, co-ops, and bungalows.

- **Ordinal variables:** Ordinal variables are variables that have two or more categories just like nominal variables, only the categories can also be ordered or ranked. So, if you asked someone if they liked the policies of the Republican Party, and they answered either *not very much, they are OK*, or *yes, a lot*, then you have an ordinal variable. Because you have 3 categories, namely, *not very much, they are OK*, and *yes, a lot*, and you can rank them from the most positive (yes, a lot), to the middle response (they are OK), to the least positive (not very much). However, even if we can rank the levels, we cannot place *value* to them; we cannot say that *they are OK* is twice as positive as *not very much* for example.

Mean, median, and mode

Mean is simply another name for average. To calculate the mean of a data set, divide the sum of all values by the number of values. We can compute the arithmetic mean along the specified axis using NumPy. Following is the Pythonic way to calculate the mean:

```
import pandas as pd
import numpy as np
a = np.array([[1, 2], [3, 4]])
print(np.mean(a))
print(np.mean(a, axis=0))
print(np.mean(a, axis=1))
```

```
2.5
[2. 3.]
[1.5 3.5]
```

Figure 8.2: Pythonic way to calculate mean

Median is the number that lies in the middle of a list of ordered numbers. The numbers may be in ascending or descending order. The median is easy to find when there is an odd number of elements in the data set. When there is an even number of elements, you need to take the average of the two numbers that fall in the center of the ordered list. Following is the way to calculate the median:

```
a = np.array([[10, 7, 4], [3, 2, 1]])
print(np.median(a))
print(np.median(a, axis=0))
print(np.median(a, axis=1))
```

```
3.5
[6.5 4.5 2.5]
[7. 2.]
```

Figure 8.3: Calculating the median

Mode is that value which appears the most number of times in a data. To calculate mode, we need another package named as `stats` from `scipy` along with `numpy`:

```
from scipy import stats
a = np.array([[1, 3, 4, 2, 2, 7],
              [5, 2, 2, 1, 4, 1],
              [3, 3, 2, 2, 1, 1]])
m = stats.mode(a)
print(m[0])

[[1 3 2 2 1 1]]
```

Figure 8.4: Calculating the mode

Now the question arises as to when to use mean, median, or mode. The answer is that it depends on your dataset. The mean is a good measure of the average when a data set contains values that are relatively evenly spread with no exceptionally high or low values. The median is a good measure of the average value when the data include exceptionally high or low values because these have little influence on the outcome. The median is the most suitable measure of average for data classified on an ordinal scale. The mode is the measure of average that can be used with nominal data. For example, late-night users of the library were classified by faculty as 14% science students, 32% social science students, and 54% biological science students. No median or mean can be calculated but the mode is that the biological science students as students from this faculty were the most common.

Basics of probability

We all must agree that our lives are full of uncertainties. We don't know the outcomes of a situation until it happens. Will it rain today? Will I pass the next math test? Will my favorite team win the toss? Will I get a promotion in the next 6 months? All these questions are examples of uncertain situations we live in. If you understand these uncertain situations, you can plan things accordingly. That's why probability plays an important role in the analysis.

We must know the following terminology related to probability – experiment is the uncertain situation which could have multiple outcomes; the outcome is the result of a single trail, the event is one or more outcome from an experiment, and probability is a measure of how likely an event is.

Statistical distributions

One of the most important things you need to know while arming yourself with prerequisite statistics for data science is the distributions. While the concept of probability gives us the mathematical calculations, distributions help us visualize what's happening underneath. Following are some important distributions we must know:

Poisson distribution

Poisson distribution is used to calculate the number of events that might occur in a continuous-time interval. For instance, how many phone calls will be received at any time period, or how many people might show up in a queue? The Poisson distribution is a `discrete` function, meaning that the event can only be measured as occurring or not as occurring, meaning the variable can only be measured in whole numbers.

To calculate this function in Python, we can use `scipy` library's `stats` package and to visualize samples, we can use `matplotlib` library as shown in the following *figure 8.5*:

```python
from scipy.stats import poisson
import matplotlib.pyplot as plt
plt.title('Probability Distribution Example')
arr = []
rv = poisson(25)
for num in range(0,40):
    arr.append(rv.pmf(num))
prob = rv.pmf(28)
plt.grid(True)
plt.plot(arr, linewidth=2.0)
plt.plot([28], [prob], marker='o', markersize=6, color="red")
plt.show()
```

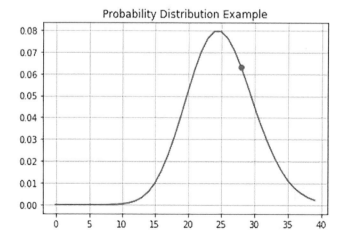

Figure 8.5: Poisson Distribution

In the preceding code cell, first we have imported the Poisson package from the `scipy.statsapi` with `matplotlib` library to plot the distribution. Then we have created a Poisson discrete random variable named `rv`. Next, we have calculated the **probability mass function (pmf)** which is a function that can predict or show the mathematical probability of a value occurring at a certain data point. In the end, we just plotted the graph using the `matplotlib` library's `plot()` and `show()` functions.

Binomial distribution

A distribution where only two outcomes are possible, such as success or failure, gain or loss, win or lose, and where the probability of success and failure is the same for all the trials is called a Binomial distribution. We can use the `matplotlib` Python library which has in-built functions to create such probability distribution graphs. Also, the `scipy` package helps in creating the binomial distribution as shown in the following *figure 8.6*:

```python
from scipy.stats import binom
import matplotlib.pyplot as plt
fig, ax = plt.subplots(1, 1)
x = range(7)
n, p = 6, 0.5
rv = binom(n, p)
ax.vlines(x, 0, rv.pmf(x), colors='k', linestyles='-', lw=1,label='Probablity of Success')
ax.legend(loc='best', frameon=False)
plt.show()
```

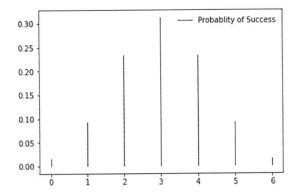

Figure 8.6: Binomial Distribution

In the preceding code cell, we have imported the `binom` package from the `scipy.statsapi`. Then we have created a binomial discrete random variable named `rv`. Now to plot vertical lines at each `x` from `ymin` to `ymax` we have used `matplotlib` library's `vlines()` function where we are passing our **probability mass function (pmf)** as one argument and then we are plotting and displaying the distribution as we did earlier.

Normal distribution

Any distribution is known as normal distribution if it has the following characteristics:

- The mean, median, and mode of the distribution coincide.

- The curve of the distribution is bell-shaped and symmetrical about the line, exactly half of the values are to the left of the center and the other half to the right.

You can calculate and draw the same using Python's `scipy` and `matplotlib` packages as shown in the following *figure 8.7*:

```
import numpy as np
import matplotlib.pyplot as plt
from scipy.stats import norm

range = np.arange(-3,3,0.001)
plt.plot(range, norm.pdf(range, 0, 1))
plt.show()
```

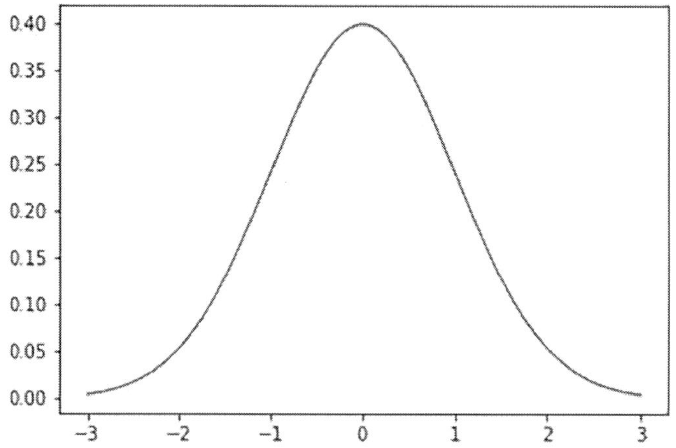

Figure 8.7: Normal Distribution

In the preceding code cell, we imported the norm package from `scipy.statsapi`, then we have passed the `probability density function (pdf)` of normal continuous – `discrete` variable as `np` argument in `plot()` function. Here a `pdf` is a function that can predict or show the mathematical probability of a value occurring between a certain interval in the function. You will know more about this function later in this chapter.

Pearson correlation coefficient

In real-world data problems, you may face hundreds of attributes and you cannot include all of them for your analysis. That's why you need to find a relationship between each variable. The Pearson correlation coefficient is a measure of the strength of a linear association between two variables and is denoted by r. It attempts to draw a line of best fit through the data of two variables, and the Pearson correlation coefficient, r, indicates how far away all these data points are to this line of best fit (i.e., how well the data points fit this new model/line of best fit).

The Pearson correlation coefficient can take a range of values from +1 to -1. A value of 0 indicates that there is no association between the two variables. A value greater than 0 indicates a positive association, that is, as the value of one variable increases, so does the value of the other variable. A value less than 0 indicates a negative association, that is, as the value of one variable increases, the value of the other variable decreases. The stronger the association of the two variables, the closer the Pearson correlation coefficient is.

Following is a guideline (depending on what you are measuring) to interpret the Pearson's correlation coefficient:

Strength of Association	Coefficient, r	
	Positive	Negative
Small	.1 to .3	-0.1 to -0.3
Medium	.3 to .5	-0.3 to -0.5
Large	.5 to 1.0	-0.5 to -1.0

Figure 8.8: Pearson correlation coefficient

Pythonic way to interpret Pearson's correlation coefficient where r_row denotes Pearson's correlation coefficient and p_value denotes the probability of an uncorrelated system producing datasets that have a Pearson correlation at least as extreme as the one computed from these datasets. The p-values are not entirely reliable but are probably reasonable for datasets larger than 500 or so:

```
import scipy
from scipy.stats import pearsonr
x = scipy.array([-0.65499887,  2.34644428, 3.0])
y = scipy.array([-1.46049758,  3.86537321, 21.0])
r_row, p_value = pearsonr(x, y)
print(r_row)
print(p_value)
```

```
0.7961701483197555
0.41371200873701036
```

Figure 8.9: Calculating Pearson correlation coefficient

Probability Density Function (PDF)

Probability Density Function (**PDF**) is used to specify the probability of the random variable falling within a range of values, as opposed to taking on anyone's value. The probability density function is nonnegative everywhere, and its integral over the entire space is equal to one.

In Python, we can interpret the PDF in the following way – first import `norm` package from `scipy.stats` library to create a normalized probability density function with NumPy and `matplotlib` libraries. In this example, we are creating a variable, `x`, and assigning it to `np.arange(-4,4,0.001)`, that range from -4 to 4 with an increment of 0.001, then we plot a normalized probability density function with the line, `plt.plot(x, norm.pdf(x))`:

```python
from scipy.stats import norm
import numpy as np
import matplotlib.pyplot as plt
x= np.arange(-4,4,0.001)
plt.plot(x, norm.pdf(x))
plt.show()
```

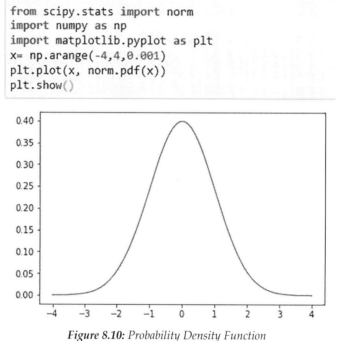

Figure 8.10: Probability Density Function

Real-world example

Pearson correlation is used in thousands of real-life situations. One recent example is – scientists in China wanted to know if there was a relationship between how weedy rice populations are different genetically. The goal was to find out the evolutionary potential of the rice. Pearson's correlation between the two groups was analyzed. It showed a positive Pearson Product Moment correlation of between 0.783 and 0.895 for weedy rice populations. This figure is quite high, which suggested a fairly strong relationship.

Statistical inference and hypothesis testing

Statistical inference is the process of deducing properties of an underlying distribution by analysis of data. Inferential statistical analysis infers properties about a population – this includes testing hypotheses and deriving estimates. Statistics prove helpful in analyzing most collections of data. Hypothesis testing can justify conclusions even when no scientific theory exists. A statistical hypothesis, sometimes called confirmatory data analysis, is a hypothesis that is testable on the basis of observing a process that is modeled via a set of random variables. Whenever we want to make claims about the distribution of data or whether one set of results are different from another set of results in applied machine learning, we must rely on statistical hypothesis tests.

In simple words, we can interpret data by assuming a specific structure of our outcome and use statistical methods to confirm or reject the assumption. The assumption is called a hypothesis and the statistical tests used for this purpose are called statistical hypothesis tests. In statistics, a hypothesis test calculates some quantity under a given assumption. The result of the test allows us to interpret whether the assumption holds or whether the assumption has been violated.

Following are two concrete examples that we will use a lot in machine learning:

- A test that assumes that data has a normal distribution.
- A test that assumes that two samples were drawn from the same underlying population distribution.

The assumption of a statistical test is called the null hypothesis, or hypothesis 0 (*H0* for short). It is often called the default assumption, or the assumption that nothing has changed. A violation of the test's assumption is often called the first hypothesis, hypothesis 1, or *H1* for short. *H1* is shorthand for *some other hypothesis*, as all we know is that the evidence suggests that the *H0* can be rejected.

The process of distinguishing between the null hypothesis and the alternative hypothesis is aided by identifying two conceptual types of errors (type 1 and type 2), and by specifying parametric limits on, for example, how much type 1 error will be permitted.

Let's understand these statistical concepts based on a real-world example. In this exercise, we will aim to study how accurately we can characterize the actual average participant experience (population mean) from the samples of data (sample mean). We can quantify the certainty of outcome through the confidence intervals. In this exercise we will first create an array of total experience in data science specialization batch of a class and store it in a variable named as `dss_exp`:

```
%matplotlib inline
import matplotlib.pyplot as plt
import numpy as np
import pandas as pd

# array containing no of total experience
dss_exp = np.array([12,  15,  13,  20,  19,  20,  11,  19,  11,  12,  19,  13,
                    12,  10,  6,  19,  3,  1,  1,  0,  4,  4,  6,  5,  3,  7,
                    12,  7,  9,  8,  12,  11,  11,  18,  19,  18,  19,  3,  6,
                    5,  6,  9,  11,  10,  14,  14,  16,  17,  17,  19,  0,  2,
                    0,  3,  1,  4,  6,  6,  8,  7,  7,  6,  7,  11,  11,  10,
                    11,  10,  13,  13,  15,  18,  20,  19,  1,  10,  8,  16,
                    19,  19,  17,  16,  11,  1,  10,  13,  15,  3,  8,  6,  9,
                    10,  15,  19,  2,  4,  5,  6,  9,  11,  10,  9,  10,  9,
                    15,  16,  18,  13])
```

Figure 8.11: a sample numpy array containing number of experience

Next, we will plot a histogram to see the distribution of experiences. For histogram plotting, we will use the `matplotlib` library's `hits()` function. In this function, we are using `bins` parameter that tells us the number of `bins` that our data will be divided into:

```
#Understanding the Underlying distribution of Experience
# Plot the distribution of Experience
plt.hist(dss_exp, range = (0,20), bins = 21)
# Add axis Labels
plt.xlabel("Experience in years")
plt.ylabel("Frequency")
plt.title("Distribution of Experience in Data Science Specialization")
# Draws the red vertical line in graph at the average experience
plt.axvline(x=dss_exp.mean(), linewidth=2, color = 'r')
plt.show()
# Statistics of DSS Batch experience
print("Mean Experience of DSS Batch: {:4.3f}".format(dss_exp.mean()))
print("Std Deviation of Experience of DSS Batch: {:4.3f}".format(dss_exp.std()))
```

Figure 8.12: Understanding underlying distribution of experience

The preceding cell will draw the following histogram:

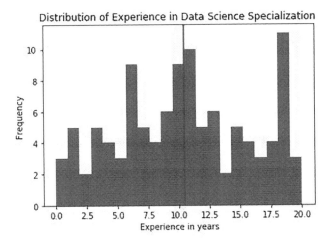

Mean Experience of DSS Batch: 10.435
Std Deviation of Experience of DSS Batch: 5.665

Figure 8.13: Distribution of experience in data science specialization

After this, we will estimate the experiences by taking the mean and standard deviation:

```
# Set the parameters for sampling
n = 10
NUM_TRIALS = 1000
#Estimating DSS Experience from samples
samp = np.random.choice(dss_exp, size = n, replace = True)#Just try for 1 iteration
samp_mean = samp.mean()
samp_sd = samp.std()
print("Samp_mean = {:4.3f} Sample_SD = {:4.3f}".format(samp_mean, samp_sd))
print("sample values:", samp)
```

Samp_mean = 10.900 Sample_SD = 5.665
sample values: [10 1 19 9 3 13 19 15 11 9]

Figure 8.14: Estimating experiences

Now, to see how the distribution of the sample mean to look like, we are drawing samples for 1000 times (NUM_TRIALS) and compute the mean each time. The distribution is plotted to identify the range of values it can take. The original data has experience raging between 0 years and 20 years and spread across it:

```
#How will the distribution of Sample Mean Look Like
np.random.seed(100)
mn_array = np.zeros(NUM_TRIALS)
sd_array = np.zeros(NUM_TRIALS)

# Extract Random Samples and compute mean & standard deviation
for i in range(NUM_TRIALS):
    samp = np.random.choice(dss_exp, size = n, replace = True)
    mn_array[i] = samp.mean()
```

Figure 8.15: How distribution of sample mean look

For computing the mean and standard deviation, we have used `mean()` and `std()` function. For computing percentile, we are using `numpy` library's `percentile()` function. This function computes the qth percentile of the data along the specified axis and returns the qth percentile(s) of the array elements:

```
mn = mn_array.mean()
sd = mn_array.std()
x5_pct = np.percentile(mn_array, 5.0)
x95_pct = np.percentile(mn_array, 95.0)
print("Mean = {:4.3f}, Std Dev = {:4.3f}, 5% Pct = {:4.3f}, 95% Pct = {:4.3f}".format(mn, sd, x5_pct, x95_pct))
# Plot Sampling distribution of Mean
plt.hist(mn_array, range=(0,20), bins = 41)
# Add axis labels
plt.xlabel("Avg Experience with n={}".format(n))
plt.ylabel("Frequency")
plt.title("Sampling Distribution of Mean")
plt.axvline(x=x5_pct, linewidth=2, color = 'r')
plt.axvline(x=x95_pct, linewidth=2, color = 'r')
plt.show()
```

Figure 8.16: Computing mean, standard deviation, and percentile

The preceding code will plot the following histogram, which tells that the original experience of students of data science is in no way a normal distribution. It has peaks around 5 years, 10 years, and 19 years' experience. The following plot is the histogram of the mean of samples for any given n:

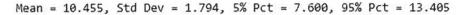

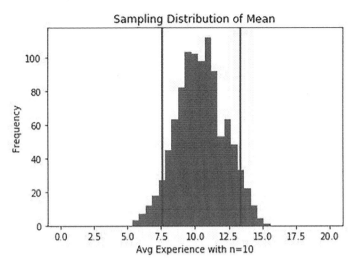

Figure 8.17: *Sampling distribution of Mean*

Now to find an estimated range of values which is likely to include an unknown population parameter, that is, the estimated range being calculated from a given set of sample data, we will select the confidence interval of our samples. In the following code cell, we are creating a function for selecting confidence interval. Always remember that the selection of a confidence level for an interval determines the probability that the confidence interval produced will contain the true parameter value. Common choices for the confidence level are 0.90, 0.95, and 0.99. These levels correspond to percentages of the area of the normal density curve. For example, a 95% confidence interval covers 95% of the normal curve – the probability of observing a value outside of this area is less than 0.05:

```
# Function to check if the true mean lies within 90% Confidence Interval
def samp_mean_within_ci(mn, l_5pct, u_95pct):
    out = True
    if (mn < l_5pct) | (mn > u_95pct):
        out = False
    return out
```

```
# Estimation and Confidence Interval
samp = np.random.choice(dss_exp, size = n, replace = True)
samp_mean = samp.mean()
samp_sd = samp.std()
# divided by sqrt(n) is done so as to compensate for the reduction in std. dev due to sample size of n
sd_ci = samp_sd/np.sqrt(n)
# Lower 90% confidence interval (This is approximate version to build intution)
samp_lower_5pct = samp_mean - 1.645 * sd_ci
# Upper 90% confidence interval (This is approximate version to build intution)
samp_upper_95pct = samp_mean + 1.645 * sd_ci
print("Pop Mean: {:4.3f} | Sample: L_5PCT = {:4.3f} | M = samp_mean = {:4.3f} | H_95PCT = {:4.3f}".format(dss_exp.mean(),
# Checking if the population mean lies within 90% Confidence Interval (CI)
mn_within_ci_flag = samp_mean_within_ci(dss_exp.mean(), samp_lower_5pct, samp_upper_95pct)
print("True mean lies with the 90% confidence Intervel = {}".format(mn_within_ci_flag))
```

```
Pop Mean: 10.435 | Sample: L_5PCT = 7.408 | M = samp_mean = 8.800 | H_95PCT = 10.192
True mean lies with the 90% confidence Intervel = False
```

Figure 8.18: *Function to select confidence interval*

This shows us that given the sample size n, we can estimate the sample mean and confidence interval. The confidence interval is estimated assuming normal distribution, which holds well when n >= 30. When n is increased, confidence interval becomes smaller, which implies that results are obtained with higher certainty:

```
Pop Mean: 10.435 | Sample: L_5PCT = 7.408 | M = samp_mean = 8.800  | H_95PCT = 10.192
True mean lies with the 90% confidence Intervel = False
```

Figure 8.19: Estimating sample mean and confidence interval

Let's apply the same concept to an array of old batch experienced so that we can perform Hypothesis testing. Firstly, let's define the Hypotheses as follows for our example:

- H0: Average Experience of Current Batch and Previous batch is the same.

- H1: Average Experience of Current Batch and Previous batch is different.

The process of distinguishing between the null hypothesis and the alternative hypothesis is aided by identifying two conceptual types of errors (type 1 and type 2), and by specifying parametric limits on, for example, how much type 1 error will be permitted:

```
# Previous Batch Data for working experience
dss_exp_prev = np.array([1, 14,  6,  7, 10, 10, 19, 15, 19, 15,
                2,  2, 14, 14, 14,  3,  0,  4, 11,  7,
                1,  2,  0,  1,  2,  2,  2,  1,  1,  2,
                4,  4,  3,  3,  3,  3,  4,  3,  3,  7,
                8,  6,  6,  6,  7,  8,  8,  8,  8,  7,
                8,  0,  0,  7,  6,  9, 10,  9,  9, 11,
                11,  9, 10, 10, 11, 10, 11,  9,  9,  9,
                12, 14, 13, 14, 18, 14, 11, 10, 17, 20,
                18,  5, 13,  4,  2,  4,  3, 12, 12, 14,
                12, 12, 10, 14,  4, 11,  9])
```

```
avg_exp_prev = dss_exp_prev.mean()
std_exp_prev = dss_exp_prev.std()
print("Previous DSS Batch: Avg Exp - {:4.3f} Std Dev - {:4.3f}".format(avg_exp_prev, std_exp_prev))

plt.hist(dss_exp_prev, range=(0,20), bins = 21)
plt.axvline(x=dss_exp_prev.mean(), linewidth=2, color = 'r')
plt.show()
```

```
Previous DSS Batch: Avg Exp - 8.041 Std Dev - 5.034
```

Figure 8.20: Performing hypothesis testing

From the output, you can easily see that the previous batch average experience is around 8 while the new batch has an average experience of 10 years. Thus, our first Hypothesis (*H1*) is fulfilled in our example, which means we can reject the null Hypothesis:

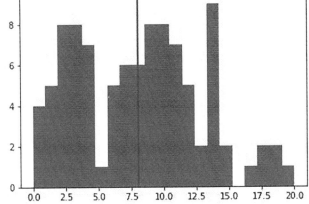

Figure 8.21: plot of hypothesis testing example

The results of a statistical hypothesis test may cause a lot of confusion to decide whether to take the result or reject it. To understand this, we need to interpret the *p-value*. P-value is a quantity that we can use to interpret or quantify the result of the test and either reject or fail to reject the null hypothesis. This is done by comparing the p-value to a threshold value chosen beforehand, called the significance level. The significance level is often referred to by the Greek lower case letter alpha. A common value used for alpha is 5% or 0.05. A smaller alpha value suggests a more robust interpretation of the null hypothesis, such as 1% or 0.1%.

In the next examples, we'll do hypothesis testing based on the intuition from the sampling distribution of mean and then we will interpret the p-value:

```
np.random.seed(100)
n = 20

dss_mean = dss_exp.mean()
dss_sd   = dss_exp.std()
print("Current DSS Batch : Population Mean - {:4.3f}".format(dss_mean))

dss_prev_samp = np.random.choice(dss_exp_prev, size = n, replace = True)
dss_prev_samp_mean = dss_prev_samp.mean()
print("Previous DSS Batch Sample Mean: {:4.3f}".format(dss_prev_samp_mean))
```

```
Current DSS Batch : Population Mean - 10.435
Previous DSS Batch Sample Mean: 8.250
```

```
from scipy import stats
t_statistic = (dss_prev_samp_mean - dss_mean)/(dss_sd/np.sqrt(n))
p_val = 2 * stats.t.cdf(t_statistic, df= (n-1))
print("T-Statistic : {:4.2f}, p-Value = {:4.2f}".format(t_statistic,p_val))
```

```
T-Statistic : -1.72, p-Value = 0.10
```

```
# For 2-tailed hypothesis testing
from scipy import stats
dss_exp_prev_samp = np.random.choice(dss_exp_prev, size = 20, replace = True)
dss_exp_samp = np.random.choice(dss_exp, size = 20, replace = True)
stats.ttest_ind(dss_exp_prev_samp, dss_exp_samp)
```

```
Ttest_indResult(statistic=-0.24857316405070548, pvalue=0.80502950101657478)
```

Figure 8.22: Hypothesis testing

In the preceding code cell, after calculating the average experiences of previous and current batches, we are performing the t-test using `stats.ttest_ind()` function. The t-test (also called Student's T-Test) compares two averages (means) and tells us if they are different from each other. The t-test also tells us how significant the differences are; In other words, it lets us know if those differences could have happened by chance. This test gives us a t-score. The t-score is a ratio of the difference between the two groups and the difference within the groups. A large t-score tells you that the groups are different. A small t-score tells you that the groups are similar.

Every t-value has a p-value to go with it. A p-value is a probability that the results from our sample data occurred by chance. P-values are from 0% to 100%. They are usually written as a decimal. For example, a p-value of 5% is 0.05. Low p-values are good; they indicate our data did not occur by chance. So, in our example, the p-value is greater than 0.05 or 1.0, so we cannot reject the null hypothesis. Since the p-value is probabilistic; when we interpret the result of a statistical test, we do not know what is true or false, only what is likely. Rejecting the null hypothesis means that there is sufficient statistical evidence that the null hypothesis does not look likely. Otherwise, it means that there is not sufficient statistical evidence to reject the null hypothesis. If we say that we *accept* the null hypothesis, the language suggests that the null hypothesis is true. Instead, it is safer to say that we *fail to reject* the null hypothesis, as in, there is insufficient statistical evidence to reject it.

Conclusion

We have covered some core concepts of statistics in this chapter and we will cover more statistical concepts related to machine learning during the course of later chapters in this book. Statistics is important in data analysis and we cannot ignore it. Framing questions statistically allows researchers to leverage data resources to extract knowledge and obtain better answers. It also allows them to establish methods for prediction and estimation, to quantify their degree of certainty, and to do all of this, using algorithms that exhibit predictable and reproducible behavior. So, practice and implement learnings from this chapter. In the next chapter, we will learn how to import various forms of data and work with data.

## CHAPTER 9

How to Import Data in Python?

Data importing is the first step you will do before analyzing. Since data is present in various forms, `.txt`, `.csv`, `.excel`, JSON, etc., importing or reading of such data is also different but quite simple in a Pythonic way. While importing external data, you need to check various points, i.e., whether header row exists in data or not, is there any missing values there, the data type of each attribute, etc. In this chapter, with the help of Pandas I/O API, you will not only learn to read the data, but also how to write data into various formats of files.

Structure

- Importing text data
- Importing CSV data
- Importing Excel data
- Importing JSON data
- Importing pickled data
- Importing a compressed data

Objective

After studying this chapter, you will become an expert in importing, reading, and refining various forms of data.

Importing text data

The simplest form of flat data you will see is in `.txt` files. To import text data, we need a dataset in this format. For this purpose, we will import a real-world dataset. In the next example, I have made use of consumer price index data obtained from the US Labor Department. You can download the data by clicking on the following URL:

https://catalog.data.gov/dataset/consumer-price-index-average-price-data

Once you copy and save the preceding data in a text file in your system, provide the path to read it. We will use `pandasread_table()` function to read the text file indicating the path where the file is stored in your system (I have stored the file in my `E:/pg/docs/BPB/data folder`), as shown in the following *figure 9.1*:

```
import pandas as pd
cpi_data = pd.read_table('E:/pg/docs/BPB/data/cpi_us.txt')
cpi_data.head()
```

	series_id	year	period	value	footnote_codes
0	APU0000701111	1995	M01	0.238	
1	APU0000701111	1995	M02	0.242	
2	APU0000701111	1995	M03	0.242	
3	APU0000701111	1995	M04	0.236	
4	APU0000701111	1995	M05	0.244	

Figure 9.1: Importing text data

Isn't that simple! The `pd.read_table()` function imports all data in a variable `cpi_data`. If you check the type of this variable, you will notice that this is a `pandas` DataFrame. The `pandas` library imports the data in `DataFrame` format which denotes row and column with index. This data type is easy to manipulate the data further:

```
type(cpi_data)
```

```
pandas.core.frame.DataFrame
```

Figure 9.2: Importing in DataFrame

We can inspect the data using the `head()` function. pandas' `read_table()` function has inbuilt functionality to filter blank columns which you can use by passing as arguments separated by a comma. For example, in the preceding `cpi` data, there is a blank column `footnote_codes`. By using the use `cols` argument as shown in the following *figure 9.3*, we can filter the unwanted columns:

```
cpi_data = pd.read_table('E:/pg/docs/BPB/data/cpi_us.txt',
                         usecols=['series_id', 'year', 'period', 'value'])
cpi_data.head()
```

	series_id	year	period	value
0	APU0000701111	1995	M01	0.238
1	APU0000701111	1995	M02	0.242
2	APU0000701111	1995	M03	0.242
3	APU0000701111	1995	M04	0.236
4	APU0000701111	1995	M05	0.244

Figure 9.3: *Using cols argument*

- Always provide correct file location to the `read_table()` function.
- Pandas `read_table()` function has a lot of arguments that are very helpful in data cleaning as per your need. You can check these by clicking on the following link: https://pandas.pydata.org/pandas-docs/stable/generated/pandas.read_table.html

Importing CSV data

CSV or comma-separated values are the favorite formats for saving data. You will see that most of the publicly available datasets for analysis/machine learning are in `.csv` format. In the next example, I have made use of crime data to analyze the crime incidents occurred in Chicago city. You can download this data by clicking on the following link or save it from the datasets provided in the GitHub repository of the book:

https://catalog.data.gov/dataset?res_format=CSV

Similar to our previous example of reading data from the .txt file, you can import and read this CSV data using the pandas read_csv() function, as shown in the following *figure 9.4*. This function also has inbuilt features which you can find in following official link: **https://pandas.pydata.org/pandas-docs/stable/generated/pandas.read_csv.html**

```
crime_data = pd.read_csv('E:\pg\docs\BPB\data\Crimes_-_2001_to_present.csv')
crime_data.head()
```

	ID	Case Number	Date	Block	IUCR	Primary Type	Description	Location Description	Arrest	Domestic	...
0	10000092	HY189866	03/18/2015 07:44:00 PM	047XX W OHIO ST	041A	BATTERY	AGGRAVATED: HANDGUN	STREET	False	False	...
1	10000094	HY190059	03/18/2015 11:00:00 PM	066XX S MARSHFIELD AVE	4625	OTHER OFFENSE	PAROLE VIOLATION	STREET	True	False	...
2	10000095	HY190052	03/18/2015 10:45:00 PM	044XX S LAKE PARK AVE	0486	BATTERY	DOMESTIC BATTERY SIMPLE	APARTMENT	False	True	...
3	10000096	HY190054	03/18/2015 10:30:00 PM	051XX S MICHIGAN AVE	0460	BATTERY	SIMPLE	APARTMENT	False	False	...
4	10000097	HY189976	03/18/2015 09:00:00 PM	047XX W ADAMS ST	031A	ROBBERY	ARMED: HANDGUN	SIDEWALK	False	False	...

Figure 9.4: Importing CSV data

Sometimes, CSV files can be loaded with numerous rows of datasets (our dataset is approximately 1.47 GB). Please be patient while the importing of data is in process. You will notice a clock icon on the top of the browser tab of your notebook indicating the system is busy.

Importing Excel data

Excel is another most widely used dataset format that contains numbers of the sheet in the form of a tab. You can use the pandas read_excel() function with its sheet_name argument to read the data from a particular sheet of Excel data. In the next example, I have used a Superstore Excel sheet with three tabs-Orders, Returns, People, which you can download by clicking on the following link: **https://community.tableau.com/docs/DOC-1236**

```
order_data = pd.read_excel('E:\pg\docs\BPB\data\Sample - Superstore.xls', sheet_name='Orders')
order_data.head()
```

	Row ID	Order ID	Order Date	Ship Date	Ship Mode	Customer ID	Customer Name	Segment	Country	City	...	Postal Code	Region	Product ID
0	1	CA-2016-152156	2016-11-08	2016-11-11	Second Class	CG-12520	Claire Gute	Consumer	United States	Henderson	...	42420	South	FUR-BO-10001798
1	2	CA-2016-152156	2016-11-08	2016-11-11	Second Class	CG-12520	Claire Gute	Consumer	United States	Henderson	...	42420	South	FUR-CH-10000454
2	3	CA-2016-138688	2016-06-12	2016-06-16	Second Class	DV-13045	Darrin Van Huff	Corporate	United States	Los Angeles	...	90036	West	OFF-LA-10000240

Figure 9.5: Importing Excel data

In the preceding *figure 9.5*, we have just imported data from the `Orders` sheet of the `Superstore.xls`.

Importing JSON data

The JSON format is the most preferred form of data exchange in today's world of API. To deal with a JSON structured data, you can use `pandas read_json()` function to read with its orient argument as shown in the following *figure 9.6*:

```
glossary_data = pd.read_json('E:\pg\docs\BPB\data\glossary.json', orient='table')
glossary_data.head()
```

	glossary
GlossDiv	{'title': 'S', 'GlossList': {'GlossEntry': {'l...
title	example glossary

Figure 9.6: Importing JSON data

Here, the orient parameter can take values as `split`, `records`, `index`, and `columns`. Try these in your notebook and see the difference in output. Please note, if you are facing error like `keyerror: 'schema'`, update your `pandas` version to v0.23, since `orient='table'` parameter has some issues in the older version of `pandas`.

Importing pickled data

Any object in Python can be pickled so that it can be saved on disk. What pickle does is that it *serializes* the object first before writing it to file. The idea is that this character stream contains all the information necessary to reconstruct the object in another Python script. When you will work on machine learning, then you will need to train your model many times, and picking will help you by saving the training time. Once you pickled your trained model, you can share this trained model to others; they don't need to waste their time in the retraining of the model. We will cover that part later; let's learn how to read a pickled file using `pandas`:

```
import pandas as pd
unpickled_data = pd.read_pickle("E:/pg/docs/BPB/data/mnist.pkl")
print("data type::", type(unpickled_data))
for index, digit in enumerate(unpickled_data):
    print(index, ":", digit)
```

```
data type:: <class 'tuple'>
0 : (array([[0., 0., 0., ..., 0., 0., 0.],
        [0., 0., 0., ..., 0., 0., 0.],
        [0., 0., 0., ..., 0., 0., 0.],
        ...,
```

Figure 9.7: Importing pickled data

Importing a compressed data

Our next type of data is in compressed form. The ZIP file format is a common archive and compression standard. So how can you unzip a file so that you can read the data? For this purpose, Python has a `zipfile` module that provides tools to create, read, write, append, and list a ZIP file. In this example, we will unzip soil data from the African region which you can download from our GitHub repository:

https://github.com/dsbyprateekg/BPB-Publications

```
import zipfile
Dataset = "africa_soil_train_data.zip"
with zipfile.ZipFile("E:/pg/bpb/BPB-Publications/Datasets/"+Dataset,"r") as z:
    z.extractall("E:/pg/bpb/BPB-Publications/Datasets")
```

Figure 9.8: Importing a compressed data

The preceding code will unzip the file in your given path; in our example, the unzipped file is in CSV format that you can easily read using pandas `read_csv()` function. There are various inbuilt parameters for this `zipfile` which you can try in your notebook by clicking on the following link: **https://docs.python.org/3.6/library/zipfile.html**

Conclusion

Data importing is the first step to get the data. In this chapter, we have learned various formats of data importing. Without loading the dataset in an appropriate data type, you cannot move further. As a data scientist, you will mostly find datasets in CSV format, so pandas `read_csv()` function will be your best friend in the data importing process. The more you practice in your notebook, the more you will learn. So, explore the data importing with different parameters and see the result. In the next chapter, we will learn about the data cleaning process.

CHAPTER 10
Cleaning of Imported Data

Before starting your analysis, you need to transform the raw data into a clean form. As a data scientist, you will spend 80% of your time cleaning and manipulating data. This process is also known as data wrangling.

A machine learning model's accuracy depends on the data it is applied to. Hence, data cleaning is a vital step for any data scientist. In this chapter, you will work on a couple of case studies and apply learnings from the previous chapters to clean the data.

Structure

- Know your data
- Analyzing missing values
- Dropping missing values
- How to scale and normalize data?
- How to parse dates?
- How to apply character encoding
- Cleaning inconsistent data

Objective

After studying this chapter, you will have applied knowledge of the data cleaning process.

Know your data

As a first step, you must understand the business problem and then look upon the data given by the business team or client. In this first case study, we are going to work on the **National Football League** (**NFL**) data. You can access the data from our GitHub repository. As a data scientist, your first task is to read the data in your notebook.

Since the data is in ZIP format, our first step will be to unzip this data and read it using Pandas `.zipfile()` function by providing the correct location of the file stored in the system as shown in the following *figure 10.1*:

```
# unzipping nfl zip data
import zipfile
Dataset = "NFL Play by Play 2009-2017 (v4).csv.zip"
with zipfile.ZipFile("E:/pg/bpb/BPB-Publications/Datasets/"+Dataset,"r") as z:
    z.extractall("E:/pg/bpb/BPB-Publications/Datasets")
```

```
# unzipping building permit zip data
import zipfile
Dataset2 = "Building_Permits.csv.zip"
with zipfile.ZipFile("E:/pg/bpb/BPB-Publications/Datasets/"+Dataset2,"r") as z:
    z.extractall("E:/pg/bpb/BPB-Publications/Datasets")
```

```
# import required modules
import pandas as pd
import numpy as np
```

```
# reading NFL data
nfl_data = pd.read_csv("E:/pg/bpb/BPB-Publications/Datasets/NFL Play by Play 2009-2017 (v4).csv", low_memory=False)
building_permits = pd.read_csv("E:/pg/bpb/BPB-Publications/Datasets/Building_Permits.csv", low_memory=False)
```

Figure 10.1: Unzipping a ZIP file

Please note, while reading the data using the pandas `read_csv()` function, I am passing `low_memory` parameter. Otherwise, you will get the `low_memory` warning because guessing dtypes (data type) for each column is very memory demanding and `pandas` tries to determine what `dtype` to set by analyzing the data in each column. The `pandas` library can only determine what `dtype` a column should have after reading the entire file. This means none of the data can be parsed before the whole file is read unless you risk having to change the `dtype` of that column when you read the last value. For now, it's ok to use a `low_memory` parameter with setting the parameter value to False.

After reading the data, we can look at it so that we get an idea about its attributes. For this, we can use `.head()` or `.sample()` function. Since you have already come across how to use the `.head()` function, I will use `.sample()` function to view the data as shown in the following *figure 10.2*:

```
# looking up the data
nfl_data.sample(5)
```

	Date	GameID	Drive	qtr	down	time	TimeUnder	TimeSecs	PlayTimeDiff	SideofField	...	yacEPA	Home_WP_pre	⁄
219237	2013-12-15	2013121507	20	4	NaN	03:07	4	187.0	0.0	NO	...	NaN	0.955040	
113588	2011-11-13	2011111302	20	4	1.0	11:16	12	676.0	1.0	HOU	...	NaN	0.010379	
214092	2013-12-05	2013120500	13	3	2.0	14:20	15	1760.0	19.0	HOU	...	0.228558	0.783278	
299928	2015-11-26	2015112601	17	4	NaN	04:17	5	257.0	4.0	DAL	...	NaN	NaN	
277934	2015-09-27	2015092703	16	3	1.0	11:45	12	1605.0	5.0	TB	...	NaN	0.482456	

5 rows × 102 columns

Figure 10.2: Viewing the data

Tada! The data is displayed in tabular form with some columns having NaN values; these values are called missing values. Let's apply the same function in `building_permits` dataframe as shown in the following *figure 10.3*:

```
building_permits.sample(5)
```

	Permit Number	Permit Type	Permit Type Definition	Permit Creation Date	Block	Lot	Street Number	Street Number Suffix	Street Name	Street Suffix	...	E: Constr
106029	201511162641	8	otc alterations permit	11/16/2015	1744	006	1237	NaN	06th	Av	...	
98590	201509116784	8	otc alterations permit	09/11/2015	0690	116	1	NaN	Daniel Burnham	Ct	...	
45517	201404213721	8	otc alterations permit	04/21/2014	1081	048	2549	NaN	Post	St	...	
136805	201609157776	8	otc alterations permit	09/15/2016	6534	010A	454	NaN	Fair Oaks	St	...	
74940	201502057581	8	otc alterations permit	02/05/2015	3538	040	63	NaN	Noe	St	...	

5 rows × 43 columns

Figure 10.3: Applying .sample() function in building_permits

Analyzing missing values

After reading the data, we have found out that both datasets have missing values. Our next step will be to calculate the number of missing values we have in each column. For counting the null values, pandas has .isnull() function. Since nfl_data has 102 columns, we will analyze the first ten columns containing missing values as shown in the following *figure 10.4*:

```
# getting the number of missing values per column
missing_values_count = nfl_data.isnull().sum()
# looking at first 10 columns missing values in nfl dataset
missing_values_count[0:10]
```

```
Date                0
GameID              0
Drive               0
qtr                 0
down            61154
time              224
TimeUnder           0
TimeSecs          224
PlayTimeDiff      444
SideofField       528
dtype: int64
```

Figure 10.4: Analyzing missing values

Each column name and the associated number indicates the number of missing values – that seems like a lot! We cannot ignore such a high number of missing values. It might be helpful to see what percentage of the values in our dataset were missing to give us a better sense of the scale of this problem. For this percentage calculation, we will take help of the combination of NumPy's .prod() and pandas shape functions as shown in the following *figure 10.5*:

```
# how many total missing values do we have in nfl_data
total_cells = np.prod(nfl_data.shape)
total_missing = missing_values_count.sum()
# percent of data that is missing
(total_missing/total_cells) * 100
```

```
24.87214126835169
```

Figure 10.5: Calculating percentage of values missing

That's amazing right, almost a quarter of the cells in this dataset are empty! Now it's your turn to apply the same steps in the building_permits dataset and check the percentage of missing values there.

In the next step, we will take a closer look at some of the columns with missing values and try to figure out what might be going on with them. This process in data science means closely looking at your data and trying to figure out why it is the way it is and how that will affect your analysis. *For dealing with missing values, you'll need to use your intuition to figure out why the value is missing*.

To help figure this out the next question that a data scientist must ask himself/herself - *Is this value missing because it wasn't recorded or because it doesn't exist?*

In the first case, if a value is missing because it doesn't exist (for example the height of the oldest child of someone who doesn't have any children), then it doesn't make any sense to try and guess what it might be. These values you probably do want to keep as NaN. In the second case, if a value is missing because it wasn't recorded, then you can try to guess what it might have been based on the other values in that column and row. This is called imputation that you will learn later in this chapter.

In our `nfl_data` dataset, if you check the `TimeSecs` column, it has a total of 224 missing values because they were not recorded. So, it would make sense for us to try and guess what they should be rather than just leaving them as NAs or NaNs. On the other hand, there are other fields, like `PenalizedTeam` that also have a lot of missing fields. In this case, though, the field is missing because if there was no penalty, then it doesn't make sense to say which team was penalized. For this column, it would make more sense to either leave it empty or to add a third value like **none** and use that to replace the NAs.

Till now you must have understood that reading and understanding through your data can be a tedious process. Imagine doing such careful data analysis daily where you have to look at each column individually until you figure out the best strategy for filling those missing values. Now it's your turn to look at the columns, street number suffix, and zip code from the `building_permits` datasets with a similar approach. Both contain missing values. Which, if either, of these are missing because they don't exist? Which, if either, are missing because they weren't recorded?

Dropping missing values

If you don't have any reason to figure out why your values are missing, the last option you could be left with is to just remove any rows or columns that contain missing values. But this is not recommended for important projects! It's usually worth taking out some time to go through your data and carefully look at all the columns with missing values one-by-one and understand your dataset. It could be frustrating at the beginning, but you'll get used to this eventually, and it will help you evolve as a better data scientist.

For dropping missing values, `pandas` do have a handy function, `dropna()` to help you do this. Stay alert! When using this function, if you don't pass any parameter, *it will remove all of the data even if every row in your dataset has at least one missing value.*

For saving ourselves from this situation, we can use axis parameter having column value with this function. We will also check before and after the effect of missing values dropping in the dataset as shown in the following *figure 10.6*:

```
# remove all columns with at least one missing value
columns_with_na_dropped = nfl_data.dropna(axis=1)
columns_with_na_dropped.head()

# checking how much data did we lose?
print("Columns in original dataset:", nfl_data.shape[1])
print("Columns with missing values dropped:", columns_with_na_dropped.shape[1])

Columns in original dataset: 102
Columns with missing values dropped: 41
```

Figure 10.6: Dropping missing values

By passing `axis=1` as parameter we were able to drop columns with one or more missing values.

We've lost quite a bit of data, but at this point we have successfully removed all the NaN's from our NFL data. Now it's your turn to try removing all the rows from the `building_permits` dataset that contains missing values and see how many are left and then try to remove all the columns with empty values and check, how much of your data is left?

Automatically fill missing values

Instead of dropping missing values, we have another option to fill these values. For this purpose, `pandas` have `fillna()` function with the option of replacing the NaN values with the value of our choice. In the case of our example data set, I will replace all the NaN values with 0 in `nfl_data` dataset, since I have already removed/dropped columns with NaN values. Before applying this function, I will pick a small subset view of data in the columns from EPA to Season so that it will print well in the notebook. For this subsetting, you can use `.loc()` function and pass the range indexes of columns after the comma inside the function. The single colon before the comma in the `.loc()` function indicates data from all rows for the subsetting:

```
# get a small subset of the NFL dataset
subset_nfl_data = nfl_data.loc[:, 'EPA':'Season'].head()
subset_nfl_data
# replace all NA's with 0
subset_nfl_data.fillna(0)
```

	EPA	airEPA	yacEPA	Home_WP_pre	Away_WP_pre	Home_WP_post	Away_WP_post	Win_Prob	WPA	airWPA	yacWPA	Season
0	2.014474	0.000000	0.000000	0.485675	0.514325	0.546433	0.453567	0.485675	0.060758	0.000000	0.000000	2009
1	0.077907	-1.068169	1.146076	0.546433	0.453567	0.551088	0.448912	0.546433	0.004655	-0.032244	0.036899	2009
2	-1.402760	0.000000	0.000000	0.551088	0.448912	0.510793	0.489207	0.551088	-0.040295	0.000000	0.000000	2009
3	-1.712583	3.318841	-5.031425	0.510793	0.489207	0.461217	0.538783	0.510793	-0.049576	0.106663	-0.156239	2009
4	2.097796	0.000000	0.000000	0.461217	0.538783	0.558929	0.441071	0.461217	0.097712	0.000000	0.000000	2009

Figure 10.7: Automatically filling missing values

In the code file, I have prepared and shared another example to check the sum and percentage of missing values in the nfl_data. I hope you'll be surprised to see the changes in the dataset after the example operations we performed in our previous examples. The second option of filling missing values automatically is by replacing missing values with the value that follows (in the next row) it in the same column. This makes a lot of sense for datasets where the observations have some sort of logical order to them. Here we are using backward filling (bfill) with fillna function for this task:

```
# replace all NaN's the value that comes directly after it in the same column,
# then replace all the remaining NaN's with 0
subset_nfl_data.fillna(method = 'bfill', axis=0).fillna(0)
```

	EPA	airEPA	yacEPA	Home_WP_pre	Away_WP_pre	Home_WP_post	Away_WP_post	Win_Prob	WPA	airWPA	yacWPA	Season
0	2.014474	-1.068169	1.146076	0.485675	0.514325	0.546433	0.453567	0.485675	0.060758	-0.032244	0.036899	2009
1	0.077907	-1.068169	1.146076	0.546433	0.453567	0.551088	0.448912	0.546433	0.004655	-0.032244	0.036899	2009
2	-1.402760	3.318841	-5.031425	0.551088	0.448912	0.510793	0.489207	0.551088	-0.040295	0.106663	-0.156239	2009
3	-1.712583	3.318841	-5.031425	0.510793	0.489207	0.461217	0.538783	0.510793	-0.049576	0.106663	-0.156239	2009
4	2.097796	0.000000	0.000000	0.461217	0.538783	0.558929	0.441071	0.461217	0.097712	0.000000	0.000000	2009

Figure 10.8: Second option to automatically filling missing value

Try the same steps in building_permits dataset and explore the automatic filling of missing values!

How to scale and normalize data?

Most of the machine learning algorithms do not take raw numerical attributes of your dataset. You need to fit the numerical values within a specific scale. For example, you might be looking at the prices of some products in both Rupee and US Dollars. One US Dollar is worth about 70 Rupees, but if you don't scale your price methods, some machine learning algorithms will consider a difference in the price of 1 Rupee as important as a difference of 1 US Dollar! This doesn't fit with our intuitions of the world. With currency, you can convert between currencies. But what if you're looking at something like height and weight? It's not entirely clear how many pounds should equal one inch (or how many kilograms should equal one meter) because these two are different measurement units.

In this example of this chapter, you will work on a Kickstarter Project dataset - ks-projects-201612.csv, which you can download from our GitHub repository. Kickstarter is a community of more than 10 million people comprising of creative, tech enthusiasts who help in bringing creative project to life. Till now, more than $3 billion dollars have been contributed by the members in fueling creative projects. The projects can be literally anything – a device, a game, an app, a film etc. Kickstarter works on all or nothing basis, i.e., if a project doesn't meet its goal, the project owner gets nothing. For example, if a projects' goal is $500, even if it gets funded until $499, the project won't be a success. In this dataset, you will transform the values of numeric variables so that the transformed data points have specific helpful properties.

These transforming techniques are known as *scaling* and *normalization*. One difference between these two techniques is that, in scaling, you're changing the range of your data while in normalization you're changing the shape of the distribution of your data. To understand the output of both techniques, we will need visualization also, so we will use some visualization libraries as well. Let's understand each of them one-by-one.

For scaling, you will first need to install the `mlxtend` library which is a Python library of useful tools for the day-to-day data science tasks. For this installation, open Anaconda Prompt and run the following command: `conda install -c conda-forge mlxtend` follow the instructions.

After installing the required library, read the download data:

```python
import pandas as pd
import numpy as np

# for Box-Cox Transformation
from scipy import stats

# for min_max scaling
from mlxtend.preprocessing import minmax_scaling

# for visualization
import seaborn as sns
import matplotlib.pyplot as plt

# reading kickstarters project data
kickstarters_2017 = pd.read_csv("E:/pg/bpb/BPB-Publications/Datasets/ks-projects-201801.csv")
# set seed for reproducibility
np.random.seed(0)
kickstarters_2017.head()
```

Figure 10.9: min max scaling example

	ID	name	category	main_category	currency	deadline	goal	launched	pledged	state	backers	country	usd pledged
0	1000002330	The Songs of Adelaide & Abullah	Poetry	Publishing	GBP	2015-10-09	1000.0	2015-08-11 12:12:28	0.0	failed	0	GB	0.0
1	1000003930	Greeting From Earth: ZGAC Arts Capsule For ET	Narrative Film	Film & Video	USD	2017-11-01	30000.0	2017-09-02 04:43:57	2421.0	failed	15	US	100.0
2	1000004038	Where is Hank?	Narrative Film	Film & Video	USD	2013-02-26	45000.0	2013-01-12 00:20:50	220.0	failed	3	US	220.0
3	1000007540	ToshiCapital Rekordz Needs Help to Complete Album	Music	Music	USD	2012-04-16	5000.0	2012-03-17 03:24:11	1.0	failed	1	US	1.0
4	1000011046	Community Film Project: The Art of Naighborhoo	Film & Video	Film & Video	USD	2015-08-29	19500.0	2015-07-04 08:35:03	1283.0	canceled	14	US	1283.0

Figure 10.10: output of the min max scaling example

By scaling your variables, you can compare different variables on equal footing. To help solidify what scaling looks like, let's start by scaling the goals of each campaign in our dataset, which is how much money they were asking for:

```
# select the usd_goal_real column
usd_goal = kickstarters_2017.usd_goal_real

# scale the goals from 0 to 1
scaled_data = minmax_scaling(usd_goal, columns = [0])

# plot the original & scaled data together to compare
fig, ax=plt.subplots(1,2)
sns.distplot(kickstarters_2017.usd_goal_real, ax=ax[0])
ax[0].set_title("Original Data")
sns.distplot(scaled_data, ax=ax[1])
ax[1].set_title("Scaled data")
plt.show()
```

Figure 10.11: Scaling the goals of each campaign

Once you run the preceding shell, the following plots will be displayed:

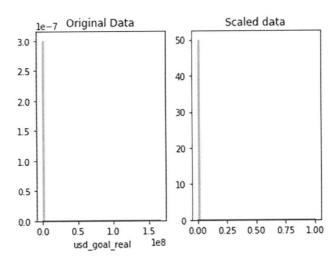

Figure 10.12: Plots that are displayed

You can see that scaling changed the scales of the plots dramatically but not the shape of the data and we can conclude that *it looks like most campaigns have small goals, but a few have very large ones.*

Scaling just changes the range of your data. Normalization is a more radical transformation. The point of normalization is to change your observations so that they can be described as a normal distribution. Remember here that normal distribution is a specific statistical distribution where roughly equal observations fall above and below the mean, the mean and the median are the same, and there are more observations closer to the mean. The normal distribution is also known as the Gaussian distribution.

The method we are using to normalize here is called the Box-Cox Transformation. In the Kickstarter data example, we're going to normalize the amount of money pledged for each campaign:

```
# get the index of all positive pledges (Box-Cox only takes postive values)
index_of_positive_pledges = kickstarters_2017.usd_pledged_real > 0

# get only positive pledges (using their indexes)
positive_pledges = kickstarters_2017.usd_pledged_real.loc[index_of_positive_pledges]

# normalize the pledges (w/ Box-Cox)
normalized_pledges = stats.boxcox(positive_pledges)[0]

# plot both together to compare
fig, ax=plt.subplots(1,2)
sns.distplot(positive_pledges, ax=ax[0])
ax[0].set_title("Original Data")
sns.distplot(normalized_pledges, ax=ax[1])
ax[1].set_title("Normalized data")
plt.show()
```

Figure 10.13: Box-Cox Transformation

Once you run the preceding shell, you will see the following plots:

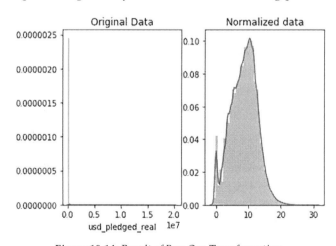

Figure 10.14: Result of Box-Cox Transformation

It's not perfect – it looks like a lot of pledges got very few pledges, but it is much closer to normal! Now it's your turn to apply the same with the *pledged* column. Does it have the same info?

How to parse dates?

Many datasets have a date column and sometimes you may have to deal with requirements like fetching transactional data for a particular month or dates of a month. In such cases, you must know how to parse date. For this you will work on the third case study, where you will work on natural disaster dataset and will learn how to parse data. Let's import the required modules and load our datasets:

```python
import pandas as pd
import numpy as np
import seaborn as sns
import datetime

# read in our data
earthquakes = pd.read_csv("E:/pg/bpb/BPB-Publications/Datasets/database.csv")
landslides = pd.read_csv("E:/pg/bpb/BPB-Publications/Datasets/catalog.csv")
volcanos = pd.read_csv("E:/pg/bpb/BPB-Publications/Datasets/database.csv")

# set seed for reproducibility
np.random.seed(0)
```

Figure 10.15: Importing required modules

If you check the landslides dataframe using `.head()` function, you will see that there is a date column on which we will build our example:

```python
landslides.head()
```

	id	date	time	continent_code	country_name	count
0	34	3/2/07	Night	NaN	United States	
1	42	3/22/07	NaN	NaN	United States	
2	56	4/6/07	NaN	NaN	United States	
3	59	4/14/07	NaN	NaN	Canada	
4	61	4/15/07	NaN	NaN	United States	

5 rows × 23 columns

Figure 10.16: Checking landslides DataFrame using .head() function

Looking at the data, we can tell that the date column contains dates, but does Python know that they're dates? Let's verify the data types of each column with the .info() function:

```
landslides.info()

<class 'pandas.core.frame.DataFrame'>
RangeIndex: 1693 entries, 0 to 1692
Data columns (total 23 columns):
id                  1693 non-null int64
date                1690 non-null object
time                629 non-null object
continent_code      164 non-null object
```

Figure 10.17: Verifying data types of each column using .info() function

Shocked to see a strange data type of the date column! Pandas, by default, use the *object* dtype for storing various types of data types. When you see a column with the dtype *object*, it will have strings in it. To convert the dtype object into date object, we will use pandas to_datetime() function for parsing date value as shown in the following *figure 10.18*:

```
# create a new column, date_parsed, with the parsed dates
landslides['date_parsed'] = pd.to_datetime(landslides['date'], format = "%m/%d/%y")
# print the first few rows
landslides['date_parsed'].head()

0    2007-03-02
1    2007-03-22
2    2007-04-06
3    2007-04-14
4    2007-04-15
Name: date_parsed, dtype: datetime64[ns]
```

Figure 10.18: Parsing date value

The dtype object is now converted into the datetime64 format, which is a standard one for storing dates. If you want to extract the day of the month from the date_parsed column, use the .dt.day function as shown in the following *figure 10.19*:

```
# get the day of the month from the date_parsed column
day_of_month_landslides = landslides['date_parsed'].dt.day
day_of_month_landslides

0     2.0
1    22.0
2     6.0
3    14.0
4    15.0
5    20.0
```

Figure 10.19: Extracting the day of the month

Apply the same approach and try your hand at fetching the day of the month from the volcanos dataset.

How to apply character encoding?

Character encodings are specific sets of rules for mapping from raw binary byte strings (that look like this: 0110100001101001) to characters that make up human-readable text (like `hello`). There are many different techniques used to encode such binary datasets and if you try converting such data in the text without knowing the encoding technique it was originally written in, you will end up with scrambled text.

While working with text in Python 3, you'll come across two main data types. One is the string, which is what text is by default. The other data is the bytes data type, which is a sequence of integers. Most datasets will probably be encoded with UTF-8. This is what Python expects by default, so most of the time you won't run into problems. However, sometimes you'll get an error like this:

UnicodeDecodeError: 'utf-8' codec can't decode byte 0x99 in position 11: invalid start byte

To understand this, let's work on the Kickstarts project again but this time try to read 2016 CSV file:

```
# try to read in a file not in UTF-8
kickstarter_2016 = pd.read_csv("E:/pg/bpb/BPB-Publications/Datasets/ks-projects-201612.csv")


---------------------------------------------------------------------------
UnicodeDecodeError                    Traceback (most recent call last)
pandas/_libs/parsers.pyx in pandas._libs.parsers.TextReader._convert_tokens (pandas\_libs\parsers.c:14858)()

pandas/_libs/parsers.pyx in pandas._libs.parsers.TextReader._convert_with_dtype (pandas\_libs\parsers.c:17119)()
```

Figure 10.20: Trying to read 2016 CSV file

To solve this error, you need to pass correct encoding while reading the file. We can check the encoding of this project's 2018 version file which you have already downloaded using chardet module as shown in the following *figure 10.21:*

```
# helpful character encoding module
import chardet

# look at the first ten thousand bytes to guess the character encoding
with open("E:/pg/bpb/BPB-Publications/Datasets/ks-projects-201801.csv", 'rb') as rawdata:
    result = chardet.detect(rawdata.read(10000))

# check what the character encoding might be
print(result)

{'encoding': 'Windows-1252', 'confidence': 0.73, 'language': ''}
```

Figure 10.21: Checking the encoding

Encoding is `Windows-125` having 73% confidence value. Let's see if that's correct:

```
# read in the file with the encoding detected by chardet
kickstarter_2016 = pd.read_csv("E:/pg/bpb/BPB-Publications/Datasets/ks-projects-201612.csv",
                               encoding='Windows-1252', low_memory=False)

# look at the first few lines
kickstarter_2016.head()
```

	ID	name	category	main_category	currency	deadline	goal	launched	pledged	state	ba
0	1000002330	The Songs of Adelaide & Abullah	Poetry	Publishing	GBP	2015-10-09 11:36:00	1000	2015-08-11 12:12:28	0	failed	
1	1000004038	Where is Hank?	Narrative Film	Film & Video	USD	2013-02-26 00:20:50	45000	2013-01-12 00:20:50	220	failed	

Figure 10.22: reading csv data with correct encoding

Cleaning inconsistent data

You may face duplicate data entry in your dataset like `Karachi` and `Karachi` where there is a space in the second or same name with case issues. These types of inconsistency need to be removed. To understand this type of situation, we will work on a dataset where suicide attacks held in Pakistan are mentioned. Let's understand this situation by importing the suicide attack dataset and explore the inconsistent column as below:

```
# read in our dat
suicide_attacks = pd.read_csv("E:/pg/bpb/BPB-Publications/Datasets/PakistanSuicideAttacks Ver 11 (30-November-2017).csv",
                              encoding='Windows-1252')
suicide_attacks.head()
```

	S#	Date	Islamic Date	Blast Day Type	Holiday Type	Time	City	Latitude	Longitude	Province	...	Targeted Sect if any	Killed Min	Killed Max	Injured Min	Injured Max	N Su B
0	1	Sunday-November 19-1995	25 Jumaada al-THaany 1416 A.H	Holiday	Weekend	NaN	Islamabad	33.7180	73.0718	Capital	...	None	14.0	15.0	NaN	60	
1	2	Monday-November 6-2000	10 SHa'baan 1421 A.H	Working Day	NaN	NaN	Karachi	24.9918	66.9911	Sindh	...	None	NaN	3.0	NaN	3	

Figure 10.23: Cleaning inconsistent data

Since our focus is on inconsistency, let's move on to the city name column:

```
# get all the unique values in the 'City' column
cities = suicide_attacks['City'].unique()

# sort them alphabetically and then take a closer look
cities.sort()
cities
```

```
array(['ATTOCK', 'Attock ', 'Bajaur Agency', 'Bannu', 'Bhakkar ', 'Buner',
       'Chakwal ', 'Chaman', 'Charsadda', 'Charsadda ', 'D. I Khan',
       'D.G Khan', 'D.G Khan ', 'D.I Khan', 'D.I Khan ', 'Dara Adam Khel',
       'Dara Adam khel', 'Fateh Jang', 'Ghallanai, Mohmand Agency ',
       'Gujrat', 'Hangu', 'Haripur', 'Hayatabad', 'Islamabad',
       'Islamabad ', 'Jacobabad', 'KURRAM AGENCY', 'Karachi', 'Karachi ',
```

Figure 10.24: Cleaning inconsistent data in City column

Let us format each cell data by converting every letter in lower case and by removing white spaces from the beginning and end of cells. You can easily do this using `str` module' `slower()` and `strip()` functions. Inconsistencies in capitalizations and trailing white spaces are very common in text data and you can fix a good 80% of your text data entry inconsistencies by doing this:

```
# convert to lower case
suicide_attacks['City'] = suicide_attacks['City'].str.lower()
# remove trailing white spaces
suicide_attacks['City'] = suicide_attacks['City'].str.strip()
```

Figure 10.25: Fixing inconsistencies using str module functions

Conclusion

If you have read this chapter carefully and applied the learning in your notebook, then at the end of this chapter you have gained practical knowledge of data cleaning process. There are many techniques to learn when it comes to mastering data science subject. After practicing the techniques covered in this chapter on different data sets, you'll gain competitive skills to stay ahead in the data science role. So, keep practicing and explore more techniques day by day. In the next chapter, we will learn about visualization in detail.

CHAPTER 11
Data Visualization

Data is very powerful. It's not easy to completely understand large data sets by looking at lots of numbers and statistics. For the ease of understanding, data needs to be classified and processed. It is a well-known fact that the human brain processes visual content better than it processes plain text. That's why data visualization is one of the core skills in data science. In simple words – visualization is nothing but, representing data in a visual form. This visual form can be charts, graphs, lists, maps, etc. In this chapter, you will work on a case study and learn different types of charts to plot with the help of Python's `matplotlib` and `seaborn` libraries along with `pandas`.

Structure

- Bar chart
- Line chart
- Histograms
- Scatter plot
- Stacked plot
- Box plot

Objective

After studying the chapter, you will become an expert in visualization using Pandas.

Bar chart

Bar charts or Bar graphs are the simplest forms of data visualization method. They map categories to numbers; that's why bar graphs are good to present the data of different groups that are being compared with each other. To understand how to plot a bar chart, you will work on the Wine Review Points dataset, which you can download in ZIP form from our repository. In this dataset, wine-producing provinces of the world (category) is compared to the number of labels of wines they produce (number). Let's load this ZIP file, unzip it, and read the file by following the same steps learned in the previous chapter:

```python
import zipfile
Dataset = "winemag-data_first150k.csv.zip"
with zipfile.ZipFile("E:/pg/bpb/BPB-Publications/Datasets/"+Dataset,"r") as z:
    z.extractall("E:/pg/bpb/BPB-Publications/Datasets")
```

Figure 11.1: Importing Zip file

The CSV file is now extracted and stored in the location mentioned in the `.extractall()` function. Read the CSV file and store data in a `pandas` library's `DataFrame` variable, as shown in the following *figure 11.2*:

```python
import pandas as pd
reviews_df = pd.read_csv("E:/pg/bpb/BPB-Publications/Datasets/winemag-data_first150k.csv", index_col=0)
reviews_df.head(5)
```

	country	description	designation	points	price	province	region_1	region_2	variety	winery
0	US	This tremendous 100% varietal wine hails from ...	Martha's Vineyard	96	235.0	California	Napa Valley	Napa	Cabernet Sauvignon	Heitz
1	Spain	Ripe aromas of fig, blackberry and cassis are ...	Carodorum Selección Especial Reserva	96	110.0	Northern Spain	Toro	NaN	Tinta de Toro	Bodega Carmen Rodríguez
2	US	Mac Watson honors the memory of a wine once ma...	Special Selected Late Harvest	96	90.0	California	Knights Valley	Sonoma	Sauvignon Blanc	Macauley
3	US	This spent 20 months in 30% new French oak, an...	Reserve	96	65.0	Oregon	Willamette Valley	Willamette Valley	Pinot Noir	Ponzi

Figure 11.2: Loading the wine review dataset into a DataFrame

Suppose you want to understand which province produces more wine than any other province in the world. For this comparison you can use the bar chart as shown in the following *figure 11.3*:

```
import matplotlib.pyplot as plt
reviews_df['province'].value_counts().head(10).plot.bar()
plt.xlabel('Province')
plt.ylabel('No of Wines')
plt.title('Provice with Wine Production Data')
plt.show()
```

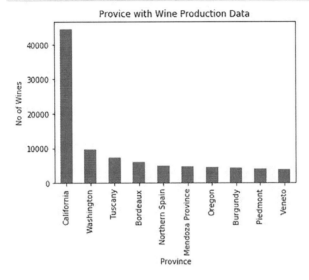

Figure 11.3: *Provinces with Wine Production Data*

Isn't it easy to clearly say that California produces more wine than any other province of the world? From this visualization, you can demonstrate a chart instead of showing statistics code to your client. That's is the beauty of data visualization. Now coming back to the actual code, we are using `matplotlib.pyplot` as our main plotting library. Next, we are using `value_counts()` function to find the frequency of the values present in the province column in descending order. For denoting the x and y axis with a name, we are using `xlabel()` and `ylabel()` functions of `pyplot`. Lastly, we have used the `show()` function to display the plots.

Line chart

A line chart or line graph is a type of chart that displays information as a series of data points called **markers** connected by straight line segments. Line graphs are used to display quantitative values over a continuous interval or time period. A line graph is most frequently used to show trends and analyze how the data has changed over time. In our example, let us draw a line graph to plot and understand wine review points using `plot.line()` function as shown in following *figure 11.4*:

```
import matplotlib.pyplot as plt
reviews_df['points'].value_counts().sort_index().plot.line()
plt.xlabel('points')
plt.ylabel('No of Wines')
plt.title('points with Wine Production Data')
plt.show()
```

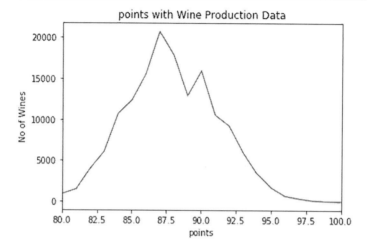

Figure 11.4: *Wine Review Points using plot.line() function*

Here, points in the wine review dataset denote the number of points *Wine Enthusiast* rated the wine on a scale of 1-100. From the preceding line chart, you can easily say that almost 20000 wines got 87 points in their reviews.

Histograms

A histogram looks like a bar plot. A histogram is a special kind of bar plot that splits your data into even intervals and displays the number of rows in each interval with bars. The only analytical difference is that instead of each bar representing a single value, it represents a range of values. However, histograms have one major shortcoming. Because they break space up into even intervals, they don't deal very well with skewed data (meaning it tends to have a long tail on one side or the other).

For example, let us check the number of wines which are priced less than $200 as shown in the following *figure 11.5*:

```
reviews_df[reviews_df['price'] < 200]['price'].plot.hist()
plt.show()
```

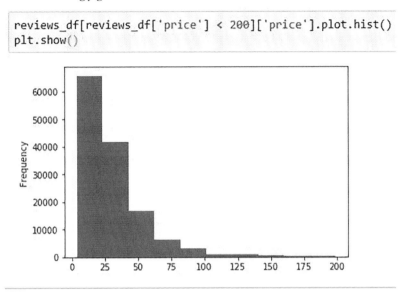

Figure 11.5: *Number of Wines priced below $200*

If you run the same code but price with greater than $200, then the plot will not break up in even interval. This is also one of the techniques to deal with skewness of the data. Histograms work best for interval variables without skew as well as for ordinal categorical variables.

Scatter plot

A scatter plot is a bivariate plot which simply maps each variable of interest to a point in two-dimensional space. If you want to see the relationship between two numerical variables, then you can use the scatter plot. In our wine dataset, suppose you want to check the relationship between price and points, then to visualize a scatter plot with the best fitting in our output cell, instead of taking all prices, we will take a sample like all the wines which have a price below $100, and then we will plot the relationship using `scatter()` function:

```
reviews_df[reviews_df['price'] < 100].sample(100).plot.scatter(x='price', y='points')
plt.show()
```

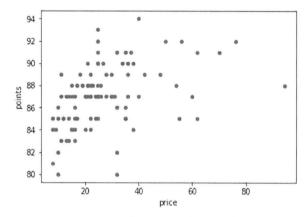

Figure 11.6: *Plotting relationship using scatter() function*

The preceding plot shows us that price and points are weakly correlated, which means that more expensive wines generally earn more points when reviewed. Scatter plot has one weakness – overplotting, therefore, scatter plots work best with relatively small datasets, and with variables which have a large number of unique values. That's why I have taken only 100 samples while plotting. Try without using the sample in the preceding code and see the difference in output.

Stacked plot

A stacked chart is one which plots the variables one on top of the other. It is like a bar graph or line chart, but it is subdivided into its components so that the comparisons, as well as the totals, can be seen. To plot a stacked plot, we will have to work on another dataset which represents the top five wine reviews:

```
wine_count_df = pd.read_csv("E:/pg/bpb/BPB-Publications/Datasets/top-five-wine-score-counts.csv", index_col=0)
wine_count_df.head()
```

points	Bordeaux-style Red Blend	Cabernet Sauvignon	Chardonnay	Pinot Noir	Red Blend
80	5.0	87.0	68.0	36.0	72.0
81	18.0	159.0	150.0	83.0	107.0
82	72.0	435.0	517.0	295.0	223.0
83	95.0	570.0	669.0	346.0	364.0
84	268.0	923.0	1146.0	733.0	602.0

Figure 11.7: *Stacked plot*

In this dataset, the review score of the top five wines is mentioned, which is a perfect example to visualize each component as a stacked plot. Let's plot a stacked plot:

```
wine_count_df.plot.bar(stacked=True)
plt.show()
```

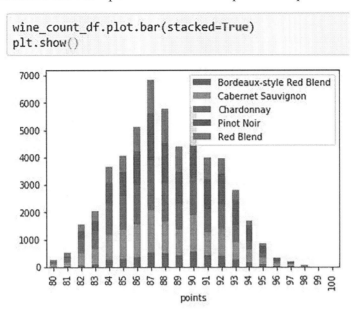

***Figure 11.8:** Plotting a stacked plot*

Doesn't it look beautiful? But this plot has the following two limitations:

- The first limitation is that the second variable in a stacked plot must be a variable with a very limited number of possible values.

- The second limitation is one of interpretability. As easy as they are to make and pretty to look at, stacked plots sometimes make it hard to distinguish concrete values. For example, looking at the preceding plots, can you tell which wine got a score of 87 more often: Red Blends (in purple), Pinot Noir (in red), or Chardonnay (in green)?

Box plot

If you want to visualize a statistics summary of a given dataset, then the box plot is your friend. As shown in the following *figure 11.9*, the left, and right of the solid-lined box are always the first and third quartiles (i.e., 25% and 75% of the data), and the band inside the box is always the second quartile (the median). The whiskers (i.e., the blue lines with the bars) extend from the box to show the range of the data:

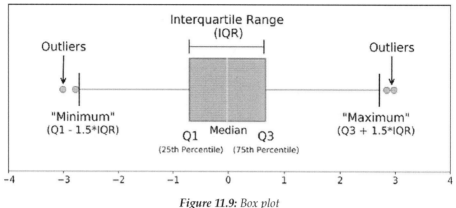

Figure 11.9: Box plot

Let's understand first these five statistical terms:

- **Median (Q2/50th Percentile)**: The middle value of the dataset.

- **First quartile (Q1/25th Percentile)**: The middle number between the smallest number (not the *minimum*) and the median of the dataset.

- **Third quartile (Q3/75th Percentile)**: The middle value between the median and the highest value (not the *maximum*) of the dataset.

- **Interquartile range (IQR)**: 25th to the 75th percentile.

- **Whiskers** (shown in blue)

- **Outlier**: The data point that is located outside the fences (*whiskers*)

- **Maximum**: Q3 + 1.5*IQR

- **Minimum**: Q1 -1.5*IQR

Let's see how to utilize a box plot on a real-world dataset – Breast Cancer Diagnostic, which you can download from our repository and read it as shown in the following *figure 11.10*:

```
import pandas as pd
cancer_df = pd.read_csv("E:/pg/bpb/BPB-Publications/Datasets/breast_cancer.csv")
cancer_df.head()
```

	id	diagnosis	radius_mean	texture_mean	perimeter_mean	area_mean	smoothness_mean	compactness_mean	concavity_mean	concave points_mean
0	842302	M	17.99	10.38	122.80	1001.0	0.11840	0.27760	0.3001	0.14710
1	842517	M	20.57	17.77	132.90	1326.0	0.08474	0.07864	0.0869	0.07017
2	84300903	M	19.69	21.25	130.00	1203.0	0.10960	0.15990	0.1974	0.12790
3	84348301	M	11.42	20.38	77.58	386.1	0.14250	0.28390	0.2414	0.10520
4	84358402	M	20.29	14.34	135.10	1297.0	0.10030	0.13280	0.1980	0.10430

5 rows × 33 columns

Figure 11.10: Utilizing a Box plot

The next task is to analyze the relationship between malignant or benign tumors (a categorical feature) and `area_mean` (continuous feature).

For this task, first, you need to separate the malignant or benign tumor data from the complete dataset based on the mean area. This time, I will use the `seaborn` library to plot my boxplot and save the plot as an image. For plotting a box plot we will use `boxplot()` function of the `seaborn` library as shown the following *figure 11.11*:

```
import seaborn as sns
malignant_tumour  = cancer_df[cancer_df['diagnosis']=='M']['area_mean']
benign_tumour  = cancer_df[cancer_df['diagnosis']=='B']['area_mean']
sns.boxplot(x='diagnosis', y='area_mean', data=cancer_df)
plt.savefig('E:/pg/bpb/BPB-Publications/Datasets/cancer_area_mean_diagnosis.png')
plt.show()
```

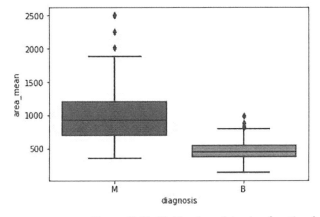

Figure 11.11: *Plotting box plot using function from seaborn library*

Using the preceding graph, we can compare the range and distribution of the area mean for malignant and benign diagnosis. We observe that there is a greater variability for malignant tumor area mean as well as larger outliers. Also, since the notches in the boxplots do not overlap, you can conclude that with 95% confidence, that the true medians do differ.

Conclusion

Data visualization is one of the core skills in data science. In order to start building useful models, we need to understand the underlying dataset. Effective data visualization is the most important tool in your arsenal for getting this done, and hence a critical skill for you to master. There are various readymade visualization tools like Tableau and QlikView present in the market, but you must know the basic plotting skills as we did in this chapter. The more you practice on actual datasets, the more you will gain your visualization knowledge; so, start practicing in your notebook and check what you can analyze from the output. In the next chapter, you will learn about the data pre-processing steps.

CHAPTER 12
Data Pre-processing

For achieving better results from the applied model in machine learning projects, properly formatted data is mandatory. Some machine learning models need the information to be in a particular format, for example, some machine learning algorithm(s) do not support null values. For such algorithms, null values have to be managed in the original raw data set. Another important reason for having formatted data is to evaluate it using more than one machine learning and deep learning algorithms and chose among the best fit algorithmic solution to the data problem. In this chapter, you will learn data pre-processing steps which will form the final step towards working with machine learning algorithms. You will learn **Feature Engineering** along with data cleaning and visualization with the help of a real-world case study.

Structure

- About the case-study
- Importing the dataset
- Exploratory data analysis
- Data cleaning and pre-processing
- Feature Engineering

Objective

After studying this chapter, you will be equipped with the skills to make your data ready to start working with machine learning algorithms.

About the case-study

In this chapter, we will analyze datasets of two pioneer e-retail merchants - *ModCloth* and *RentTheRunWay*. Both retailers want to improve their catalog size recommendation process and thus they asked data scientists to help. The following type of information is available in the datasets:

- Ratings and reviews
- Fit feedback (small/fit/large)
- Customer/product measurements
- Category information

These datasets are highly sparse, with most products and customers having only a single transaction. Note that, here a `product` refers to a specific size of a product, as your goal is to predict fitness for associated catalog sizes. Also, since different clothing products use different sizing conventions, you will standardize sizes into a single numerical scale preserving the order.

Importing the dataset

You can download the two datasets of each merchant from the link provided in the book for downloading the dataset. Both datasets are in the ZIP format. So before reading the actual file, you need to unzip it first, as shown in the following code block:

```
import zipfile
Dataset = "modcloth_final_data.json.zip"
with zipfile.ZipFile("E:/pg/bpb/BPB-Publications/Datasets/"+Dataset,"r") as z:
    z.extractall("E:/pg/bpb/BPB-Publications/Datasets")
```

Figure 12.1: Unzipping the datafile

Once you run the preceding code, it unzips the datafile which is in JSON format. Use the `pandas` library's `.read_json()` function to read this JSON file and store it in a dataframe for processing later:

```
modcloth_df = pd.read_json('E:/pg/bpb/BPB-Publications/Datasets/modcloth_final_data.json', lines=True)
modcloth_df.head()
```

	bra size	bust	category	cup size	fit	height	hips	item_id	length	quality	review_summary	review_text	shoe size	shoe width	size	user_id	user_name	waist
0	34.0	36	new	d	small	5ft 6in	38.0	123373	just right	5.0	NaN	NaN	NaN	NaN	7	991571	Emily	29.0
1	36.0	NaN	new	b	small	5ft 2in	30.0	123373	just right	3.0	NaN	NaN	NaN	NaN	13	587883	sydneybraden2001	31.0
2	32.0	NaN	new	b	small	5ft 7in	NaN	123373	slightly long	2.0	NaN	NaN	9.0	NaN	7	395665	Ugggh	30.0
3	NaN	NaN	new	dd/e	fit	NaN	NaN	123373	just right	5.0	NaN	NaN	NaN	NaN	21	875643	alexmeyer626	NaN
4	36.0	NaN	new	b	small	5ft 2in	NaN	123373	slightly long	5.0	NaN	NaN	NaN	NaN	18	944840	dberrones1	NaN

Figure 12.2: Using pandas library's function to read file

Exploratory data analysis

From the preceding head view of our case-study dataset, you will notice the following points:

- There are missing values (NaN) across the dataframe, which need to be handled.

- Cup-size contains some multiple preferences, which will need handling if we wish to define cup sizes as `category` datatype.

- `Height` column needs to be parsed for extracting the height in a numerical quantity – it looks like a `string` (object) right now.

Let's explore the columns and information of the dataset in details:

```
modcloth_df.columns
```

```
Index(['bra size', 'bust', 'category', 'cup size', 'fit', 'height', 'hips',
       'item_id', 'length', 'quality', 'review_summary', 'review_text',
       'shoe size', 'shoe width', 'size', 'user_id', 'user_name', 'waist'],
      dtype='object')
```

Figure 12.3: Exploring columns and information of dataset

It looks like there are spaces between some column names. So, let's rename the space with an underscore as shown in the following *figure 12.4*:

```
modcloth_df.columns = ['bra_size', 'bust', 'category', 'cup_size', 'fit', 'height', 'hips',
        'item_id', 'length', 'quality', 'review_summary', 'review_text',
        'shoe_size', 'shoe_width', 'size', 'user_id', 'user_name', 'waist']
modcloth_df.columns
```
```
Index(['bra_size', 'bust', 'category', 'cup_size', 'fit', 'height', 'hips',
        'item_id', 'length', 'quality', 'review_summary', 'review_text',
        'shoe_size', 'shoe_width', 'size', 'user_id', 'user_name', 'waist'],
       dtype='object')
```

Figure 12.4: Renaming space with an underscore

Let's move further and check the data types of each column so that you can make more observations:

```
modcloth_df.info()

<class 'pandas.core.frame.DataFrame'>
RangeIndex: 82790 entries, 0 to 82789
Data columns (total 18 columns):
bra_size          76772 non-null float64
bust              11854 non-null object
category          82790 non-null object
cup_size          76535 non-null object
fit               82790 non-null object
height            81683 non-null object
hips              56064 non-null float64
item_id           82790 non-null int64
length            82755 non-null object
quality           82722 non-null float64
review_summary    76065 non-null object
review_text       76065 non-null object
shoe_size         27915 non-null float64
shoe_width        18607 non-null object
size              82790 non-null int64
user_id           82790 non-null int64
user_name         82790 non-null object
waist              2882 non-null float64
dtypes: float64(5), int64(3), object(10)
memory usage: 11.4+ MB
```

Figure 12.5: Checking datatypes of each column

Once again if you analyze the data type of each column, you will find the following points:

- There is a total of 18 columns but out of 18, only 6 columns have complete data (82790).

- There is a lot of data missing in various columns like – bust, shoe width, shoe size, and waist.

- You need to especially look at the items which have shoe size and shoe width available – these could be shoes!

- A lot of the columns have strings (object) datatype, which need to be parsed into the category datatype for memory optimization.

Next, you can check the missing values in each column as shown in the following block of code:

```
missing_data = pd.DataFrame({'total_missing': modcloth_df.isnull().sum(),
                    'percentage_missing': (modcloth_df.isnull().sum()/82790)*100})
missing_data
```

Figure 12.6: Checking for missing values

	percentage_missing	total_missing
bra_size	7.268994	6018
bust	85.681846	70936
category	0.000000	0
cup_size	7.555260	6255
fit	0.000000	0
height	1.337118	1107
hips	32.281677	26726
item_id	0.000000	0
length	0.042276	35
quality	0.082136	68
review_summary	8.122962	6725
review_text	8.122962	6725
shoe_size	66.282160	54875
shoe_width	77.525063	64183
size	0.000000	0
user_id	0.000000	0
user_name	0.000000	0
waist	96.518903	79908

Figure 12.7: Analyzing the missing values

Further analyzing the output under that waist column, we surprisingly found a lot of NULL values (97%) – consider also that Modcloth is an online retail merchant and most of the data from Modcloth comes from the 3 categories of *dresses, tops, and bottoms*.

Let's dig more into the data before you dive into performing the pre-processing tasks as shown in the following *figure 12.8*:

```
modcloth_df.describe()
```

	bra_size	hips	item_id	quality	shoe_size	size	user_id	waist
count	76772.000000	56064.000000	82790.000000	82722.000000	27915.000000	82790.000000	82790.000000	2882.000000
mean	35.972125	40.358501	469325.229170	3.949058	8.145818	12.661602	498849.564718	31.319223
std	3.224907	5.827166	213999.803314	0.992783	1.336109	8.271952	286356.969459	5.302849
min	28.000000	30.000000	123373.000000	1.000000	5.000000	0.000000	6.000000	20.000000
25%	34.000000	36.000000	314980.000000	3.000000	7.000000	8.000000	252897.750000	28.000000
50%	36.000000	39.000000	454030.000000	4.000000	8.000000	12.000000	497913.500000	30.000000
75%	38.000000	43.000000	658440.000000	5.000000	9.000000	15.000000	744745.250000	34.000000
max	48.000000	60.000000	807722.000000	5.000000	38.000000	38.000000	999972.000000	50.000000

Figure 12.8: Analyzing the data

From the preceding statistical description, you can infer the following:

- Most of the shoe sizes are around 5-9, but the maximum shoe size is 38! It is surprising because if you check their website, you will find that they use UK shoe sizing.

- Size has a minimum of 0 and maximum size matches the maximum shoe size.

Keeping in mind the basic statistical analysis we have done till now, let's check the outliers in our dataset by plotting a box plot using numerical columns of the dataset:

```
num_cols = ['bra_size','hips','quality','shoe_size','size','waist']
plt.figure(figsize=(10,5))
modcloth_df[num_cols].boxplot()
plt.title("Numerical variables in Modcloth dataset", fontsize=20)
plt.show()
```

Figure 12.9: Plotting a box plot using numerical columns

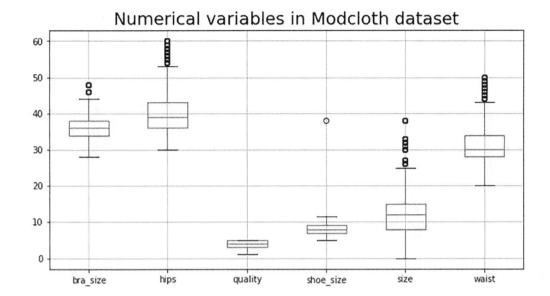

Figure 12.10: Numerical variables in Modcloth dataset

You can analyze the following key points from the preceding box plot:

- The single maximum value of shoe size (38) is an outlier, and you should ideally remove that row or handle that outlier value. Since it is a single value in the whole dataset, it could be wrongly entered by the customer or it could be a simple noise. As of now, you can enter this as a null value.

- In the bra-size, you can see that boxplot shows 2 values as outliers, as per the **Inter-Quartile Range** (**IQR**). Thus, you can visualize the distribution of bra_size vs. size (bivariate) to arrive at an understanding of the values.

The next step will be to handle the null values in shoe size and then visualize the bra_size vs. size:

```
modcloth_df.at[37313,'shoe_size'] = None
```

```
plt.figure(figsize=(10,5))
plt.xlabel("bra_size")
plt.ylabel("size")
plt.suptitle("Joint distribution of bra_size vs size")
plt.plot(modcloth_df.bra_size, modcloth_df['size'], 'bo', alpha=0.2)
plt.show()
```

Figure 12.11: Handling null values

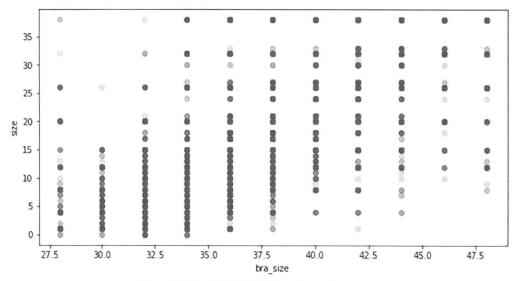

Figure 12.12: Joint distribution of bra_size vs. size

From the plot we can't see any significant deviation from usual behavior for bra-size; in fact for all other numerical variables as well, you can expect the *apparent* outliers, from the boxplot to behave similarly. Now, we 'll head to pre-processing the dataset for suitable visualizations.

Data cleaning and pre-processing

Let's handle the variables and change the data type to the appropriate type for each column. For this purpose, you will define a function first for creating the distribution plot of different variables as shown in the following *figure 12.13*:

```
# function for initial distribution of features
def plot_features(col, ax):
    modcloth_df[col][modcloth_df[col].notnull()].value_counts().plot('bar', facecolor='b', ax=ax)
    ax.set_xlabel('{}'.format(col), fontsize=20)
    ax.set_title("{} on Modcloth Dataset".format(col))
    return ax

f, ax = plt.subplots(3,3, figsize = (20,13))
f.tight_layout(h_pad=9, w_pad=2, rect=[0, 0.03, 1, 0.93])
cols = ['bra_size','bust', 'category', 'cup_size', 'fit', 'height', 'hips', 'length', 'quality']
k = 0
for i in range(3):
    for j in range(3):
        plot_features(cols[k], ax[i][j])
        k += 1
__ = plt.suptitle("Initial Distributions of features")
plt.show()
```

Figure 12.13: Defining the function for creating distribution plot

Once you run the preceding function, it will draw the following, which looks like the plot in your notebook:

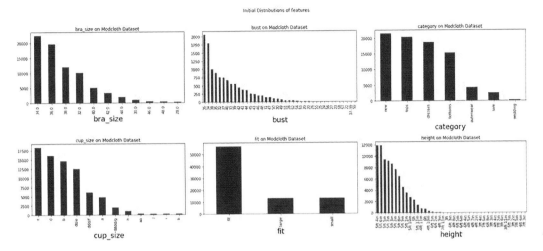

Figure 12.14: *Initial distribution of features*

Looking at the individual plots from the output, you can analyze and infer the following:

- **bra_size**: Although it looks numerical, it only ranges from 28 to 48, with most of the sizes lying around 34-38. You can see here that most of the buyers have a bra-sizing of 34 or 36. It makes sense to convert this to the categorical data type. You can further refine the analysis by filling the NaN values into an Unknown category.

- **bust**: You can see by looking at the values which are not null, that bust should be an integer data type. You can further refine the data where the bust is given as, '37-39' and replace the entry of '37-39' with its mean, i.e., 38, for analysis purposes. Later convert the data type into int.

- **category**: None missing; you can change it to the data type category.

- **cup size**: Change the data type to the category for this column. This column has around 7% missing values.

- **fit**: Change the data type to the category for this column. You can see that a vast majority of customers gave good fit feedback for the items on Modcloth!

- **height**: You need to parse the height column as currently, it is a string object, of the form - Xft. It will make sense to convert height to centimeters. We also take a look at the rows where the height data is missing.

Let's apply these observations one by one as shown in the following *figure 12.15*:

```
modcloth_df.cup_size.fillna('Unknown', inplace=True)
modcloth_df.cup_size = modcloth_df.cup_size.astype('category').cat.as_ordered()
modcloth_df.fit = modcloth_df.fit.astype('category')
```

```
def change_in_cms(x):
    # function to chnage height in cm
    if type(x) == type(1.0):
        return
    try:
        return (int(x[0])*30.48) + (int(x[4:-2])*2.54)
    except:
        return (int(x[0])*30.48)
modcloth_df.height = modcloth_df.height.apply(change_in_cms)
```

Figure 12.15: Applying the observations

Feature Engineering

Creating new features from existing ones is called *feature engineering*. This step improves your model accuracy amazingly. To extract a new feature, you must understand the actual business problem, it's dataset and you must think out of the box sometimes. In the given dataset, we will try to do the same, so let's start this approach by creating a new feature of first_time_user.

You can use the following logic to identify first time buyer:

- If bra_size/cup_size has a value and height, hips, shoe_size, shoe_width, and waist do not - it is a first-time buyer of lingerie.

- If shoe_size/shoe_width has a value and bra_size, cup_size, height, hips, and waist do not - it is a first-time buyer of shoes.

- If hips/waist have a value and bra_size, cup_size, height, shoe_size, and shoe_width do not - it is a first-time buyer of a dress/tops.

You can verify the above logic as the following, before creating the new feature:

- Looking at the few rows where either bra_size or cup_size exists, but no other measurements are available.

- Looking at the few rows where either shoe_size or shoe_width exists, but no other measurements are available.

- Looking at the few rows where either hips or waist exists, but no other measurements are available.

Now we can add a new column to the original data - `first_time_user`, with Boolean data type which will indicate if a user / a transaction, is a first-time user or not. This is based on the grounds that Modcloth has no previous information about the person; in fact, it is possible that the new user did multiple transactions for the first time!

```
lingerie_logic = (((modcloth_df.bra_size != 'Unknown') | (modcloth_df.cup_size != 'Unknown'))
                & (modcloth_df.height.isnull()) & (modcloth_df.hips.isnull()) &
                (modcloth_df.shoe_size.isnull()) & (modcloth_df.shoe_width.isnull()) & (modcloth_df.waist.isnull()))

shoe_logic = ((modcloth_df.bra_size == 'Unknown') & (modcloth_df.cup_size == 'Unknown') & (modcloth_df.height.isnull())
            & (modcloth_df.hips.isnull()) & ((modcloth_df.shoe_size.notnull()) | (modcloth_df.shoe_width.notnull()))
            & (modcloth_df.waist.isnull())))

dress_logic = ((modcloth_df.bra_size == 'Unknown') & (modcloth_df.cup_size == 'Unknown') &
            (modcloth_df.height.isnull()) & ((modcloth_df.hips.notnull()) | (modcloth_df.waist.notnull())) &
            (modcloth_df.shoe_size.isnull()) & (modcloth_df.shoe_width.isnull()))

modcloth_df['first_time_user'] = (lingerie_logic | shoe_logic | dress_logic)
print("Column is added!")
print("Total transactions by first time users who bought bra, shoes, or a dress: " + str(sum(modcloth_df.first_time_user)))
print("Total first time users: " + str(len(modcloth_df[(lingerie_logic | shoe_logic | dress_logic)].user_id.unique())))
```

```
Column is added!
Total transactions by first time users who bought bra, shoes, or a dress: 903
Total first time users: 565
```

Figure 12.16: Adding a new column

Let's move further and observe other columns; you will find the following analysis result:

- `hips`: **Hips column has a lot of missing values** ~ 32.28%! Maybe Modcloth never got this data from the user. **You cannot remove** such a significant chunk of the data, so you need another way of handling this feature. You will learn how to bin the data - based on quartiles.

- `length`: **There are only 35 missing rows in length**. Most probably the customers did not leave behind the feedback or the data was corrupted in these rows. However, you should be able to impute these values using review related fields (if they are filled!). Or you could also simply choose to remove these rows. For the sake of this analysis, we will remove these rows.

- `quality`: **There are only 68 missing rows in quality**. Just like we assumed the possibility for length column, the customers did not leave behind the feedback or the data was corrupted in these rows. We will remove these rows and convert the data type to an ordinal variable (ordered categorical).

```
# cleaning hips column
modcloth_df.hips = modcloth_df.hips.fillna(-1.0)
bins = [-5,0,31,37,40,44,75]
labels = ['Unknown','XS','S','M', 'L','XL']
modcloth_df.hips = pd.cut(modcloth_df.hips, bins, labels=labels)

# cleaning length column
missing_rows = modcloth_df[modcloth_df.length.isnull()].index
modcloth_df.drop(missing_rows, axis = 0, inplace=True)

# cleaning quality
missing_rows = modcloth_df[modcloth_df.quality.isnull()].index
modcloth_df.drop(missing_rows, axis = 0, inplace=True)
modcloth_df.quality = modcloth_df.quality.astype('category').cat.as_ordered()
```

Figure 12.17: Cleaning the columns

Let's analyze the remaining columns:

- review_summary/review_text: The NaN values are there because these reviews are simply not provided by customers. Let's just fill those as Unknown.

- shoe_size: Roughly 66.3% of the shoe_size data is missing. We will have to change the shoe_size into category data type and fill the NaN values as Unknown.

- shoe_width: Roughly 77.5% of the shoe_width data is missing. We will have to fill the NaN values as Unknown.

- waist: Waist column has the highest number of missing values - 96.5%! We will have to drop this column.

- bust: 85.6% missing values and highly correlated to bra_size. We'll have to remove them.

- user_name: user_name itself is not needed with the user_id given. We'll have to remove them.

Let's apply the above analysis to our dataframe:

```
modcloth_df.review_summary = modcloth_df.review_summary.fillna('Unknown')
modcloth_df.review_text = modcloth_df.review_text.fillna('Unkown')
modcloth_df.shoe_size = modcloth_df.shoe_size.fillna('Unknown')
modcloth_df.shoe_size = modcloth_df.shoe_size.astype('category').cat.as_ordered()
modcloth_df.shoe_width = modcloth_df.shoe_width.fillna('Unknown')
modcloth_df.drop(['waist', 'bust', 'user_name'], axis=1, inplace=True)
missing_rows = modcloth_df[modcloth_df.height.isnull()].index
modcloth_df.drop(missing_rows, axis = 0, inplace=True)
```

Figure 12.18: Applying the analysis

Now if you check the dataset using `.info()`, you will find that there are no more missing values! You can move onto visualizing and gaining more insight into the data.

Here, you will **visualize how the items of different categories fared in terms of - fit, length, and quality**. This will tell Modcloth which categories need more attention! For this, you can plot 2 distributions in categories like the following:

- **Unnormalized distributions**: Viewing the frequency counts directly - for comparison across categories. We also include the best fit, length, or quality measure in this plot.

- **Normalized distributions**: Viewing the distribution for the category after normalizing the counts, amongst the category itself - it will help us compare what the major reason was for return amongst the category itself. We exclude the best sizing and quality measures, to focus on the predominant reasons for return per category (if any).

For this purpose, I have used various functions in the next code block as shown in the following *figure 12.19*:

```python
# functions for Unnormalized and Normalized distributions
def plot_barh(df,col, cmap = None, stacked=False, norm = None):
    df.plot(kind='barh', colormap=cmap, stacked=stacked)
    fig = plt.gcf()
    fig.set_size_inches(24,12)
    plt.title("Category vs {}-feedback -  Modcloth {}".format(col, '(Normalized)' if norm else ''))
    plt.ylabel('Category', fontsize = 18)
    plot = plt.xlabel('Frequency', fontsize=18)


def norm_counts(t):
    norms = np.linalg.norm(t.fillna(0), axis=1)
    t_norm = t[0:0]
    for row, euc in zip(t.iterrows(), norms):
        t_norm.loc[row[0]] = list(map(lambda x: x/euc, list(row[1])))
    return t_norm
```

Figure 12.19: Using various functions

Let's apply our functions to visualize the comparison of `category` and fit:

```python
# Category vs. Fit
group_by_category = modcloth_df.groupby('category')
cat_fit = group_by_category['fit'].value_counts()
cat_fit = cat_fit.unstack()
cat_fit_norm = norm_counts(cat_fit)
cat_fit_norm.drop(['fit'], axis=1, inplace=True)
plot_barh(cat_fit, 'fit')
plt.show()
```

Figure 12.20: Visualizing comparison of category and fit

The output will look like below:

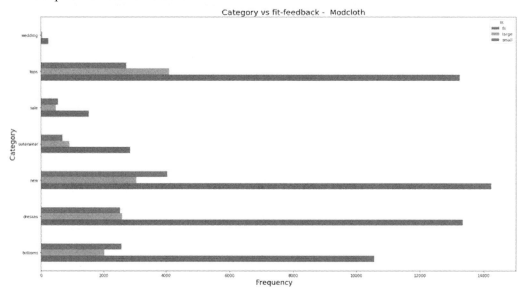

Figure 12.21: Output of comparison

Analyze the preceding plot, and you can find the following observation:

- **Best-fit response (fit)** has been highest for new, dresses, and tops categories.
- Overall maximum bad-fit feedback has belonged mostly to 2 categories - new and tops! Dresses and bottoms categories follow.
- Weddings, outerwear, and sale are not prominent in our visualization - mostly due to the lack of transactions in these categories.

You can draw the same plot to see the comparison between category and length; try at your end and analyze what observation you can make! There is another dataset of *RentTheRunWay* merchant, which I have provided in the datasets for your practice. Try implementing the learnings from this chapter to the dataset and see what observations you can make.

Conclusion

Feature Engineering and visualization are very impactful skills in data analysis. If done in the right way, they can push your machine learning modeling in a very positive way. Achieving the expertise in both skills requires practicing all the previous chapters, as well as this chapter learning in different datasets. Don't just load the dataset in your notebook - try to understand the actual business problem first, explore each attributes of the dataset, think how you can extract a new feature from the existing one, and what will be the impact of it on analysis. Keep practicing and in the next chapter you will start your machine learning journey.

CHAPTER 13
Supervised Machine Learning

In the previous chapters of this book, you have gained all the required skills to jump into the **machine learning (ML)** world. ML is the field of teaching machines and computers to learn from existing data to make predictions on new data without being explicitly programmed. In this chapter, you will learn about different types of machine learning, deep dive into some supervised machine learning techniques, and how to use Python to perform supervised learning. You will also learn how to build predictive models, tune their parameters, and tell how well they will perform on unseen data, all this while using real-world datasets. You will do so using `scikit-learn`, one of the most popular and user-friendly machine learning libraries for Python.

Structure

- Some common ML terms
- Introduction to machine learning (ML)
- List of common ML algorithms
- Supervised ML fundamentals
- Solving a classification ML problem
- Solving a regression ML problem

- How to tune your ML model?
- How to handle categorical variables in Sklearn?
- The advance technique to handle missing data

Objective

After studying and practicing this chapter, you will be an expert in solving supervised ML problems.

Some common ML terms

- **Dataset**: It is a collection of data that is organized into some types of data structure.

- **Model**: The representation of what an ML system has learned from the training data. To generate a machine learning model, you will need to provide training data to a machine learning algorithm to learn from.

- **Training**: The process of determining the ideal parameters comprising a model.

- **Learning**: The output of the training process is a machine learning model that you can then use to make predictions. This process is called learning.

- **Training dataset**: The subset of the data set used to train a model.

- **Validation dataset**: A subset of the data set; disjunct from the training dataset that you use to adjust hyperparameters.

- **Testing dataset**: The subset of the data set that you use to test your model after the model has gone through initial vetting by the validation set.

- **Hyperparameter**: It is a parameter whose value is set before training a machine learning or deep learning model. Different models require different hyperparameters and some require none.

- **Parameter**: A variable of a model that the ML system trains on its own.

- **Target**: The target is the output of the input variables. A target variable is also called a **dependentvariable** or **responsevariable**.

- **Feature**: They are individual independent variables that act as the input in your system. You can consider one column of your data set to be one feature. Sometimes these are also called **predictorvariables** or **independentvariables** or attributes and the number of features is called dimensions.

- **Label**: Labels are the final output. You can also consider the output classes to be the labels.

- **Fit**: Capture patterns from provided data. This is the heart of modeling.

- **Evaluate**: Determine how accurate the model's predictions are.
- **Regularization**: It is the method to estimate a preferred complexity of the machine learning model so that the model generalizes, and the over-fit/under-fit problem is avoided.

Introduction to machine learning (ML)

Machine learning algorithms are divided into the following four categories according to their purpose:

- Supervised learning
- Unsupervised learning
- Semi-supervised learning
- Reinforcement learning

Supervised learning

Supervised ML learning algorithms try to model relationships and dependencies between the target prediction output and the input features such that we can predict the output values for new data based on those relationships which it learns from the original data set. Supervised ML algorithm is further divided into the following two categories based on two types of problems:

- **Classification**: The classification problem can be defined as the problem that brings output variable, which falls just in particular categories, such as the "red" or "blue", "male" or "female" or it could be "disease" and "no disease". Some examples are - A mail is spam or not? Is this a picture of a car or a bus?

- **Regression**: Regression problem is when the output variable is a real value, such as "dollars", "Rupees" or it could be "weight". Some examples are - What is the price of a house in a specific city? What is the value of the stock?

Unsupervised learning

Unsupervised ML Learning algorithms are used when computer/system is trained with unlabelled data - meaning the training data does not include targets or in other sense, we don't tell the system where to go. On the contrary, a system will arrive at an understanding by itself from the data we provide. These algorithms are useful in cases where the human expert doesn't know what to look for in the data. Clustering is the most important unsupervised ML problem, where we group similar things. For the grouping of data, we don't provide the labels, the system understands from data itself and clusters the data. Some examples are - given a set of tweets, cluster data based on the content of tweets, or based on a set of images or clusters into different objects.

Semi-supervised learning

The semi-supervised ML Learning algorithm falls in between the two types of algorithms mentioned earlier. In many practical situations, the cost to label is quite high, since it requires skilled human experts to do that. So, in the absence of labels in most of the observations (but present in few), semi-supervised algorithms are the best candidates for the model building. Speech analysis and web content classification are two classic examples, of semi-supervised learning models.

Reinforcement learning

The reinforcement ML learning algorithm allows machines/software agents to automatically determine the ideal behavior within a specific context, in order to maximize its performance. In this process-input state, which is observed by the agent, the decision-making function is used to make the agent perform an action; after the action is performed, the agent receives reward or reinforcement from the environment and then the state-action pairing information about the reward is stored. Some applications of the reinforcement learning algorithms are computer played board games (Chess, Go), robotic hands, and self-driving cars.

List of common ML algorithms

The following is a list of must-know algorithms:

- Linear regression
- Logistic regression
- Decision tree
- SVM
- Naive Bayes
- kNN
- K-Means
- Random Forest
- Dimensionality Reduction algorithms
- Gradient Boosting algorithms
- GBM
- XGBoost

- LightGBM
- CatBoost

In the next few chapters, we will learn to apply these algorithms, like Logistic Regression, Linear Discriminant Analysis, k-Nearest Neighbors, Decision Trees, Gradient Boosting, and Support Vector Machine to real-life case studies, and understand how they help provide human-like solutions.

Supervised ML fundamentals

In supervised ML problems, we act as the teacher where we feed the computer with training data containing the input/predictors. We show the system correct answers (output) obtained from analyzing the data and from the analysis the computer should be able to learn the patterns to predict the output values for new input data based on relationships it learned by analyzing the original datasets. In more simple words, we first train the model with lots of training data (inputs and targets), then with new data and the logic we got earlier, we predict the output.

The following image shows thumb rule to distinguish between two types of supervised ML problems:

- **Classification**: The target variable consists of categories
- **Regression**: The target variable is continuous.

The first type of supervised ML algorithm - classification algorithms, are used when the desired output is a discrete label. In other words, they're helpful when the answer to your question about your business falls under a finite set of possible outcomes. Many use cases, such as determining whether an email is a spam or not, have only two possible outcomes. This is called a binary classification.

Multi-label classification captures everything else and is useful for customer segmentation, audio and image categorization, and text analysis for mining customer sentiment.

Following is a list of some common classification ML algorithms:

- **Linear Classifiers:** Logistic Regression and Naive Bayes Classifier
- Support Vector Machines
- Decision Trees
- Boosted Trees
- Random Forest
- Neural Networks
- Nearest Neighbor

The second type of Supervised ML algorithm – regression, is useful for predicting continuous outputs. That means the answer to your question is represented by a quantity that can be flexibly determined based on the inputs of the model rather than being confined to a set of possible labels. Linear regression is one form of regression algorithm. The representation of linear regression is an equation that describes a line that best fits the relationship between the input variables (x) and the output variables (y), by finding specific weightings for the input variables called coefficients (B). For example: $y = B0 + B1 * x$

We will predict y given the input x as the goal of the linear regression learning algorithm is to find the values for the coefficients $B0$ and $B1$.

> In machine learning, there's something called the "No Free Lunch" theorem. In a nutshell, it states that no one algorithm works best for every problem, and it's especially relevant for supervised learning (i.e., predictive modeling).

Logistic Regression

Don't confuse with the name, it is a classification model. **Logistic regression (LR)** is used to describe data and to explain the relationship between one dependent binary variable and one or more nominal, ordinal, interval, or ratio-level independent variables. Behind the scenes, the logistic regression algorithm uses a linear equation with independent predictors to predict a value. The predicted value can be anywhere between negative infinity to positive infinity. We need the output of the algorithm to be class variable, i.e., 0-no, 1-yes. LR is based on the probability (p) so if the probability > 0.5, the data is labeled as '1', otherwise data is labeled as '0'. By default, the value of the probability threshold (p) in LR is 0.5.

Decision Tree Classifier

The decision tree classifiers organized a series of test questions and conditions in a tree structure. In the decision tree, the root and internal nodes contain attribute test conditions to separate records that have different characteristics. All the terminal node is assigned a class label - Yes or No. Once the decision tree has been constructed, classifying a test record is straightforward. Starting from the root node, we apply the test condition to the record and follow the appropriate branch based on the outcome of the test. It then leads us either to another internal node, for which a new test condition is applied or to a leaf node. When we reach the leaf node, the class label associated with the leaf node is then assigned to the record. Various efficient algorithms have been developed to construct a reasonably accurate, albeit suboptimal, decision tree in a reasonable amount of time. For example, Hunt's algorithm, ID3, C4.5, CART, SPRINT are greedy decision tree induction algorithms.

K-Nearest Neighbor Classifier

The principle behind the nearest neighbor classification consists of finding a predefined number, i.e., the 'k' - of training samples closest in distance to a new sample, which has to be classified. The label of the new sample will be defined by these neighbors. L-nearest neighbor classifiers have a fixed user-defined constant for the number of neighbors which has to be determined. There are also radius-based neighbor learning algorithms, which has a varying number of neighbors based on the local density of points, all the samples inside of a fixed radius. The distance can, in general, be any metric measure; standard Euclidean distance is the most common choice. Neighbors-based methods are known as non-generalizing machine learning methods since they simply *remember* all of its training data. Classification can be computed by a majority vote of the nearest neighbors of the unknown sample.

Linear Discriminant Analysis (LDA)

Linear Discriminant Analysis is a dimensionality reduction technique but can also be used as a linear classifier technique. Since Logistic regression can become unstable when the classes are well separated or when there are few examples from which to estimate the parameters; LDA is a better technique in such cases. LDA model consists of the statistical properties of your data, calculated for each class. For a single input variable (x), this is the mean and the variance of the variable for each class. For multiple variables, these are the same properties calculated over the multivariate Gaussian, namely the means and the covariance matrix.

These statistical properties are estimated from your data and plug into the LDA equation to make predictions. These are the model values that you would save to file for your model.

Gaussian Naive Bayes Classifier

A **Gaussian Naive Bayes (NB)** algorithm is a special type of NB algorithm. It's specifically used when the features have continuous values. It's also assumed that all the features are following a Gaussian distribution, i.e., normal distribution. Remember that Bayes' theorem is based on conditional probability. The conditional probability helps us in calculating the probability that something will happen, given that something else has already happened.

Support Vector Classifier

Support Vector Machine (SVM) is a supervised machine learning algorithm that can be used for either classification or regression challenges. In the SVM Classifier algorithm, we plot each data item as a point in n-dimensional space (where *n* is the number of features you have) with the value of each feature being the value of a particular coordinate. Then, we perform classification by finding the hyper-plane that differentiates the two classes very well. SVMs are simply the coordinates of individual observation. SVM is a frontier that best segregates the two classes (hyper-plane/line).

Solving a classification ML problem

For solving a supervised machine learning problem, you need labeled data. You can get labeled data either in the form of a historical data with labels or you can perform experiments like A/B testing to get labeled data or get from crowdsourcing labeled data. In all cases, our goal is to learn from the data and then make a prediction on new data based on past learning. To understand this in our next example, we will use Python's `sci-kit learn` or `sklearn` library to solve a classification problem. Except for `sklearn`, there are `TensorFlow` and `keras` libraries also widely used in solving ML problems.

> **Sklearnapi expects inputs in numpy array, so always check the data type of the data and convert it accordingly. Also, it expects that the data should not have missing values so handle the missing values before training the model.**

About the dataset

You will work on the best known and simple dataset named Iris, to be found in the pattern recognition. Iris is a plant that has three species. This dataset was introduced by the British statistician *Ronald Fisher* in 1936. Based on the features of this plant, Fisher developed a linear discriminant model to distinguish the Iris species with each other. The data set contains 3 classes of 50 instances each, where each class refers to a type of iris plant. One class is linearly separable from the other 2; the latter are NOT linearly separable from each other.

Attribute information
- sepal length in cm
- sepal width in cm
- petal length in cm
- petal width in cm
- class:
    - Iris Setosa
    - Iris Versicolour
    - Iris Virginica

Goal: Your goal is to predict the class of an iris plant.

From the above description of the problem, you can understand that sepal length/ width and petal length/width are the features, whereas Species is the Target variable. Species have three possibilities - Versicolor, Virginica, Setosa. This is a multi-class classification problem. Along with many datasets, the iris dataset is also present in the sklearn library, so you don't need to download it. The complete solution of this exercise has been done as a notebook for your reference, named as Solving a classification ML problem.ipynb. Let's start our step-by-step process to solve the problem:

1. Loading the dataset from sklearn library:

```
from sklearn import datasets
import pandas as pd
import numpy as np
import matplotlib.pyplot as plt
plt.style.use('ggplot')
```

```
#load the iris dataset
iris = datasets.load_iris()
```

Figure 13.1: Loading dataset

2. After importing the dataset, check the type of the dataset as shown in the following *figure 13.2*:

```
print(type(iris))
```

```
<class 'sklearn.utils.Bunch'>
```

Figure 13.2: Checking type of dataset

It will show that the datatype is of class Bunch, which is like a dictionary containing key-value; each key will be unique in the key-value pair and the values can be accessed if you know the keys. To find out the list of keys present in the dataset iris, you can print the keys with .keys() function as shown in the following *figure 13.3*:

```
print(iris.keys())
```

```
dict_keys(['data', 'target', 'target_names', 'DESCR', 'feature_names'])
```

Figure 13.3: Printing keys with .keys() function

3. After diagnosis of a data key with the **shape** attribute, you will notice that there are a total of **150** samples (observations) and 4 features in iris data:

```
#check rows(samples) and columns(features) in iris data
iris.data.shape
```

```
(150, 4)
```

Figure 13.4: Diagnosis of the data key

4. Let's look at the values associated with the **target** variable as shown in the following *figure 13.5*:

```
#check target variables
iris.target_names
```

```
array(['setosa', 'versicolor', 'virginica'], dtype='<U10')
```

Figure 13.5: Values associated with target variable

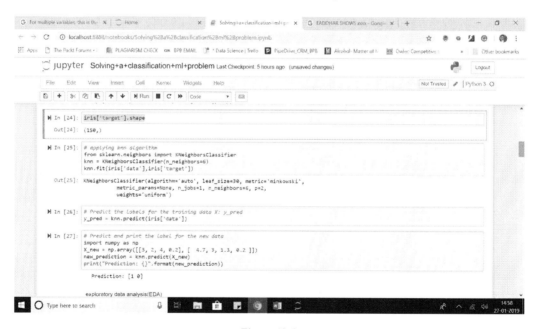

Figure 13.6

5. In the next step, we will store iris plant's length/width and species in separate variables so that you can pass these two variables in further processing. Here, you can also convert the iris data, which is in n-dimensional array data type, into a Pandas data frame using Pandas `DataFrame()` function:

```
X = iris.data
y = iris.target
#converting data in Pandas Dataframe
iris_df = pd.DataFrame(X, columns=iris.feature_names)
#check first five rows of iris dataframe
print(iris_df.head())
```

	sepal length (cm)	sepal width (cm)	petal length (cm)	petal width (cm)
0	5.1	3.5	1.4	0.2
1	4.9	3.0	1.4	0.2
2	4.7	3.2	1.3	0.2
3	4.6	3.1	1.5	0.2
4	5.0	3.6	1.4	0.2

Figure 13.7: Converting iris data

6. Next, to visualize the relationship between samples, we can plot a histogram plot as shown in the following *figure 13.8* and *13.9*:

```
#plotting histogram of features
_ = pd.plotting.scatter_matrix(iris_df, c=y, figsize=[8,8], s=150, marker='D')
plt.show()
```

Figure 13.8: Plotting histogram of features

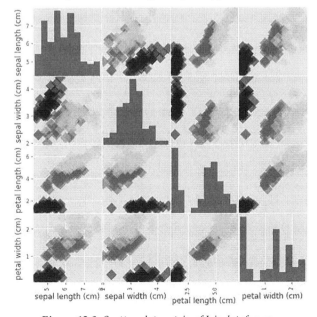

Figure 13.9: Scatter plot matrix of Iris dataframe

Here, we have created a scatter plot matrix of our Iris dataframe using the `scatter_matrix` method in `pandas.plotting`. In simple words, the scatter matrix is plotting each of the columns specified against other columns which you can see as the diagonal of the matrix.

7. As a next step, we will split the loaded dataset into two sets - 80% of which we will use to train our models and 20% of which we will hold back as a validation dataset. Splitting a dataset is an important and highly recommended step while testing and applying a machine learning solution to a problem:

```
validation_size = 0.20
seed = 7
from sklearn import model_selection
X_train, X_validation, Y_train, Y_validation = model_selection.train_test_split(X, y,
                                                          test_size=validation_size,
                                                          random_state=seed)
```

Figure 13.10: Splitting a dataset

Here, we have used `train_test_split()` function of sklearn's `model_selection` package. This function splits arrays or matrices into a random train, and test subsets. In this function we pass the feature data as the first argument, target as the second argument, and proportion of the original data for testing as `test_size` and last the seed for random number generations. This function returns four arrays - the training data, the test data, the training labels, and the test labels; so we have unpacked these four into variables named as `X_train, X_validation, Y_train, Y_validation` respectively. Now you have training data in the `X_train` and `Y_train` for preparing models and an `X_validation` and `Y_validation` sets that we can use later as validation.

8. Next, for estimating the accuracy of your model, you can use the Cross-validation technique which is a statistical method used to estimate the skill of machine learning models. It is commonly used in applied machine learning to compare and select a model for a given predictive modeling problem. Here we used 10 in place of k so 10-fold cross-validation will split our dataset into 10 parts - train on 9 and test on 1 and repeat for all combinations of train-test splits.

Why train/test split and cross-validation?

For understanding the importance of train/test split and cross-validation, we need to first understand the two types of problems in ML - **Overfitting** and **Underfitting** a model. Overfitting means that the model we trained has been trained *too well* and is now, well, fit too closely to the training dataset. This usually happens when the model is too complex (i.e., too many features/variables compared to the number of observations). This model will be very accurate on the training data but will probably be not very accurate on untrained or new data. It is because this model is not generalized, meaning you can generalize the results, and can't make any inferences on other data, which is, ultimately, what you are trying to do. In contrast to overfitting, underfitting is when a model is underfitted, which means that the model does not fit the training data and therefore misses the trends in the data. It also means the model cannot be generalized to new data.

Train/test split and cross-validation help to avoid overfitting more than underfitting. But train/test split does have its dangers—what if the split we make isn't random? In order to avoid this, we perform cross-validation. It's very similar to train/test split, but it's applied to more subsets. Meaning, we split our data into k subsets, and train on k-1 one of those subsets. What we do is to hold the last subset for the test. We're able to do it for each of the subsets.

1. Next, we will use the metric of `accuracy` to evaluate models. In classification, accuracy is a commonly used metric for measuring the performance of a model. This is a ratio of the number of correctly predicted instances divided by the total number of instances in the dataset multiplied by 100 to give a percentage (e.g., 95% accurate). We will be using the scoring variable when we run to build and evaluate each model next:

```
seed = 7
scoring = 'accuracy'
```

Figure 13.11: *Using scoring variable*

2. Before testing out any algorithm(s), we would not know which would be good to use for a problem or what configurations to use. We get an idea from the plots that some of the classes are partially linearly separable in some dimensions, so we are expecting generally good results. So here we will apply some classification algorithms and evaluate each model. For this purpose, we will reset the random number seed before each run to ensure that the evaluation of each algorithm is performed using the same data splits. It ensures the results are directly comparable. Since we have to repeat the logic for all algorithms we are going to use, we will take the help of `for` loop in this case. Import the required algorithms like Logistic Regression, Linear

Discriminant Analysis, K Nearest Neighbors, Decision Trees Classifier, Gaussian Naïve Bayes, and Support Vector Classifier, then follow this code cell:

```
#Check Algorithms
models = []
models.append(('LR', LogisticRegression()))
models.append(('LDA', LinearDiscriminantAnalysis()))
models.append(('KNN', KNeighborsClassifier()))
models.append(('CART', DecisionTreeClassifier()))
models.append(('NB', GaussianNB()))
models.append(('SVM', SVC()))
# evaluate each model in turn
results = []
names = []
for name, model in models:
    kfold = model_selection.KFold(n_splits=10, random_state=seed)
    cv_results = model_selection.cross_val_score(model, X_train, Y_train, cv=kfold, scoring=scoring)
    results.append(cv_results)
    names.append(name)
    msg = "%s: %f (%f)" % (name, cv_results.mean(), cv_results.std())
    print(msg)
```

```
LR: 0.966667 (0.040825)
LDA: 0.975000 (0.038188)
KNN: 0.983333 (0.033333)
CART: 0.975000 (0.038188)
NB: 0.975000 (0.053359)
SVM: 0.991667 (0.025000)
```

Figure 13.12: Code cell

Code explanation: Here we have first initialized an empty list where we can store our models. Next, we are adding six classification algorithms in these models so that we can compare the result of each. For evaluating each model one by one and saving the result of each model, we have defined `results` variable for storing the model's `accuracy` and `names` variable for storing algorithm name. Both these variables are of type list.

In the next step inside the `for` loop, we are iterating the models' list. In this iteration, we are using the `KFold()` function of `model_selection` which provides train/test indices to split data into train/test sets. It split the dataset into k consecutive folds (without shuffling by default).

For evaluating our metrics by cross-validation and also recording fit/score times, we are using `cross_val_score()` function. From the output, it looks like the SVM classifier has the highest estimated accuracy score (99%).

3. You can also create a plot of the model evaluation results and compare the spread and the mean accuracy of each model. There is a population of accuracy measures for each algorithm because each algorithm was evaluated 10 times (10-fold cross-validation):

```
fig = plt.figure()
fig.suptitle('Compare Algorithm Accuracy')
ax = fig.add_subplot(111)
plt.boxplot(results)
ax.set_xticklabels(names)
plt.show()
```

Figure 13.13: Code snippet for accuracy comparison

Once you run the preceding cell, you will see below result:

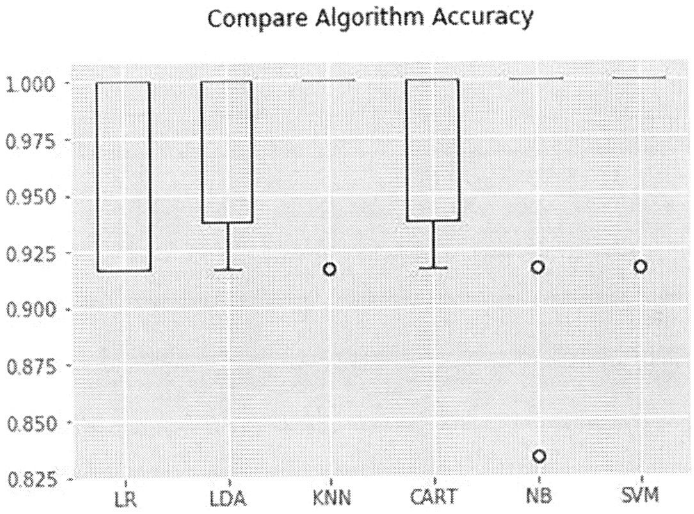

Figure 13.14: Plot of accuracy comparison

4. Now we can run the SVM model directly on the validation set and summarize the results as a final accuracy score, a confusion matrix, and a classification report. Always remember accuracy is not always an informative metric, that's why evaluate the performance of your binary classifiers by computing the confusion matrix and generating a classification report. **For generating our accuracy score and report we will use the sklearn's classification metrics module**. Here `metrics.classification_report()` will build a text report showing the main classification `metrics`, `metrics.confusion_matrix()` will compute confusion matrix to evaluate the accuracy of a classification

and `metrics.accuracy_score()` will tell us the accuracy classification score of our model:

```
#import required matrics
from sklearn.metrics import classification_report
from sklearn.metrics import confusion_matrix
from sklearn.metrics import accuracy_score
```

```
svm = SVC()
svm.fit(X_train, Y_train)
predictions = svm.predict(X_validation)
print(accuracy_score(Y_validation, predictions))
print(confusion_matrix(Y_validation, predictions))
print(classification_report(Y_validation, predictions))
```

```
0.9333333333333333
[[ 7  0  0]
 [ 0 10  2]
 [ 0  0 11]]
             precision    recall  f1-score   support

          0       1.00      1.00      1.00         7
          1       1.00      0.83      0.91        12
          2       0.85      1.00      0.92        11

avg / total       0.94      0.93      0.93        30
```

Figure 13.15: Generating accuracy score and report

To train our model, we have used `.fit()` function which is a default function in many algorithms for training. After training the model, to make predictions, we have used `.predict()`function call. Inside `fit()` method, we pass two required arguments - `features` and `target` as numpy array. The `sklearnapi` requires data in numpy array format only. Another point to remember is that there should be no missing values in data, otherwise you will face unexpected errors.

From the output, we can deduce that the accuracy is 0.933333 or 93%. The confusion matrix provides an indication of the three errors made. Finally, the classification report provides a breakdown of each class by precision, recall, f1-score, and support, showing excellent results (granted the validation dataset was small). The support gives the number of samples of the true response that lie in that class (no. of species in our case on the test dataset).

Details of the report: Here, the classification report is a report of Precision/ Recall/F1-score - for each element in your test data. In multiclass problems, it is not a good idea to read Precision/Recall and F1-score over the whole data because any imbalance would make you feel you've reached better results. The confusion matrix is a much-detailed representation of what's going on with your labels. So, there are 7 [7+0+0] points in the first class (label 0). Out of these, your model was successful in identifying 7 of those correctly in label 0. Similarly, look at the second row. There were 12 [0+10+2] points in class 1, but 10 of them were marked correctly.

Coming to Recall/Precision: They are some of the most used measures in evaluating how good your system works. Now you had 7 points in the first species (call it 0 species). Out of them, your classifier was able to get 7 elements correctly. That's your recall. $7/7 = 1$. Now look only at the first column in the table. There is one cell with entry 7, rest all are zeros. This means your classifier marked 7 points in species 0, and all 7 of them were actually in species 0. This is precision. $7/7 = 1$. Look at the column marked 2. In this column, there are elements scattered in two rows. 11 of them [0+2+11=13] were marked correctly. Rest [2] is incorrect. So that reduces your precision.

5. Save your model in your disk so that the next time you don't need to run all steps again in your notebook, instead you can predict any new iris species directly. For this purpose, you can use Python's `pickle` library. The `pickle` library serializes your machine learning algorithms and saves the serialized format to a file as shown in the following *figure 13.16*:

```
# save the model to disk
import pickle
filename = 'finalized_model.sav'
pickle.dump(svm, open(filename, 'wb'))
# load the model from disk for next time you open this notebook
loaded_model = pickle.load(open(filename, 'rb'))
result = loaded_model.score(X_validation, Y_validation)
print(result)
```

0.9333333333333333

Figure 13.16: Pickle library serializes ML algorithms

Running the example saves the model to `finalized_model.sav` in your local working directory. Load the saved model; evaluating it provides an estimate of the accuracy of the model on unseen data. Later you can load this file to deserialize your model and use it to make new predictions.

Solving a regression ML problem

There are many different types of regression problems based on different data. The specific type of regressions we are going to learn is called *generalized linear models*. The important thing for you to know is that with this family of models, you need to pick a specific type of regression you're interested in. The different type of data with respect to regression is shown in the following *figure 13.17*:

- **Linear**: When you are predicting a continuous value. (What temperature will it be today?)

- **Logistic**: When you are predicting which category, your observation is in. (Is this a car or a bus?)

- **Poisson**: When you are predicting a count value. (How many cats will I see in the park?)

	Family	Type of data
Linear	Gaussian	Continuous
Logistic	Binomial	Categorical
Poisson	Poisson	Count

A quick guide to the three types of regression we've talked about.

Figure 13.17: Three types of regression

About the problem – you are going to work on the GapMinder dataset. This dataset is already in a clean state. *GapMinder* is a non-profit venture promoting sustainable global development and achievement of the *United Nations Millennium Development Goals*. It seeks to increase the use and understanding of statistics about social, economic, and environmental development at local, national, and global levels.

Goal: Your goal will be to use this data to predict the life expectancy in a given country based on features such as the country's GDP, fertility rate, and population.

1. Load the dataset into Pandas dataframe and inspect the columns and data types:

```
gapminder_df = pd.read_csv("E:/pg/bpb/BPB-Publications/Datasets/regression/gm_2008_region.csv")
```

```
gapminder_df.info()
<class 'pandas.core.frame.DataFrame'>
RangeIndex: 139 entries, 0 to 138
Data columns (total 10 columns):
population       139 non-null float64
fertility        139 non-null float64
HIV              139 non-null float64
CO2              139 non-null float64
BMI_male         139 non-null float64
GDP              139 non-null float64
BMI_female       139 non-null float64
life             139 non-null float64
child_mortality  139 non-null float64
Region           139 non-null object
```

Figure 13.18: Inspecting columns and data types

Always remember, `scikit-learn` does not accept non-numerical features. In our case, **Region** is a categorical variable, so you cannot include it in your training process until you handle it. You will learn how to handle this later.

2. In this dataset, our target variable is `life` and the features variable is `fertility`. Both these variables are of a float data type but `sklearnapi` accepts numpy array input. We need to convert our variables into arrays:

```
# Create arrays for features and target variable
y = gapminder_df['life'].values
X = gapminder_df['fertility'].values
```

Figure 13.19: Creating arrays for features and target variable

3. If you check the dimension of the variables, you will notice that you are working on only one `feature` variable. With `sklearnapi`, you will need to reshape it:

```
# Print the dimensions of X and y before reshaping
print("Dimensions of target variable before reshaping: {}".format(y.shape))
print("Dimensions of feature variable before reshaping: {}".format(X.shape))
```

```
Dimensions of target variable before reshaping: (139,)
Dimensions of feature variable before reshaping: (139,)
```

Figure 13.20: Reshaping the variables

After reshaping both variables, dimension will be changed:

```
# Reshape X and y
y = y.reshape(-1,1)
X = X.reshape(-1,1)
# Print the dimensions of X and y after reshaping
print("Dimensions of target after reshaping: {}".format(y.shape))
print("Dimensions of feature variable after reshaping: {}".format(X.shape))
```

```
Dimensions of target after reshaping: (139, 1)
Dimensions of feature variable after reshaping: (139, 1)
```

Figure 13.21: Changing the dimension

4. Now to check co-relation between different features of our dataframe, we can take the help of `heatmap` function. For this, instead of `matplotlib` library, we will use the `seaborn` library because it generates more beautiful plots; so first import the `seaborn` library and then follow this code cell:

```
sns.heatmap(gapminder_df.corr(), square=True, cmap='RdYlGn')
plt.show()
```

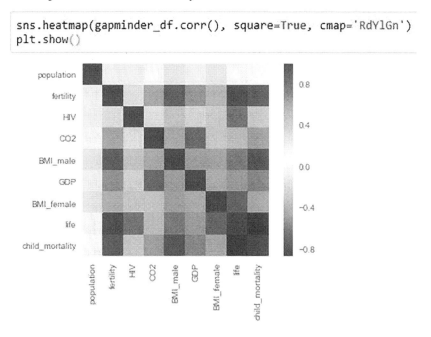

Figure 13.22: Heat map

In the preceding heat map, green cells show a positive correlation, while cells that are in red show a negative correlation. Here, we can say that `life` and `fertility` are poorly correlated. Linear regression should be able to capture this trend.

Next, we will solve our problem using linear regression. Before applying this, let's know some fundamentals of this algorithm. In this algorithm, we try to fit a line to the data in such a way that it follows the equation: $y=ax+b$ or for higher dimensions: $y=a1x1+a2x2+b$. Here y is the target, x is the single feature, a and b are the parameters of the model that you want to learn. So here the first question is how to choose a and b?

For this, we define an error function (loss or cost function) for any given line and choose the line that minimizes the error function. In the `sklearn` library, when we train the data using the `fit()` method, it automatically applies this `loss` function behind the scene. This function is also called **ordinary least squares** (**OLS**). The default accuracy metrics of this algo is R^2 (R square) instead of accuracy in classification problem.

5. Let's apply Linear Regression to our dataset without splitting it first:

```python
# Import LinearRegression
from sklearn.linear_model import LinearRegression
# Create the regressor: reg
reg = LinearRegression()
# Create the prediction space
prediction_space = np.linspace(min(X), max(X)).reshape(-1,1)
# Fit the model to the data
reg.fit(X, y)
# Compute predictions over the prediction space: y_pred
y_pred = reg.predict(prediction_space)
# Print R^2
print(reg.score(X, y))
# Plot regression line
plt.plot(prediction_space, y_pred, color='black', linewidth=3)
plt.show()
```

0.6192442167740035

Figure 13.23: Applying Linear Regression

6. Now you will split the GapMinder dataset into training and testing sets and then fit and predict a linear regression's overall features, just like we did for our classification problem. In addition to computing the R^2 score, you will also compute the **Root Mean Squared Error** (RMSE), which is another commonly used metric to evaluate regression models. Here R^2 score (R square) is a regression metric for evaluating predictions on regression machine learning problems:

```python
# Import necessary modules
from sklearn.linear_model import LinearRegression
from sklearn.metrics import mean_squared_error
from sklearn.model_selection import train_test_split
# Create training and test sets
X_train, X_test, y_train, y_test = train_test_split(X, y, test_size = 0.3, random_state=42)
# Create the regressor: reg_all
reg_all = LinearRegression()
# Fit the regressor to the training data
reg_all.fit(X_train, y_train)
# Predict on the test data: y_pred
y_pred = reg_all.predict(X_test)
# Compute and print R^2 and RMSE
print("R^2: {}".format(reg_all.score(X_test, y_test)))
rmse = np.sqrt(mean_squared_error(y_test, y_pred))
print("Root Mean Squared Error: {}".format(rmse))
```

R^2: 0.7298987360907494
Root Mean Squared Error: 4.194027914110243

Figure 13.24: Evaluating predictions on regression ML problems

If you compare this output with the output of the previous cell, you can easily say that all features have improved the model score, because our model fit is increased from 0.619 to 0.729. Model performance is dependent on the way the data is split. This makes sense, as the model has more information to learn from.

7. But as said earlier, it is important to do cross-validation because it maximizes the amount of data that is used to train the model. During the course of training, the model is not only trained but also tested on all of the available data as explained in the following *figure 13.25*:

```
# Import the necessary modules
from sklearn.linear_model import LinearRegression
from sklearn.model_selection import cross_val_score
# Create a linear regression object: reg
reg = LinearRegression()
# Compute 5-fold cross-validation scores: cv_scores
cv_scores = cross_val_score(reg, X, y, cv=5)
# Print the 5-fold cross-validation scores
print(cv_scores)
# Print the average 5-fold cross-validation score
print("Average 5-Fold CV Score: {}".format(np.mean(cv_scores)))
```

```
[0.71001079 0.75007717 0.55271526 0.547501   0.52410561]
Average 5-Fold CV Score: 0.6168819644425119
```

Figure 13.25: Cross validation code snippet

In the preceding example, we have applied 5-fold cross-validation on the GapMinder data. By default, the `scikit-learn` library's `cross_val_score()` function uses R^2 (R square) as the metric of choice for regression. Since we are performing 5-fold cross-validation, the function will return 5 scores. Hence, we have computed these 5 scores and then taken their averages.

> **Cross-validation is essential, but do not forget, the more folds you use, the more computationally expensive cross-validation becomes. Define the k as per your system capabilities.**

Since linear regression minimizes a loss function by choosing a coefficient for each feature variable, largely chosen coefficients can lead your model to overfit. To avoid this situation, we can alter the loss function; this technique is known as regularization. In this technique, we try to find out the most important features and shrink the large coefficients to almost zero, so that only important ones remain. Two regularization techniques are widely used in ML - Lasso Regression and Ridge regression. Let's understand each one by one:

- **Lasso Regression**: Performs L1 regularization, i.e., adds penalty equivalent to the absolute value of the magnitude of coefficients. Along with shrinking coefficients, lasso performs feature selection as well. Here some of the coefficients become exactly zero, which is equivalent to a particular feature being excluded from the model. It is majorly used to prevent overfitting as well as feature selection. The default value of the regularization parameter in Lasso regression (given by alpha) is 1

- **Ridge Regression**: Performs L2 regularization, i.e., adds penalty equivalent to the square of the magnitude of coefficients. It includes all (or none) of the features in the model. Thus, the major advantage of ridge regression is coefficient shrinkage and reducing model complexity. It is majorly used to prevent overfitting. It generally works well even in the presence of highly correlated features, as it will include all of them in the model, but the coefficients will be distributed among them depending on the correlation.

Let's understand how you can apply Lasso with Python in the breast cancer research dataset. This dataset is already there in `sklearnapi`. First, we will import the Lasso package from the `sklearn.linear_model` library followed by the breast cancer dataset from `sklearnapi`, and then we will apply the Lasso in our dataset as shown in the following *figure 13.26*:

```
from sklearn.linear_model import Lasso
from sklearn.datasets import load_breast_cancer
cancer = load_breast_cancer()
print(cancer.keys())
print(cancer.data.shape)
cancer_df = pd.DataFrame(cancer.data, columns=cancer.feature_names)
X = cancer.data
Y = cancer.target
X_train,X_test,y_train,y_test=train_test_split(X,Y, test_size=0.3, random_state=31)
lasso = Lasso()
lasso.fit(X_train,y_train)
train_score=lasso.score(X_train,y_train)
test_score=lasso.score(X_test,y_test)
coeff_used = np.sum(lasso.coef_!=0)
print("training score:", train_score )
print("test score: ", test_score)
print("number of features used: ", coeff_used)
plt.xlabel('Coefficient Index',fontsize=16)
plt.ylabel('Coefficient Magnitude',fontsize=16)
plt.legend(fontsize=13,loc=4)
plt.subplot(1,2,2)
plt.plot(lasso.coef_,alpha=0.7,linestyle='none',marker='*',markersize=5,color='red',label=r'Lasso; $\alpha = 1$',zorder=7)
plt.tight_layout()
plt.show()
```

Figure 13.26: Applying Lasso package

Once you run the preceding cell, you will see the following output:

```
dict_keys(['data', 'target', 'target_names', 'DESCR', 'feature_names'])
(569, 30)
training score: 0.5600974529893079
test score:   0.5832244618818156
number of features used:  4
```

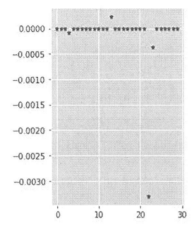

Figure 13.27: Output of running Lasso package

In our dataset, there are a total of 30 features initially, but on the application of Lasso regression, only 4 features are used; rest are all shrunk to zero (see the red stars on the preceding plot). The training and test scores are 56% and 58% respectively, which are very low -- it means our model is underfitting. Now you can reduce this under-fitting by increasing the number of iteration and reducing the alpha. Try with alpha=0.0001 and number of *feature =22 [lasso = Lasso(alpha=0.0001, max_iter=10e5)]* and see how much accuracy you get!

Next, we will learn how to apply Ridge Regression in Python. Here we will use Boston house price dataset from `sklearnapi`:

```
from sklearn.datasets import load_boston
from sklearn.linear_model import Ridge
boston=load_boston()
boston_df=pd.DataFrame(boston.data,columns=boston.feature_names)
boston_df['Price']=boston.target
newX=boston_df.drop('Price',axis=1)
newY=boston_df['Price']
```

Figure 13.28: Applying Ridge Regression

Here `axis=1` means we are applying logic row-wise. We have separated the target column - `Price` from the dataframe and stored it as `target` column:

```
X_train,X_test,y_train,y_test=train_test_split(newX,newY,test_size=0.3,random_state=3)
print(len(X_test), len(y_test))
lr = LinearRegression()
lr.fit(X_train, y_train)
rr = Ridge(alpha=0.01)
rr.fit(X_train, y_train)
train_score=lr.score(X_train, y_train)
test_score=lr.score(X_test, y_test)
Ridge_train_score = rr.score(X_train,y_train)
Ridge_test_score = rr.score(X_test, y_test)
print("linear regression train score:", train_score)
print("linear regression test score:", test_score)
print("ridge regression train score low alpha:", Ridge_train_score)
print("ridge regression test score low alpha:", Ridge_test_score)
plt.plot(rr.coef_,alpha=0.7,linestyle='none',marker='*',markersize=5,color='red',label=r'Ridge; $\alpha = 0.01$',zorder=7)
plt.plot(lr.coef_,alpha=0.4,linestyle='none',marker='o',markersize=7,color='green',label='Linear Regression')
plt.xlabel('Coefficient Index',fontsize=16)
plt.ylabel('Coefficient Magnitude',fontsize=16)
plt.legend(fontsize=13,loc=4)
plt.show()
```

Figure 13.29: Separating a column and storing as target column

Here, in X-axis, we plot the coefficient index, which is the features of our dataset. In our case, `Boston` data has 13 features. Once you run the preceding code, you will see the following output:

```
152 152
linear regression train score: 0.7419034960343789
linear regression test score: 0.7146895989294312
ridge regression train score low alpha: 0.7419030253527293
ridge regression test score low alpha: 0.7145115044376255
```

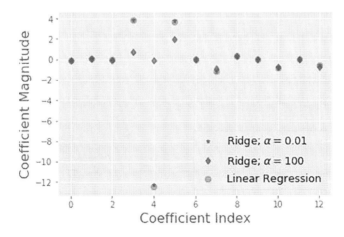

Figure 13.30: Plot of coefficient index vs magnitude

You will notice in the preceding plot, that the low value of alpha (0.01) is denoted as a red star, and when the coefficients are less restricted, the coefficient magnitudes are almost the same as of linear regression. Try with `alpha=100` and you will see that for this higher value of `alpha` (`100`), for coefficient indices 3,4,5, the magnitudes are considerably less compared to linear regression case. From the preceding exercises, you can say that Lasso is great for feature selection, but when building regression models, ridge regression should be your first choice.

If you noticed, the steps we have followed to solve classification and regression problems have a similarity. We can summarize the common steps in the following simple words:

1. Perform the necessary imports.

2. Instantiate your classifier or regressor.

3. Split your dataset into training and test sets.

4. Fit the model on your training data.

5. Predict on your test set.

How to tune your ML model?

Till now you have learned the required steps to build an ML model. But sometimes, implementing a model is not the ultimate solution. You may be required to fine-tune your model for better accuracy. For the example explained earlier, you can tune your models:

- By choosing the right `alpha` parameter value in Lasso/Ridge regression.

- By choosing the right `n_neighbors` parameter value in K-NN.

The preceding parameters are chosen before training the model and are called *hyperparameters*. These parameters cannot be learned by fitting the model. So how can you choose the right one? Till now only one possible solution is found - try with different hyperparameters values, fit all of them separately, do cross-validation, and then choose the right one after comparing the results.

Now, you will learn how to do the same using `GridSearchCV` library which exhaustive searches over specified parameter values for an estimator. Here you only need to specify the hyperparameter as a dictionary in which keys are the hyperparameter's name like `alpha` or `n_neighbors` and the values in this dictionary area list containing the values for which we choose the relevant hyperparameters.

Let's see how to use the `GridSearchCV` with logistic regression. Logistic Regression has a parameter - `C` which controls the inverse of the regularization strength, so a large `C` can lead to an overfit model, while a small `C` can lead to an underfit model. Now see how you can set up the hyperparameter grid (`c_space`) and perform grid-search cross-validation on a diabetic dataset. This dataset was prepared on diabetes patients for the use of participants for the 1994 *AAAI Spring Symposium on Artificial Intelligence in Medicine*:

```
from sklearn.linear_model import LogisticRegression
from sklearn.model_selection import GridSearchCV

df = pd.read_csv("E:/pg/bpb/BPB-Publications/Datasets/diabetes.csv")
print(df.columns)

y=df['diabetes']
X=df.drop('diabetes',axis=1)

#Setup the hyperparameter grid
c_space = np.logspace(-5, 8, 15)
param_grid = {'C': c_space}

logreg = LogisticRegression()
logreg_cv = GridSearchCV(logreg, param_grid, cv=5)
logreg_cv.fit(X, y)

print("Tuned Logistic Regression Parameters: {}".format(logreg_cv.best_params_))
print("Best score is {}".format(logreg_cv.best_score_))
```

Figure 13.31: Setting up hyperparameter grid and performing grid-search cross-validation

Here in `param_grid` variable, you can also use `penalty` argument along with C to specify what you want, to use l1 or l2 regularization:

```
Index(['pregnancies', 'glucose', 'diastolic', 'triceps', 'insulin', 'bmi',
       'dpf', 'age', 'diabetes'],
      dtype='object')
Tuned Logistic Regression Parameters: {'C': 163789.3706954068}
Best score is 0.7721354166666666
```

Figure 13.32: Using penalty argument with C

In the preceding output cell, you can see the different properties of diabetes patients as columns. With proper hyperparameter grid setup, we have achieved the best score of our logistic regression model.

One drawback of `GridSearchCV` is - it can be computationally expensive, especially if you are searching over a large hyperparameter space and dealing with multiple hyperparameters. As an alternative, you can also use `RandomizedSearchCV` in which a fixed number of hyperparameter settings is sampled from specified probability distributions. Let's understand how to use this in a decision tree classifier. As the name suggests, the decision tree classifiers organized a series of test questions and conditions in a tree structure. Decision Tree Classifier poses a series of carefully crafted questions about the attributes of the test record. Each time it receives an answer, a follow-up question is asked until a conclusion about the class label of the record is reached:

```python
# Import necessary modules
from scipy.stats import randint
from sklearn.tree import DecisionTreeClassifier
from sklearn.model_selection import RandomizedSearchCV

param_dist = {"max_depth": [3, None],
              "max_features": randint(1, 9),
              "min_samples_leaf": randint(1, 9),
              "criterion": ["gini", "entropy"]}

tree = DecisionTreeClassifier()
tree_cv = RandomizedSearchCV(tree, param_dist, cv=5)

tree_cv.fit(X, y)

print("Tuned Decision Tree Parameters: {}".format(tree_cv.best_params_))
print("Best score is {}".format(tree_cv.best_score_))
```

```
Tuned Decision Tree Parameters: {'criterion': 'entropy', 'max_depth': 3, 'max_features': 7, 'min_samples_leaf': 4}
Best score is 0.7447916666666666
```

Figure 13.33: Decision Tree Classifier example

In the preceding code cell, we have set the hyperparameter grid using RandomizedSearchCV to find the best parameters and as a result, we found the best hyperparameters criterion, max_depth, and min_simple_leaf as entropy, 3, and 4 respectively. You have now understood that hyperparameter tuning skill depends on your practice. The more you try with different parameters with different algorithms, the more you will be able to understand.

How to handle categorical variables in sklearn?

If you recollect, in one of the preceding examples, there is a categorical variable Region in GapMider dataset which is not accepted by sklearnapi. You need to learn how to handle this case because sometimes it is not good to just leave such variables. One way to convert a non-numeric variable in the desired format of sklearn is to binarize using Pandas get_dummies() function. Let's see how to do the same:

```python
# handling categorical variable 'Region' by binarizing it(creating dummy variables)
# Create dummy variables: df_region
df_region = pd.get_dummies(df)

# Print the columns of df_region
print(df_region.columns)

# Drop 'Region_America' from df_region
df_region = pd.get_dummies(df, drop_first=True)

# Print the new columns of df_region
print(df_region.columns)
```

Figure 13.34: Converting non-numeric variable in desired format

Here `pd.get_dummies(df)` is converting the categorical variable of our dataframe into `dummy`/`indicator` variable. Once you run the preceding cell, you will see that `Region` column is suffixed by region names:

```
Index(['population', 'fertility', 'HIV', 'CO2', 'BMI_male', 'GDP',
       'BMI_female', 'life', 'child_mortality', 'Region_America',
       'Region_East Asia & Pacific', 'Region_Europe & Central Asia',
       'Region_Middle East & North Africa', 'Region_South Asia',
       'Region_Sub-Saharan Africa'],
      dtype='object')
```

Figure 13.35: Region DataFrame columns

Now you can perform regression technique on the whole GapMinder dataset as shown in the following *figure 13.36*:

```
from sklearn.model_selection import cross_val_score
from sklearn.linear_model import Ridge

ridge = Ridge(alpha=0.5, normalize=True)
y=df_region['life'].values
X=df_region.drop('life', axis=1).values

# Perform 5-fold cross-validation: ridge_cv
ridge_cv = cross_val_score(ridge, X, y, cv=5)
print(ridge_cv)
```

```
[0.86808336 0.80623545 0.84004203 0.7754344  0.87503712]
```

Figure 13.36: Regression technique on GapMinder dataset

Here `axis=1` means we are applying logic row-wise; for column-wise operation, change it to `axis=0`.

The advanced technique to handle missing data

You have already learned to handle the missing data either by removing it or replacing it with mean, median, or mode or forward/backward values in previous chapters. But what about if your dataset has many zero values? Here you will learn how to use `sklearnapi` to handle such values. The `sklearn.preprocessing` has `imputer` package and `imputer` has `transform()` function, which we can use in the following way to fill zero/missing values in the Pima Indians Diabetes Dataset that involves predicting the onset of diabetes within 5 years in Pima Indians given medical details:

```
df = pd.read_csv('E:/pg/bpb/BPB-Publications/Datasets/pimaindians-diabetes.data.csv',header = None)
df.info()
```

```
<class 'pandas.core.frame.DataFrame'>
RangeIndex: 768 entries, 0 to 767
Data columns (total 9 columns):
0    768 non-null int64
1    768 non-null int64
2    768 non-null int64
3    768 non-null int64
4    768 non-null int64
5    768 non-null float64
6    768 non-null float64
7    768 non-null int64
8    768 non-null int64
dtypes: float64(2), int64(7)
```

Figure 13.37: Handling missing data

Once you check the count of the dataset, you will find that there are no missing values here:

```
missing_values_count = df.isnull().sum()
print("count of missing values:\n", missing_values_count)
```

```
count of missing values:
 0    0
 1    0
 2    0
 3    0
 4    0
 5    0
 6    0
 7    0
 8    0
```

Figure 13.38: Counting missing values

But you should not blindly believe the preceding output; you must perform statistical analysis as shown in the following *figure 13.39*:

```
df.describe()
```

	0	1	2	3	4	5	6	7	8
count	768.000000	768.000000	768.000000	768.000000	768.000000	768.000000	768.000000	768.000000	768.000000
mean	3.845052	120.894531	69.105469	20.536458	79.799479	31.992578	0.471876	33.240885	0.348958
std	3.369578	31.972618	19.355807	15.952218	115.244002	7.884160	0.331329	11.760232	0.476951
min	0.000000	0.000000	0.000000	0.000000	0.000000	0.000000	0.078000	21.000000	0.000000
25%	1.000000	99.000000	62.000000	0.000000	0.000000	27.300000	0.243750	24.000000	0.000000
50%	3.000000	117.000000	72.000000	23.000000	30.500000	32.000000	0.372500	29.000000	0.000000
75%	6.000000	140.250000	80.000000	32.000000	127.250000	36.600000	0.626250	41.000000	1.000000
max	17.000000	199.000000	122.000000	99.000000	846.000000	67.100000	2.420000	81.000000	1.000000

Figure 13.39: Performing statistical analysis

Since this is a diabetic data, many attributes of this data cannot be zero, for example, blood pressure or Body mass index. Hence, you must replace such zero values with logical ones. This observation is very important, and you must review carefully your data and the problem.

Let's first replace zeros of some columns with actual missing value - NaN and then we will handle NaN:

```
# mark some columns zero values as missing or NaN
import numpy as np
df[[1,2,3,4,5]] = df[[1,2,3,4,5]].replace(0, np.NaN)
print(df.isnull().sum())
```

```
0      0
1      5
2     35
3    227
4    374
5     11
6      0
7      0
8      0
```

Figure 13.40: Replacing zero with actual missing value

As you already know that missing values in a dataset can cause errors with some machine learning algorithms like LDA algorithm, let's impute these values and then we will apply LDA:

```
from sklearn.preprocessing import Imputer
# fill missing values with mean column values
values = df.values
imputer = Imputer()
transformed_values = imputer.fit_transform(values)
# count the number of NaN values in each column
print(np.isnan(transformed_values).sum())
```

0

Figure 13.41: Imputing missing values

Now you can easily apply LDA algorithm on imputed data:

```
# evaluate an LDA model on the dataset using k-fold cross validation
model = LinearDiscriminantAnalysis()
kfold = KFold(n_splits=3, random_state=7)
result = cross_val_score(model, transformed_values, y, cv=kfold, scoring='accuracy')
print(result.mean())
```

0.7669270833333334

Figure 13.42: Applying LDA algorithm

That's it! It is quite easy to impute zero values, right? Let's see another example of Impute with pipeline with another algorithm known as SVM Classifier:

```
from sklearn.preprocessing import Imputer
from sklearn.svm import SVC
imp = Imputer(missing_values='NaN', strategy='most_frequent', axis=0)

# Instantiate the SVC classifier: clf
clf = SVC()

# Setup the pipeline with the required steps: steps
steps = [('imputation', imp),
         ('SVM', clf)]
```

Figure 13.43: Example of imputing

Here steps variable is a list of tuples where the first tuple consists of the imputation step and the second consists of the classifier. This is the pipeline concept for imputing.

After setting it up you can use it for classification as shown in the following *figure 13.44*:

```
from sklearn.preprocessing import Imputer
from sklearn.pipeline import Pipeline
from sklearn.svm import SVC
from sklearn.model_selection import train_test_split
from sklearn.metrics import classification_report

# Setup the pipeline steps: steps
steps = [('imputation', Imputer(missing_values='NaN', strategy='most_frequent', axis=0)),
         ('SVM', SVC())]

# Create the pipeline: pipeline
pipeline = Pipeline(steps)

# Create training and test sets
X_train, X_test, y_train, y_test = train_test_split(X, y, test_size=0.3, random_state=42)

# Fit the pipeline to the train set
pipeline.fit(X_train, y_train)

# Predict the labels of the test set
y_pred = pipeline.predict(X_test)

# Compute metrics
print(classification_report(y_test, y_pred))
```

Figure 13.44: *Using for classification*

	precision	recall	f1-score	support
0.0	0.65	1.00	0.79	151
1.0	0.00	0.00	0.00	80
avg / total	0.43	0.65	0.52	231

Figure 13.45: *classification report result*

See, how easy it is to handle such data with pipeline!

Conclusion

You have now learned the fundamentals, as well as some advanced techniques of supervised machine learning algorithms. You have also solved a real-world supervised problem. But there is so much to explore and learn in this field. That can be only done if you try different approaches and algorithms by your own; so try as much as you can. Until then go chase your dreams, have an awesome day, make every second count. See you later in next chapter of this book, where you will learn about unsupervised machine learning.

CHAPTER 14
Unsupervised Machine Learning

The main feature of unsupervised learning algorithms, when compared to classification and regression methods, is that input data are unlabeled (i.e., no labels or classes given), and the algorithm learns the structure of the data without any assistance. This is the world of unsupervised learning - you are not guiding or supervising the pattern discovery by some prediction task, but instead uncovering hidden structure from unlabeled data. Unsupervised learning encompasses a variety of techniques in machine learning, from clustering to dimension reduction to matrix factorization. In this chapter, you will learn the fundamentals of unsupervised learning and implement the essential algorithms using `scikit-learn` and `scipy`.

Structure

- Why unsupervised learning?
- Unsupervised learning techniques
- K-means clustering
- Principal Component Analysis (PCA)
- Case study
- Validation of unsupervised Ml

Objective

After studying and practicing this chapter, you will be familiar with unsupervised learning, and will be able to cluster, transform, visualize, and extract insights from unlabeled datasets.

Why unsupervised learning?

The unsupervised learning inputs (training data) are unlabeled and we have no output results to validate the efficiency of the learning process. However, once the training process is complete, we are able to label our data. The described process is similar to how humans acquire knowledge through experience. Even though the machine works in the dark, it somehow manages to extract features and patterns from the probability distributions of data (e.g., images, texts), which are fed to it.

However, why would we even need unsupervised learning if we have so many efficient and tested supervised ML methods around? There are several reasons for the growing popularity of unsupervised methods:

- Sometimes we don't know in advance as to which class/type our data belongs to. For example, in the consumer segmentation problem, we don't know what similarities consumers share and how they differ as groups.

- Structured data can be expensive and not always available. Supervised learning requires properly labeled, cleaned up, and regularized data. What's worse is that many AI start-ups might not have access to structured data at all. To acquire the data needed to train their AI systems, start-up has to buy the license from commercial platforms.

- Supervised methods are a good fit for classification and prediction, but not as suitable for content generation. Unsupervised learning is an excellent option when we want to generate content (e.g., images, videos) similar to the original training data.

- Now, thanks to the cheaper cloud-based computing power and new deep learning techniques, we may efficiently use unsupervised learning in combination with neural networks trained on powerful GPUs.

Unsupervised learning techniques

Some applications of unsupervised machine learning techniques include the following:

- **Clustering** allows you to automatically split the dataset into groups according to similarity. Often, however, cluster analysis overestimates the similarity between groups and doesn't treat data points as individuals. For this reason, cluster analysis is a poor choice for applications like customer segmentation and targeting.

- **Anomaly detection** can automatically discover unusual data points in your dataset. This is useful in pinpointing fraudulent transactions, discovering faulty pieces of hardware, or identifying an outlier caused by a human error during data entry.

- **Association mining** identifies sets of items that frequently occur together in your dataset. Retailers often use it for basket analysis, because it allows analysts to discover goods often purchased at the same time, and develop more effective marketing and merchandising strategies.

- **Latent variable models** are commonly used for data pre-processing, such as reducing the number of features in a dataset (dimensionality reduction) or decomposing the dataset into multiple components.

The two unsupervised learning techniques that we will explore are clustering the data into groups by similarity and reducing dimensionality to compress the data while maintaining its structure and usefulness.

Clustering

Clustering is the process of grouping similar entities together. The goal of this unsupervised machine learning technique is to find similarities in the data point and group similar data points together. Grouping similar entities together gives us insight into the underlying patterns of different groups. For example, you can identify different groups/segments of customers and market each group in a different way to maximize the revenue. Clustering is also used to reduce the dimensionality of the data when you are dealing with a copious number of variables. The most popular and widely used clustering algorithms are K-mean clustering and hierarchical clustering.

K-mean clustering

In K-mean clustering, *K means the input, which is how many clusters you want to find*. In this algorithm, you place K centroids in random locations in your space, rather than using the Euclidean distance between data points and centroids. You assign each data point to the cluster which is close to it, then recalculate the cluster centers as a mean of data points assigned to it, and then again repeat the preceding steps until no further changes occur. In mathematics, the **Euclidean distance** or **Euclidean metric** is the *ordinary* straight-line distance between two points in Euclidean space. With this distance, Euclidean space becomes a metric space and the centroids are like the heart of the cluster; they capture the points closest to them and add them to the cluster.

You might be thinking, how I decided the value of K in the first step? One of the methods is called the **Elbow method** – which can be used to decide an optimal number of clusters. The idea is to run K-mean clustering on a range of K values and plot the *percentage of variance explained* on the Y-axis and *K* on X-axis. For example, in the following screenshot, you will notice that as we add more clusters after 3, though it doesn't give much better modeling on the data. The first cluster adds a lot of information, but at some point, the marginal gain will start dropping:

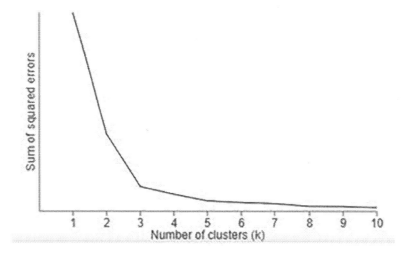

Figure 14.1: Elbow method plot

See the preceding plot - it almost looks like a human elbow structure. Let's see how to apply k-means on an actual dataset and evaluate a cluster. To understand and practice the code examples, kindly load the unsupervised learning notebook provided inside the code bundle.

In this exercise you will get the poker training/testing dataset from a `url` and then perform k-means with Elbow method:

```
# read training and test data from the url link and save the file to your working directory
url = "http://archive.ics.uci.edu/ml/machine-learning-databases/poker/poker-hand-training-true.data"

urllib.request.urlretrieve(url, "E:/pg/bpb/BPB-Publications/Datasets/unsupervised/poker_train.csv")

url2 = "http://archive.ics.uci.edu/ml/machine-learning-databases/poker/poker-hand-testing.data"

urllib.request.urlretrieve(url2, "E:/pg/bpb/BPB-Publications/Datasets/unsupervised/poker_test.csv")

# read the data in and add column names
data_train = pd.read_csv("E:/pg/bpb/BPB-Publications/Datasets/unsupervised/poker_train.csv", header=None,
                  names=['S1', 'C1', 'S2', 'C2', 'S3', 'C3','S4', 'C4', 'S5', 'C5', 'CLASS'])

data_test = pd.read_csv("E:/pg/bpb/BPB-Publications/Datasets/unsupervised/poker_test.csv", header=None,
                  names=['S1', 'C1', 'S2', 'C2', 'S3', 'C3','S4', 'C4', 'S5', 'C5', 'CLASS'])
```

Figure 14.2: Performing k-means with elbow method

In the preceding code cell, first, we read the train and test data from a `url` using `urllib.request.urlretrieve()` function, which takes `url` as one required argument. This function is the easiest way to store the content of a page in a variable; so, we will do the same by storing the train and test data in `url` and `url2` variables.

Here, we have saved the train and test CSV files in our local directory. From there, we will read and store them in Pandas `Dataframe` for further processing. Next, we subset the training dataset:

```
# subset clustering variables
cluster=data_train[['S1', 'C1', 'S2', 'C2', 'S3', 'C3','S4', 'C4', 'S5', 'C5']]
```

Figure 14.3: Subset clustering variables

Next, in order to cluster the data effectively, you'll need to standardize these features first. For equally contributing to the variables, we will scale them using `preprocessing.scale()` function as shown in the following screenshot:

```
from sklearn import preprocessing
# standardize clustering variables to have mean=0 and sd=1 so that card suit and
# rank are on the same scale as to have the variables equally contribute to the analysis
clustervar = cluster.copy() # create a copy
clustervar['S1']=preprocessing.scale(clustervar['S1'].astype('float64'))
clustervar['C1']=preprocessing.scale(clustervar['C1'].astype('float64'))
clustervar['S2']=preprocessing.scale(clustervar['S2'].astype('float64'))
clustervar['C2']=preprocessing.scale(clustervar['C2'].astype('float64'))
clustervar['S3']=preprocessing.scale(clustervar['S3'].astype('float64'))
clustervar['C3']=preprocessing.scale(clustervar['C3'].astype('float64'))
clustervar['S4']=preprocessing.scale(clustervar['S4'].astype('float64'))
clustervar['C4']=preprocessing.scale(clustervar['C4'].astype('float64'))
clustervar['S5']=preprocessing.scale(clustervar['S5'].astype('float64'))
clustervar['C5']=preprocessing.scale(clustervar['C5'].astype('float64'))

# The data has been already split data into train and test sets
clus_train = clustervar
```

Figure 14.4: Scaling variables

The `preprocessing.scale()` function standardizes a dataset along any axis **[Center to the mean and component-wise scale to unit variance]**.

Next, for computing distance between each pair of the two collections of inputs, you don't need to do any calculation. Using `scipy.spatial.distance` object's `cdist` library, we can do that. After calculating the distance, we will loop through each cluster and fit the model to the train set, and then we will generate the predicted cluster assignment and append the mean distance by taking the sum divided by the shape, as shown in the following screenshot:

```python
from sklearn.cluster import KMeans

# k-means cluster analysis for 1-10 clusters due to the 10 possible class outcomes for poker hands
from scipy.spatial.distance import cdist
clusters=range(1,20)
meandist=[]

# loop through each cluster and fit the model to the train set
# generate the predicted cluster assingment and append the mean distance my taking the sum divided
for k in clusters:
    model=KMeans(n_clusters=k)
    model.fit(clus_train)
    clusassign=model.predict(clus_train)
    meandist.append(sum(np.min(cdist(clus_train, model.cluster_centers_, 'euclidean'), axis=1))
    / clus_train.shape[0])

"""
Plot average distance from observations from the cluster centroid
to use the Elbow Method to identify number of clusters to choose
"""
plt.plot(clusters, meandist)
plt.xlabel('Number of clusters')
plt.ylabel('Average distance')
plt.title('Selecting k with the Elbow Method') # pick the fewest number of clusters that reduces th
```

```
Text(0.5,1,'Selecting k with the Elbow Method')
```

Figure 14.5: Finding value of k with Elbow method

Once you run the preceding cell, you will see, as shown in the following output plot, that 3 (see X-axis in the plot) will be the right choice of k as after this you will not get a better model. The number of clusters = the X-axis value of the point, that is, the corner of the elbow (the plot looks often like an elbow):

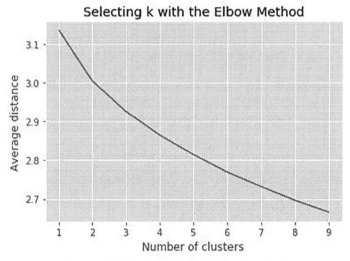

Figure 14.6: Selecting k with the elbow method

Hierarchical clustering

Unlike K-mean clustering, hierarchical clustering starts by assigning all data points as their cluster. As the name suggests, it builds the hierarchy, and in the next step, it combines the two nearest data points and merges it to one cluster. Following are the steps to implement this technique:

1. Start with N clusters, assign each data point to its cluster.

2. Find the closest pair of clusters using Euclidean distance and merge them into a single cluster.

3. Calculate distance between two nearest clusters and combine until all items are clustered into a single cluster.

In a nutshell, you can decide the optimal number of clusters by noticing which vertical lines can be cut by horizontal lines without intersecting a cluster and cover the maximum distance. Let's see how you can use hierarchical clustering on Iris dataset:

```python
# calculate full dendrogram
from scipy.cluster.hierarchy import dendrogram, linkage
# generate the linkage matrix
Z = linkage(iris, 'ward')
# set cut-off to 50
max_d = 7.08                    # max_d as in max_distance

plt.figure(figsize=(25, 10))
plt.title('Iris Hierarchical Clustering Dendrogram')
plt.xlabel('Species')
plt.ylabel('distance')
dendrogram(
    Z,
    truncate_mode='lastp',    # show only the last p merged clusters
    p=150,                     # Try changing values of p
    leaf_rotation=90.,         # rotates the x axis labels
    leaf_font_size=8.,         # font size for the x axis labels
)
plt.axhline(y=max_d, c='k')
plt.show()
```

Figure 14.7: Using hierarchical clustering on Iris dataset

Here, we are using `linkage()` function with `ward` argument to obtain a hierarchical clustering of the iris samples, and `dendrogram()` to visualize the result. Here, `ward` is a `linkage` method that minimizes the variant between the clusters. Once you run the preceding cell, it will display the following plot:

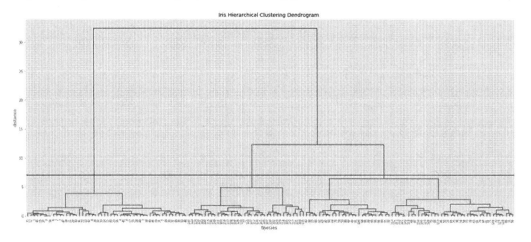

Figure 14.8: dendogram plot example

See, dendrograms are a great way to illustrate the arrangement of the clusters produced by hierarchical clustering! In our example, you can see a straight black horizontal line between the clusters. This line is currently crossing the 3 clusters, so the number of clusters will be three in this case.

Remember, hierarchical clustering can't handle big data well, but K-means clustering can. In K-means clustering, as we start with an arbitrary choice of clusters, the results generated by running the algorithm multiple times might differ, while results are reproducible in hierarchical clustering.

t-SNE

Another clustering technique often used in visualization is t-distributed stochastic neighbor embedding (**t-SNE**). It maps higher dimension space to 2D or 3D space so that we can visualize higher-dimensional data. It's a dimensionality reduction technique.

In the case of the Iris dataset, which has four measurements, its samples are 4D. For this dataset, t-SNE technique can map samples to 2D for easy visualization. In `sklearnapi`, you can use t-SNE from `sklearn.ma` library and then can use its `fit_transform()` method for fitting the model and transforming the data simultaneously. But it has one limit - you cannot extend it to include new samples, you have to start over each time. One important parameter of t-SNE is the learning rate, which you choose according to the dataset but a value between 50-200 is often a fine choice.

One strange behavior of this technique is that every time you apply t-SNE, you will get different visualization results on the same dataset, so don't be confused with this behavior. In fact, it is perfectly fine to run t-SNE a number of times (with the same data and parameters), and to select the visualization with the lowest value of the objective function as your final visualization. One drawback of using this technique is that it is a memory consuming technique; so, be careful to apply on a simple computer, otherwise you may get memory errors.

Let's see how you can use `sklearnapi` to apply t-SNE in the MNIST digit dataset. You can load this dataset from the `sklearn.datasetsapi` using `fetch_mldata` function as shown in the following code cell:

```
from sklearn.datasets import fetch_mldata
mnist = fetch_mldata("MNIST original")
X = mnist.data / 255.0
y = mnist.target
print(X.shape, y.shape)
```

```
(70000, 784) (70000,)
```

Figure 14.9: Using fetch_mldata function

If you face any issue while loading the data from `sklearnapi`, you can then download the dataset from any other resources like Google or GitHub or the download link provided in the book. Next, import the basic libraries - numpy and `pandas` and then convert the preceding training data (X) into a `pandas` dataframe. From this newly created dataframe, extract the target variable as shown in the following code cell:

```
#convert the matrix and vector to a Pandas DataFrame
feat_cols = [ 'pixel'+str(i) for i in range(X.shape[1]) ]

df = pd.DataFrame(X,columns=feat_cols)
df['label'] = y
df['label'] = df['label'].apply(lambda i: str(i))

X, y = None, None

print('Size of the dataframe: {}'.format(df.shape))
```

```
Size of the dataframe: (70000, 785)
```

Figure 14.10: Extracting target variable

Next, we will take a random subset of the digits. The randomization is important as the dataset is sorted by its label (i.e., the first seven thousand or so are zeros, etc.). To ensure randomization, we'll create a random permutation of the number 0 to 69,999, which allows us later to select the first five or ten thousand for our calculations and visualizations:

```
rndperm = np.random.permutation(df.shape[0])
```

Figure 14.11: Random selecting the permutations

We now have our dataframe and our randomization vector. Let's first check what these numbers look like. To do this, we'll generate 30 plots of randomly selected images. Don't forget to import the `matplotlib.pyplot` as `plt` before running the following code:

```
plt.gray()
fig = plt.figure( figsize=(16,7) )
for i in range(0,30):
    ax = fig.add_subplot(3,10,i+1, title='Digit: ' + str(df.loc[rndperm[i],'label']) )
    ax.matshow(df.loc[rndperm[i],feat_cols].values.reshape((28,28)).astype(float))
plt.show()
```

Figure 14.12: code snippet for plotting the numbers

These are 28-by-28-pixel images and therefore have a total of 784 `dimensions`, each holding the value of one specific pixel. What we can do is reduce the number of dimensions drastically, whilst trying to retain as much of the `variation` in the information as possible:

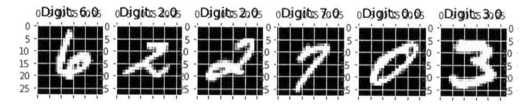

Figure 14.13: result of the plotting code snippet

In case if you are not seeing the actual image as output or seeing the object as output; you need to put a semicolon after the `plt.show()` line, i.e., `plt.show()`. To make sure that we don't burden our machine in terms of memory and power/time, we will only use the first 7,000 samples to run the algorithm on:

```
import time
from sklearn.manifold import TSNE

n_sne = 7000

time_start = time.time()
tsne = TSNE(n_components=2, verbose=1, perplexity=40, n_iter=300)
tsne_results = tsne.fit_transform(df.loc[rndperm[:n_sne],feat_cols].values)

print('t-SNE done! Time elapsed: {} seconds'.format(time.time()-time_start))
```

Figure 14.14: use of TSNE

In the preceding code cell, we have taken the 7000 samples as a variable `n_sne` and then in the `TSNE()` function, we are passing *Dimension of the embedded space* as `n_components`, *Verbosity level* as verbose, *Number of nearest neighbors* as perplexity and the *Maximum number of iterations for the optimization* as `n_iter` arguments. The `fit_transform()` method fits the data into an embedded space and returns that transformed output.

Based on my system configuration, the output looks like the following screenshot:

```
[t-SNE] Computing 121 nearest neighbors...
[t-SNE] Indexed 7000 samples in 0.329s...
[t-SNE] Computed neighbors for 7000 samples in 59.903s...
[t-SNE] Computed conditional probabilities for sample 1000 / 7000
[t-SNE] Computed conditional probabilities for sample 2000 / 7000
[t-SNE] Computed conditional probabilities for sample 3000 / 7000
[t-SNE] Computed conditional probabilities for sample 4000 / 7000
[t-SNE] Computed conditional probabilities for sample 5000 / 7000
[t-SNE] Computed conditional probabilities for sample 6000 / 7000
[t-SNE] Computed conditional probabilities for sample 7000 / 7000
[t-SNE] Mean sigma: 2.239101
[t-SNE] KL divergence after 250 iterations with early exaggeration: 83.187843
[t-SNE] Error after 300 iterations: 2.422179
t-SNE done! Time elapsed: 135.07717204093933 seconds
```

Figure 14.15: Result of the TSNE code snippet

We can visualize the two dimensions by creating a scatter plot and coloring each sample by its respective label. This time we will use `ggplot` to visualize our data. To install this package with `conda`, run one of the following in the Anaconda prompt:

```
conda install -c conda-forge ggplot
```

```
conda install -c conda-forge/label/gcc7 ggplot
```

```
conda install -c conda-forge/label/cf201901 ggplot
```

```
from ggplot import *
df_tsne = df.loc[rndperm[:n_sne],:].copy()
df_tsne['x-tsne'] = tsne_results[:,0]
df_tsne['y-tsne'] = tsne_results[:,1]

tsne_plot = ggplot( df_tsne, aes(x='x-tsne', y='y-tsne', color='label') ) \
        + geom_point(size=70,alpha=0.1) \
        + ggtitle("tSNE dimensions colored by digit")
tsne_plot
```

Figure 14.16: ggplot code snippet

Once you run the preceding code, you will see the following beautiful plot. In case if you are getting an object instead of plot, you need to add and run following code-`tsne_plot.show();`

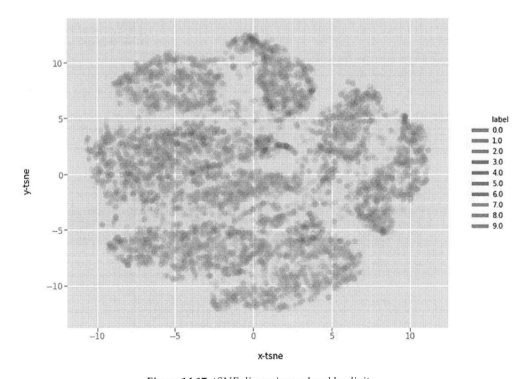

Figure 14.17: tSNE dimensions colored by digit

We can see that the digits are very clearly clustered in their little group (see the label colors as each color is denoting a separate color). The same visualization you cannot do without t-SNE, if you include higher dimensions.

Principal Component Analysis (PCA)

One of the most common tasks in unsupervised learning is dimensionality reduction. On one hand, dimensionality reduction may help with data visualization (e.g., t-SNA method) while, on the other hand, it may help deal with the multicollinearity of your data and prepare the data for a supervised learning method (e.g., decision trees). Multicollinearity of data is a type of disturbance in the data, and if present in the data, the statistical inferences made about the data may not be reliable. PCA is one of the easiest, most intuitive, and most frequently used methods for dimensionality reduction.

PCA aligns the data with axes, which means that it rotates data samples to be aligned with axes in such a way that no information is lost. Here you can understand a principal component as the direction of variance. Let's see how we can apply PCA on a student details dataset. Don't forget to rerun the required packages like pandas before running the following line if you are starting your work:

```
student_data_mat  = pd.read_csv("E:/pg/bpb/BPB-Publications/Datasets/unsupervised/PCA/student-mat.csv",delimiter=";")
student_data_por  = pd.read_csv("E:/pg/bpb/BPB-Publications/Datasets/unsupervised/PCA/student-por.csv",delimiter=";")
student_data = pd.merge(student_data_mat,student_data_por,how="outer")
student_data.head()
```

	school	sex	age	address	famsize	Pstatus	Medu	Fedu	Mjob	Fjob	...	famrel	freetime	goout	Dalc	Walc	health	absences	G1	G2	G3
0	GP	F	18	U	GT3	A	4	4	at_home	teacher	...	4	3	4	1	1	3	6	5	6	6
1	GP	F	17	U	GT3	T	1	1	at_home	other	...	5	3	3	1	1	3	4	5	5	6
2	GP	F	15	U	LE3	T	1	1	at_home	other	...	4	3	2	2	3	3	10	7	8	10
3	GP	F	15	U	GT3	T	4	2	health	services	...	3	2	2	1	1	5	2	15	14	15
4	GP	F	16	U	GT3	T	3	3	other	other	...	4	3	2	1	2	5	4	6	10	10

5 rows × 33 columns

Figure 14.18: Loading example datasets

This dataset contains the details about student achievement in secondary education of two Portuguese schools. The data attributes include student grades, demographic, social, and school-related features, and it was collected by using school reports and questionnaires. Two datasets are provided regarding the performance in two distinct subjects: Mathematics (mat) and Portuguese language (por). Here the target attribute **G3** has a strong correlation with attributes **G2** and **G1**. **G3** is the final year grade (issued at the 3rd period), while **G1** and **G2** correspond to the 1st and 2nd-period grades.

Here, some columns look like categorical variables, so let's handle such columns:

```
student_data.isnull().values.any()
```

```
False
```

```
col_str = student_data.columns[student_data.dtypes == object]
```

```
from sklearn.preprocessing import LabelEncoder
lenc = LabelEncoder()
student_data[col_str] = student_data[col_str].apply(lenc.fit_transform)
```

Figure 14.19: Handling categorical columns

Let's check the correlation between G1, G2, and G3 columns of the dataset, using .corr() function:

```
print(student_data[["G1","G2","G3"]].corr())

          G1        G2        G3
G1  1.000000  0.858739  0.809142
G2  0.858739  1.000000  0.910743
G3  0.809142  0.910743  1.000000
```

Figure 14.20: Using .corr() function

From the preceding output cell, you can easily say that G1, G2, and G3 are highly correlated, so we can drop G1 and G2 for further analysis:

```
# Since, G1,G2,G3 have very high correlation, we can drop G1,G2
student_data.drop(axis = 1,labels= ["G1","G2"])
```

Figure 14.21: Dropping G1 and G2

The next step is to separate targets and samples from the dataset, and then apply PCA using the sklearn.decomposition package. Here, our target variable is G3, so we will separate it from the dataset. In the following code cell, we are putting the target in label variable and rest of the data in the predictor variable. Later, we import the PCA library from the sklearn.decompositionapi and initialize it using PCA() function. Then, we use .fit() method to train our data, and explained_variance_ration() method to get the percentage of variance explained by each of the selected components. Next, we will use numpy' `cumsum()` method, which returns the cumulative sum of the elements along a given axis:

```
label = student_data["G3"].values
predictors = student_data[student_data.columns[:-1]].values
```

```
from sklearn.decomposition import PCA
pca = PCA(n_components=len(student_data.columns)-1)
pca.fit(predictors)
variance_ratio = pca.explained_variance_ratio_
variance_ratio_cum_sum=np.cumsum(np.round(pca.explained_variance_ratio_, decimals=4)*100)
print(variance_ratio_cum_sum)
plt.plot(variance_ratio_cum_sum)
plt.show()
```

Figure 14.22: PCA code snippet example

Here, `variance` means summative variance or multivariate variability or overall variability or total variability. PCA replaces original variables with new variables, called principal components, which are orthogonal (i.e., they have zero covariations), and has variances (called eigenvalues) in decreasing order. Once you run the preceding cell, the following plot will be displayed:

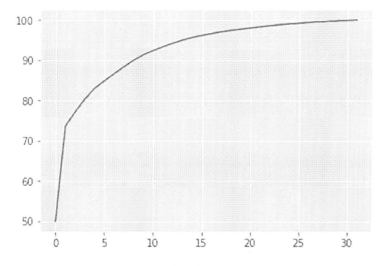

Figure 14.23: Plot of the code snippet

In the preceding output, the red line is the regression line or the set of the predicted values from the model. The variance explained, can be understood as the ratio of the vertical spread of the regression line (i.e., from the lowest point on the line to the highest point on the line) to the vertical spread of the data (i.e., from the lowest data point to the highest data point).

Case study

By now, you must have grasped the basic knowledge of regression techniques. It's time to apply your knowledge to a real problem. Here, you will work on the MNIST computer vision dataset, which consists of 28 x 28 pixel images of digits. Let's import the train data first:

```
train = pd.read_csv("E:/pg/bpb/BPB-Publications/Datasets/regression/MNIST/train.csv")
print(train.shape)
train.head()
```

(42000, 785)

	label	pixel0	pixel1	pixel2	pixel3	pixel4	pixel5	pixel6	pixel7	pixel8	...	pixel774	pixel775	pixel776
0	1	0	0	0	0	0	0	0	0	0	...	0	0	0
1	0	0	0	0	0	0	0	0	0	0	...	0	0	0

Figure 14.24: Importing train data

The MNIST set consists of 42,000 rows and 785 columns. There are 784 columns, as well as one extra label column, which is essentially a class label to state whether the row-wise contribution to each digit gives a 1 or a 9. Each row component contains a value between one and zero, which describes the intensity of each pixel.

Let's conduct some cleaning of the train data by saving the label feature and then removing it from the dataframe:

```
# save the labels to a Pandas series target
target = train['label']
# Drop the label feature
train = train.drop("label",axis=1)
```

Figure 14.25: target column handling

Since our dataset consists of a relatively large number of features (columns), it is a perfect time to apply the Dimensionality Reduction method (PCA). For this, it may be informative to observe how the variances look like for the digits in the MNIST dataset. Therefore, to achieve this, let us calculate the eigenvectors and eigenvalues of the covariance matrix as follows:

```
# Standardizing MNIST dataset features by removing the mean and scaling to unit variance
from sklearn.preprocessing import StandardScaler
train_X = train.values
train_X_std = StandardScaler().fit_transform(train_X)

# Calculating Eigenvectors and Eigenvalues of Covariance matrix
covariance_matrix = np.cov(train_X_std.T)
eigen_values, eigen_vectors = np.linalg.eig(covariance_matrix)

# Creating a list of (eigenvalue, eigenvector)
eigen_pairs = [ (np.abs(eigen_values[i]),eigen_vectors[:,i]) for i in range(len(eigen_values))]

# Sorting the eigenvalue, eigenvector pair from high to low
eigen_pairs.sort(key = lambda x: x[0], reverse= True)

# Calculating Individual and Cumulative explained variance
total_eigen_values = sum(eigen_values)
indivisual_exp_var = [(i/total_eigen_values)*100 for i in sorted(eigen_values, reverse=True)]
cumulative_exp_var = np.cumsum(indivisual_exp_var)
```

Figure 14.26: Calculating eigenvectors and eigenvalues of covariance matrix

After calculating Individual Explained Variance and Cumulative Explained Variance values, let's use the `plotly` visualization package to produce an interactive chart to showcase this. The first import required `plotly` libraries. If this library is not installed in your notebook, install it using the command, `conda install -c plotlyplotly`:

```
import plotly.offline as py
py.init_notebook_mode(connected=True)
from plotly.offline import init_notebook_mode, iplot
import plotly.graph_objs as go
import plotly.tools as tls
import seaborn as sns
```

Figure 14.27: Installing plotly libraries

Next, we will plot a simple scatter plot using `plotly`. Since these plots are interactive, you can move up and down over it. In the following code cell, first, we will set the scatter plot parameters like name, mode, and color for cumulative and individual explained variances, then we will append these two scatter plot variables into a subplot using `make_subplots()` function:

```
cumulative_plot = go.Scatter(
    x=list(range(784)),
    y= cumulative_exp_var,
    mode='lines+markers',
    name="'Cumulative Explained Variance'",
    line=dict(
        shape='spline',
        color = 'limegreen'
    )
)
individual_plot = go.Scatter(
    x=list(range(784)),
    y= indivisual_exp_var,
    mode='lines+markers',
    name="'Individual Explained Variance'",
    line=dict(
        shape='linear',
        color = 'black'
    )
)
fig = tls.make_subplots(insets=[{'cell': (1,1), 'l': 0.7, 'b': 0.5}],
                        print_grid=True)

fig.append_trace(cumulative_plot, 1, 1)
fig.append_trace(individual_plot,1,1)
fig.layout.title = 'Explained Variance plots - Full and Zoomed-in'
fig.layout.xaxis = dict(range=[0, 50], title = 'Feature columns')
fig.layout.yaxis = dict(range=[0, 40], title = 'Explained Variance')
iplot(fig)
```

Figure 14.28: scatter plot code snippet

Once you run the preceding cell, you will get the following plot:

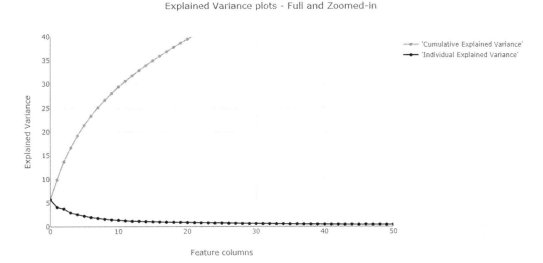

Figure 14.29: *Explained variance plots*

As we can see, out of our 784 features or columns, approximately 90% of the Explained Variance can be described by using just over 200 features. So, if you want to implement a PCA on this, extracting the top 200 features would be a very logical choice, as they already account for the majority of the data.

The PCA method seeks to obtain the optimal directions (or eigenvectors) that captures the most variance (spreads out the data points the most). Therefore, it may be informative to visualize these directions and their associated eigenvalues. For speed, I will invoke PCA to only extract the top 30 eigenvalues (using sklearn's `.components_` call) from the digit dataset and visually compare the top 5 eigenvalues to some of the other smaller ones to see if we can glean any insights. Import the PCA package from `sklearn.decompositionapi`, if you are restarting your work, and then follow this code:

```
# Invoke SKLearn's PCA method
n_components = 30
pca = PCA(n_components=n_components).fit(train.values)
eigenvalues = pca.components_.reshape(n_components, 28, 28)
# Extracting the PCA components ( eignevalues )
eigenvalues = pca.components_
```

Figure 14.30: *checking eigenvalues*

```
n_row = 4
n_col = 7
# Plot the first 8 eignenvalues
plt.figure(figsize=(13,12))
for i in list(range(n_row * n_col)):
    offset =0
    plt.subplot(n_row, n_col, i + 1)
    plt.imshow(eigenvalues[i].reshape(28,28), cmap='jet')
    title_text = 'Eigenvalue ' + str(i + 1)
    plt.title(title_text, size=6.5)
    plt.xticks(())
    plt.yticks(())
plt.show()
```

Figure 14.31: code snippet for plotting eigen values

The preceding cell will draw the following plots:

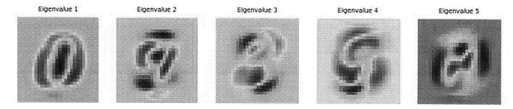

Figure 14.32: plot of different eigen values

The preceding subplots portray the top 5 optimal directions or principal component axes that the PCA method has decided to generate for our digit dataset. If you compare the first component *Eigenvalue 1* to the 25th component *Eigenvalue 5*, it is obvious that more complicated directions or components are being generated in the search to maximize variance in the new feature subspace.

Now using the sklearn toolkit, we implement the PCA algorithm as follows:

```
# Delete our earlier created train_X object
del train_X
# Taking only the first N rows to speed things up
X= train[:6000].values
del train
# Standardising the values
X_std = StandardScaler().fit_transform(X)

# Call the PCA method with 5 components.
pca = PCA(n_components=5)
pca.fit(X_std)
X_5d = pca.transform(X_std)

# Restrict the target values also for speed up
Target = target[:6000]
```

Figure 14.33: Implementing PCA algorithm

In the preceding code, we are first normalizing the data (actually no need to do so for this data set, as they are all 1's and 0's) using sklearn's convenient `StandardScaler()` call. Next, we invoke the `sklearn` library's inbuilt PCA function by providing into its argument `n_components`, the number of components/dimensions we would like to project the data on. As a general practice, for selecting the number of components or dimensions, always look at the proportion of cumulative variance and the individual variance, which you have already done earlier in this chapter.

Finally, we'll call both fits and transform methods that fit the PCA model with the standardized digit data set, and then perform a transformation by applying the dimensionality reduction on the data.

Imagine just for a moment that we were not provided with the class labels to this digit set, because PCA is an unsupervised method. How will we be able to separate our data points in the new feature space? We can apply a clustering algorithm on our new PCA projection data, and hopefully arrive at distinct clusters that would tell us something about the underlying class separation in the data.

To start, we set up a KMeans clustering method with Sklearn's KMeans call, and use the `fit_predict` method to compute cluster centers, and predict cluster indices for the first and second PCA projections (to see if we can observe any appreciable clusters):

```
from sklearn.cluster import KMeans
# Set a KMeans clustering with 9 components
kmeans = KMeans(n_clusters=9)
# Compute cluster centers and predict cluster indices
X_clustered = kmeans.fit_predict(X_5d)

trace_Kmeans = go.Scatter(x=X_5d[:, 0], y= X_5d[:, 1], mode="markers",
                  showlegend=False,
                  marker=dict(
                        size=8,
                        color = X_clustered,
                        colorscale = 'Portland',
                        showscale=False,
                        line = dict(
            width = 2,
            color = 'rgb(255, 255, 255)'
    )
                )
            ))
```

Figure 14.34: KMeans clustering code snippet

```
layout = go.Layout(
    title= 'KMeans Clustering',
    hovermode= 'closest',
    xaxis= dict(
        title= 'First Principal Component',
        ticklen= 5,
        zeroline= False,
        gridwidth= 2,
    ),
    yaxis=dict(
        title= 'Second Principal Component',
        ticklen= 5,
        gridwidth= 2,
    ),
    showlegend= True
)
data = [trace_Kmeans]
fig1 = dict(data=data, layout= layout)
# fig1.append_trace(contour_list)
py.iplot(fig1, filename="svm")
```

Figure 14.35: clustering plot code snippet

The output of the preceding input looks like as shown in the following screenshot:

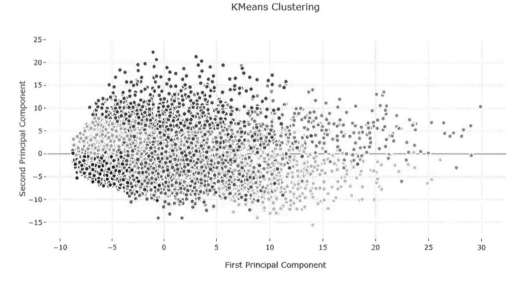

Figure 14.36: K-means clustering

Visually, the clusters generated by the K-Means algorithm appear to provide a clearer demarcation amongst clusters, as compared to naively adding in class labels into our PCA projections. This should come as no surprise as PCA is meant to be an unsupervised method, and therefore not optimized for separating different class labels.

Validation of unsupervised ML

Validation of an unsupervised ML depends on which class of unsupervised algorithms you are referring to.

For example, **dimensionality reduction techniques are generally evaluated by computing the reconstruction error**. You can do this, using similar techniques with respect to supervised algorithms, for example, by applying a k-fold cross-validation procedure.

Clustering algorithms are more difficult to evaluate. Internal metrics use only information on the computed clusters to evaluate whether clusters are compact and well-separated. Also, you can have external metrics that perform statistical testing on the structure of your data.

Density estimation is also rather difficult to evaluate, but there is a wide range of techniques that are mostly used for model tuning, for example, cross-validation procedures.

In addition, unsupervised strategies are sometimes used in the context of a more complex workflow, in which an extrinsic performance function can be defined. For example, if clustering is used to create meaningful classes (e.g., clustering documents), it is possible to create an external dataset by hand-labeling and testing the accuracy (the so-called gold standard). Similarly, if dimensionality reduction is used as a pre-processing step in a supervised learning procedure, the accuracy of the latter can be used as a proxy performance measure for the dimensionality reduction technique.

Conclusion

This chapter has taught you the basic concepts of unsupervised learning along with practical use cases of dimensionality reduction techniques. It is strongly recommended that you apply the learnings from this chapter, as well as other supervised dimensionality reduction techniques – LDA, and compare the results with each other. As always said, practice more and more on different datasets and you will find new insights in every practice. In the next chapter, you will learn how to handle time-series data.

## CHAPTER 15

Handling Time-Series Data

In previous chapters, you have learned how to solve supervised and unsupervised machine learning problems. In this chapter, you will gain knowledge to understand and work with time-series data. Whether it is analyzing business trends, forecasting company revenue, or exploring customer behavior, every data scientist is likely to encounter time series data at some point during their work. Time series is a series of data points indexed (or listed or graphed) in time order. Therefore, the data is organized by relatively deterministic timestamps, and compared to random sample data, may contain additional information that we can extract.

Structure

- Why time-series is important?
- How to handle date and time?
- Transforming a time-series data
- Manipulating a time-series data
- Comparing time-series growth rates
- How to change time-series frequency?
- Conclusion

Objective

After studying this chapter, you will be able to manipulate and visualize the time-series data in order to extract meaningful statistics and other characteristics of the data.

Why time-series is important?

Since time-series is a collection of data points collected at constant time intervals, they are analyzed to determine the long-term trend. Time-series forecasting is the use of a model to predict future values based on previously observed values. In business scenarios, that's like predicting stock price or predicting the weather conditions for tomorrow, time-series has a significant role. In your day-to-day job, you will come across situations with time series-connected tasks. For example, think about the following frequent question a person may think daily—What will happen with our metrics in the next day/week/month?How many people will install the app? How much time will a user spend online? How many actions will the users do? Analyzing such kind of data can reveal things that at first were not clear, such as unexpected trends, correlations, and forecast trends in the future bringing a competitive advantage to anyone who uses it. For these reasons, time-series can be applied to a wide range of fields.

How to handle date and time?

Pandas have dedicated libraries for handling time-series objects, particularly the `datatime64[ns]` class, which stores time information and allows us to perform some operations fast. Here `ns` means nano-seconds. Besides `pandas`, you will need `statsmodels` library that has tons of statistical modeling functions, including time series. You can install the `statsmodels` by running the following command in Anaconda prompt:

```
conda install -c anaconda statsmodels
```

When you load the data in a pandas `Dataframe`, any column can contain the date for time information, but it is most important as a `Dataframe` index, because it converts the entire dataframe into a Time Series. The complete examples of this chapter are in `Time Series Data.ipynb` as a notebook. First, let's understand the `pandas` capability of handling time-series data by importing basic libraries:

```
import pandas as pd
from datetime import datetime # for manually creating dates
```

Figure 15.1: Importing basic libraries

Now, we will create a `pandas` dataframe and check its datatype as shown in the following screenshot:

```
# creating pandas timestamp
time_stamp = pd.Timestamp(datetime(2019,1,1))

# using a date string as datetime object
pd.Timestamp(datetime(2019,1,1)) == time_stamp

True
```

```
time_stamp

Timestamp('2019-01-01 00:00:00')
```

Figure 15.2: Creating pandas dataframe and checking datatype

In the preceding cells, the type of our `time_stamp` variable is `Timestamp` and a default time with midnight value is added, and date string also generates the same result, which means that you can use the date as string also. Pandas `Timestamp` has various attributes like a `year`, `month`, `day`, `weekday_name`, etc., to store time-specific information which you can access as shown in the following screenshot:

```
time_stamp.year

2019
```

```
time_stamp.month

1
```

```
time_stamp.day

1
```

Figure 15.3: Accessing time-specific information

Pandas has also a data type for handling time periods. The `Period` object always has a frequency with month as default. It also has a method to convert between frequencies, as well as the `period` object to convert back in its timestamp format. You can also convert a `Timestamp` object to `period` and vice versa. What more to say! You can even perform basic date arithmetic operations. Let's understand how you can practically implement this:

```python
period = pd.Period('2019-01')
print("period:: ", period)

#convert period to daily from month
print(period.asfreq('D'))

#convert period to timestamp back
print(period.to_timestamp().to_period('M'))

#basic date arithmetic operation
print(period + 3)
```

```
period::   2019-01
2019-01-31
2019-01
2019-04
```

Figure 15.4: Handling time periods

Next, you will create a time-series with sequences of `Dates` using the pandas `date_range()` function. This function returns a fixed frequency `DatetimeIndex`. You can also convert the index to period index just like `Timestamp`. See the following cells for each one and notice the data type in output cells:

```python
index = pd.date_range(start='2018-1-1', periods=12, freq='M')
index
```

```
DatetimeIndex(['2018-01-31', '2018-02-28', '2018-03-31', '2018-04-30',
               '2018-05-31', '2018-06-30', '2018-07-31', '2018-08-31',
               '2018-09-30', '2018-10-31', '2018-11-30', '2018-12-31'],
              dtype='datetime64[ns]', freq='M')
```

```python
index[0]
```

```
Timestamp('2018-01-31 00:00:00', freq='M')
```

```python
index.to_period()
```

```
PeriodIndex(['2018-01', '2018-02', '2018-03', '2018-04', '2018-05', '2018-06',
             '2018-07', '2018-08', '2018-09', '2018-10', '2018-11', '2018-12'],
            dtype='period[M]', freq='M')
```

Figure 15.5: How to use date_range()

Now we can easily create a time-series (Pandas `DatetimeIndex`). For example, we will create a random 12 rows with 2 columns using `numpy.random.rand()` to match the date-time index and then create our first time-series as shown in the following screenshot:

```
pd.DataFrame({'date' : index}).info()
print("========================================")
import numpy as np
my_data = np.random.rand(12, 2)
pd.DataFrame(data = my_data, index = index).info()

<class 'pandas.core.frame.DataFrame'>
RangeIndex: 12 entries, 0 to 11
Data columns (total 1 columns):
date    12 non-null datetime64[ns]
dtypes: datetime64[ns](1)
memory usage: 176.0 bytes
========================================
<class 'pandas.core.frame.DataFrame'>
DatetimeIndex: 12 entries, 2018-01-31 to 2018-12-31
Freq: M
Data columns (total 2 columns):
0    12 non-null float64
1    12 non-null float64
dtypes: float64(2)
memory usage: 608.0 bytes
```

Figure 15.6: Creating a time series data with DataFrame

In the preceding output cells, you can see that each date in the resulting `pd.DatetimeIndex` is a `pd.Timestamp` and since this `Timestamp` has various attributes, you can easily access and obtain information about the date. In the following example, we will create a week of data, iterate over the result, and obtain the `dayofweek` and `weekday_name` for each date:

```
# Create the range of dates here
seven_days = pd.date_range('2019-1-1', periods=7)

# Iterate over the dates and print the number and name of the weekday
for day in seven_days:
    print(day.dayofweek, day.weekday_name)

1 Tuesday
2 Wednesday
3 Thursday
4 Friday
5 Saturday
6 Sunday
0 Monday
```

Figure 15.7: Creating a week of data to obtain result

The preceding examples will help you to handle and manipulate time-series data with `statsmodel` library very easily. Next, you will learn how to transform a time-series data.

Transforming a time-series data

While analyzing the time-series data, it is common to transform your data into a better one. For example, your date column is in object form and you will need to parse this `string` object and then convert it to `datetime64` datatype, or you may need to generate new data from the existing time-series data. That's why it is important to know all these transformations. Let's understand the importance of transformation by working on Google's stock price data, which you can download from the download link provided at the start of the book:

```
google_df = pd.read_csv("E:/pg/bpb/BPB-Publications/Datasets/timeseries/stock_data/google.csv")
google_df.head()
```

	Date	Close
0	2014-01-02	556.00
1	2014-01-03	551.95
2	2014-01-04	NaN
3	2014-01-05	NaN
4	2014-01-06	558.10

Figure 15.8: Understanding importance of transformation

The `Date` column looks fine at first, but when you check its data type, it's a string:

```
google_df.info()
<class 'pandas.core.frame.DataFrame'>
RangeIndex: 1094 entries, 0 to 1093
Data columns (total 2 columns):
Date     1094 non-null object
Close    756 non-null float64
dtypes: float64(1), object(1)
memory usage: 17.2+ KB
```

Figure 15.9: Datatype is a string

Since many machine learning algorithms don't accept `string` input, you must convert data column datatype to correct data type. You can convert a `string` data type to `dateTime64[ns]` using pandas as shown in the following screenshot:

```
google_df.Date = pd.to_datetime(google_df.Date)
google_df.info()

<class 'pandas.core.frame.DataFrame'>
RangeIndex: 1094 entries, 0 to 1093
Data columns (total 2 columns):
Date     1094 non-null datetime64[ns]
Close     756 non-null float64
dtypes: datetime64[ns](1), float64(1)
```

Figure 15.10: Converting string datatype to dateTime64[ns]

Now, our `Date` column is an incorrect datatype and we can set it as the index as shown in the following screenshot:

```
google_df.set_index('Date', inplace=True)
google_df.info()

<class 'pandas.core.frame.DataFrame'>
DatetimeIndex: 1094 entries, 2014-01-02 to 2016-12-30
Data columns (total 1 columns):
Close     756 non-null float64
dtypes: float64(1)
```

Figure 15.11: How to set date as index

If you get an error like `keyerror: ['Date']`, add `drop=False'` argument in the preceding code cell. So your new code will be `google_df.set_index('Date', inplace=True, drop=False)`.

Here, we are setting the `Date` column as index and the argument- `inplace=True` means don't create a new copy of the `DataFrame`.

Once you have corrected the datatype, you can easily visualize the stock price data as shown in the following screenshot:

```
import matplotlib.pyplot as plt
%matplotlib inline
google_df.Close.plot(title='Google Stock closing Price')
plt.tight_layout()
plt.show()
```

Figure 15.12: Visualizing stock price data

You might have noticed here that there is no frequency in our date time index; the calendar day frequency can be set, as shown in the following screenshot:

```
google_df.asfreq('D').info()

<class 'pandas.core.frame.DataFrame'>
DatetimeIndex: 1094 entries, 2014-01-02 to 2016-12-30
Freq: D
Data columns (total 1 columns):
Close     756 non-null float64
dtypes: float64(1)
```

Figure 15.13: Setting calendar day frequency

After this transformation, let's check the new data, because there may be some null values added. It's good to check the head of the dataset, as shown in the following screenshot:

```
google_df.asfreq('D').head()
```

Date	Close
2014-01-02	556.00
2014-01-03	551.95
2014-01-04	NaN
2014-01-05	NaN
2014-01-06	558.10

Figure 15.14: Head of dataset

As you can see, these new dates have missing values; this is called upsampling. This means, higher frequency implies new dates, therefore the missing values. We will handle this later in this chapter.

Manipulating a time-series data

Time-series data manipulation means shifting or lagging values back or forward in time, getting the difference in value for a given time period, or computing the percent change over any number of periods. The pandas library has built-in methods to achieve all such manipulations.

In the next example, we will explore the power of the pandas. We will reload Google stock price data using Pandas DataFrame, but with some additional parameters, as shown in the following screenshot:

```
google_df = pd.read_csv("E:/pg/bpb/BPB-Publications/Datasets/timeseries/stock_data/google.csv",
                        parse_dates=['Date'],
                        index_col='Date')
google_df.head()
```

Date	Close
2014-01-02	556.00
2014-01-03	551.95
2014-01-04	NaN
2014-01-05	NaN
2014-01-06	558.10

Figure 15.15: Reloading Google stock price data with additional parameters

In this case, while loading the dataset, you will notice the date column is automatically transformed in the correct format. Here, `pandas` does all parsing for you and provides us with the properly formatted time series dataset!

Let's understand the different methods of `pandas` for manipulating our time-series data. First, we will see the `shift()` method, which by default, shifts by 1 period into the future, as shown in the following screenshot:

```
google_df['shifted'] = google_df.Close.shift()
google_df.head()
```

Date	Close	shifted
2014-01-02	556.00	NaN
2014-01-03	551.95	556.00
2014-01-04	NaN	551.95
2014-01-05	NaN	NaN
2014-01-06	558.10	NaN

Figure 15.16: Using shift() method

Similarly, there is `alagged()` method, which by default, shifts by 1 period into the past. You can try this in your notebook!

You can also calculate one-period finance change or financial return using `div()` method and some arithmetic operation on it, as shown in the following screenshots:

```
google_df['change'] = google_df.Close.div(google_df.shifted)
google_df.head()
```

Date	Close	shifted	change
2014-01-02	556.00	NaN	NaN
2014-01-03	551.95	556.00	0.992716
2014-01-04	NaN	551.95	NaN
2014-01-05	NaN	NaN	NaN
2014-01-06	558.10	NaN	NaN

Figure 15.17: Calculating one period finance using div()

```
google_df['return'] = google_df.change.sub(1).mul(100)
google_df.head()
```

Date	Close	shifted	change	return
2014-01-02	556.00	NaN	NaN	NaN
2014-01-03	551.95	556.00	0.992716	-0.728417
2014-01-04	NaN	551.95	NaN	NaN
2014-01-05	NaN	NaN	NaN	NaN
2014-01-06	558.10	NaN	NaN	NaN

Figure 15.18: Peek of the DataFrame

You can also calculate the difference in value for two adjacent periods using `diff()` method. Try this in your notebook! Since you are able to use the preceding knowledge to visually compare a stock price series for Google, let us now shift 90 business days into both past and future, as shown in the following screenshot:

```
# Set data frequency to business daily
google = google_df.asfreq('B')

# Create 'lagged' and 'shifted'
google['lagged'] = google.Close.shift(periods=-90)
google['shifted'] = google.Close.shift(periods=90)

# Plot the google price series
google.plot()
plt.show()
```

Figure 15.19: Visually comparing time series

Thus, you can visually compare the time series to itself at different points in time.

Comparing time-series growth rates

Comparing the time-series growth rate is a very common task, and you will come across it in your time series analysis. For example, comparing the stock performance. However, this is not a piece of cake, because stock price series are very hard to compare at different levels. There is a solution to tackle this problem - normalize price series to start at 100. To achieve this solution, you just need to divide all prices in series and then multiply the same by 100. As a result, you will get the first value as 1 and all prices relative to the starting point. Let's apply this solution in our Google stock price data, as shown in the following screenshot:

```
first_price = google.Close.iloc[0]
# normalize a single series
normalized = google.Close.div(first_price).mul(100)
normalized.plot(title='Google Normalized Price')
plt.show()
```

Figure 15.20: Comparing time-series growth

Notice the output plot here! It is starting at 100.

In the same way, you can normalize multiple series as well. We just need to ensure that row labels of our series align with the columns headers of the `DataFrame`. For this confirmation, you don't need to worry, because the `div()` method will take care of this. For example, we will normalize different companies' stock price, as shown in the following screenshot:

```
price_df = pd.read_csv("E:/pg/bpb/BPB-Publications/Datasets/timeseries/stock_data/stock_data.csv",
                        parse_dates=['Date'],
                        index_col='Date')
price_df.head(3)
```

Date	AAPL	AMGN	AMZN	CPRT	EL	GS	ILMN	MA	PAA	RIO	TEF	UPS
2010-01-04	30.57	57.72	133.90	4.55	24.27	173.08	30.55	25.68	27.00	56.03	28.55	58.18
2010-01-05	30.63	57.22	134.69	4.55	24.18	176.14	30.35	25.61	27.30	56.90	28.53	58.28
2010-01-06	30.14	56.79	132.25	4.53	24.25	174.26	32.22	25.56	27.29	58.64	28.23	57.85

Figure 15.21: *Normalizing stock price of different companies*

Now, we will plot different stock prices of different companies using the `plot()` method. Here, we will again use `div()` method to ensure that row labels of our series align with the column headers of the `price_df`, as shown in the following screenshot:

```
normalized = price_df.div(price_df.iloc[0])
normalized.plot(title='Stocks Normalized Price')
plt.show()
```

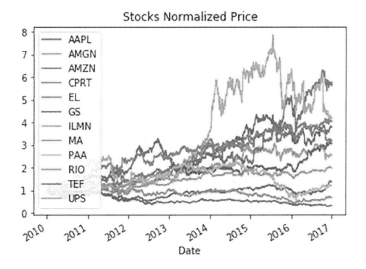

Figure 15.22: *Using div() method*

Once you normalize the price of the stocks, as shown in the preceding screenshot, you can also compare the performance of various stocks against a benchmark. Let's learn this by comparing the three largest stocks from the NYSE to the Dow Jones Industrial Average datasets, which contain the 30 largest US companies, as shown in the following screenshots:

```python
# Import stock prices and index here
stocks = pd.read_csv('E:/pg/bpb/BPB-Publications/Datasets/timeseries/stock_data/nyse.csv',
                     parse_dates=['date'], index_col='date')
dow_jones = pd.read_csv('E:/pg/bpb/BPB-Publications/Datasets/timeseries/stock_data/dow_jones.csv',
                        parse_dates=['date'], index_col='date')

# Concatenate data and inspect result
data = pd.concat([stocks, dow_jones], axis=1)
print(data.info())

# Normalize and plot your data
data.div(data.iloc[0]).mul(100).plot()
plt.show()
```

Figure 15.23: Comparing various stocks data

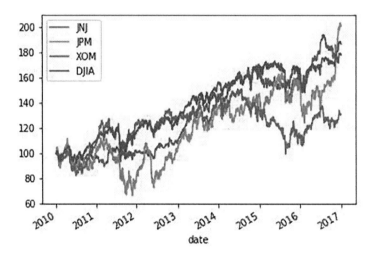

Figure 15.24: Plot of the stocks comparison

Next, we will learn how to compare the performance of Microsoft (MSFT) and Apple (AAPL) to the S&P 500 dataset over the last 10 years, as shown in the following screenshots:

```
# Create tickers
tickers = ['MSFT', 'AAPL']

# Import stock data here
stocks = pd.read_csv('E:/pg/bpb/BPB-Publications/Datasets/timeseries/stock_data/msft_aapl.csv',
                      parse_dates=['date'], index_col='date')

# Import index here
sp500 = pd.read_csv('E:/pg/bpb/BPB-Publications/Datasets/timeseries/stock_data/sp500.csv',
                    parse_dates=['date'], index_col='date')

# Concatenate stocks and index here
data = pd.concat([stocks, sp500], axis=1).dropna()

# Normalize data
normalized = data.div(data.iloc[0]).mul(100)

# Subtract the normalized index from the normalized stock prices, and plot the result
normalized[tickers].sub(normalized['SP500'], axis=0).plot()
plt.show()
```

Figure 15.25: Comparing performances of Apple and Microsoft stock data

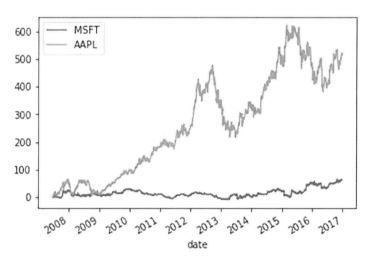

Figure 15.26: Plot of the comparison

Now you can compare these stocks to the overall market, so that you can easily spot trends and outliers.

How to change time-series frequency?

Change in frequency also affects the data. If you are doing upsampling, then you should fill or handle the missing values, and if you are doing downsampling, then you should aggregate the existing data. First, we will find out the quarterly frequency of the time series data, then from this quarterly frequency, we will take out the monthly frequency so that in the end, we can use this monthly frequency for upsampling and downsampling:

```
dates = pd.date_range(start='2018', periods=4, freq='Q')
my_data = range(1,5)
quaterly = pd.Series(data=my_data, index=dates)
quaterly
```

```
2018-03-31    1
2018-06-30    2
2018-09-30    3
2018-12-31    4
Freq: Q-DEC, dtype: int64
```

```
# upsampling quaterly to Month
monthly = quaterly.asfreq('M')
monthly
```

```
2018-03-31    1.0
2018-04-30    NaN
2018-05-31    NaN
2018-06-30    2.0
2018-07-31    NaN
2018-08-31    NaN
2018-09-30    3.0
2018-10-31    NaN
2018-11-30    NaN
2018-12-31    4.0
Freq: M, dtype: float64
```

Figure 15.27: Using monthly frequency for upsampling and downsampling

Now let's see how we can achieve this in each case:

```
monthly = monthly.to_frame('baseline')
# handling missing values using forward fill
monthly['ffill'] = quaterly.asfreq('M', method='ffill')
# handling missing values using backward fill
monthly['bfill'] = quaterly.asfreq('M', method='bfill')
# handling missing values with 0
monthly['ffill'] = quaterly.asfreq('M', fill_value=0)
monthly
```

	baseline	ffill	bfill
2018-03-31	1.0	1	1
2018-04-30	NaN	0	2
2018-05-31	NaN	0	2
2018-06-30	2.0	2	2
2018-07-31	NaN	0	3

Figure 15.28: Handling missing values

Now you will learn about the `interpolate()` method. Pandas `dataframe.interpolate()` function is basically used to fill NA values in the dataframe or series. But this is a very powerful function to fill the missing values. It uses various interpolation techniques to fill the missing values, rather than hard-coding the value. To understand the Pandas `interpolate()` method, which Interpolates values according to different methods, let's take an example of a new dataset:

```
# Import & inspect data
data_df = pd.read_csv('E:/pg/bpb/BPB-Publications/Datasets/timeseries/stock_data/debt_unemployment.csv',
                parse_dates=['date'],
                index_col='date')
data_df.info()

<class 'pandas.core.frame.DataFrame'>
DatetimeIndex: 89 entries, 2010-01-01 to 2017-05-01
Data columns (total 2 columns):
Debt/GDP        29 non-null float64
Unemployment    89 non-null float64
dtypes: float64(2)
```

Figure 15.29: Understanding interpolate() method

Now we will interpolate debt/GDP and compare to unemployment, as shown in the following screenshot:

```
interpolated = data_df.interpolate()
interpolated.info()

<class 'pandas.core.frame.DataFrame'>
DatetimeIndex: 89 entries, 2010-01-01 to 2017-05-01
Data columns (total 2 columns):
Debt/GDP        89 non-null float64
Unemployment    89 non-null float64
dtypes: float64(2)
```

Figure 15.30: Interpolating dept/GDP

Later, we can visualize this as shown in the following screenshot:

```
interpolated.plot(secondary_y='Unemployment');
plt.show()
```

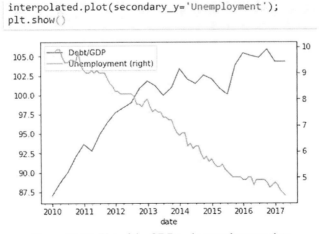

Figure 15.31: Plot of the GDP and unemployment data

In the preceding plot, you can see Debt/GDP column of our dataframe as a blue line, whereas Unemployment as a brown line. From the plot, you can understand that Debt/GDP rate is increasing with some variation between 2015 and 2016, while Unemployment is decreasing steadily since 2010.

So far, we have done upsampling, fill logic, and interpolation. Now we will learn how to do downsampling. For downsampling, you can choose options like mean, median, or last value to fill the missing values. For understanding this, let's work on the air quality dataset:

```
ozone_df = pd.read_csv('E:/pg/bpb/BPB-Publications/Datasets/timeseries/air_quality_data/ozone_nyla.csv',
            parse_dates=['date'], index_col='date')
ozone_df.info()
```

```
<class 'pandas.core.frame.DataFrame'>
DatetimeIndex: 6291 entries, 2000-01-01 to 2017-03-31
Data columns (total 2 columns):
Los Angeles    5488 non-null float64
New York       6167 non-null float64
dtypes: float64(2)
```

Figure 15.32: To understand how to do downsampling

First, we calculate and plot the monthly average ozone trend, as shown in the following screenshot:

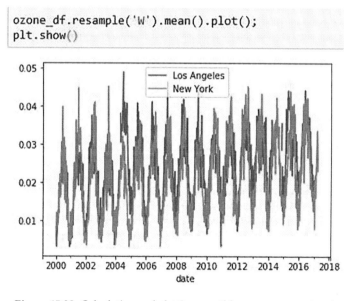

Figure 15.33: Calculating and plotting monthly average ozone trend

Next, we calculate and plot the annual average ozone trend, as shown in the following screenshot:

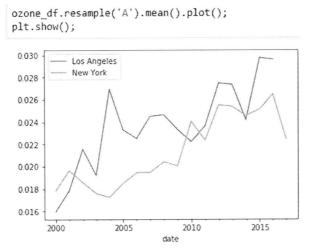

Figure 15.34: Calculating and plotting annual average ozone trend

You can easily see how changing the resampling period changes the plot of the time series.

Now you can compare higher-frequency stock price series to lower-frequency economic time series easily. As a first example, let's compare the quarterly GDP growth rate to the quarterly rate of return on the (resampled) *Dow Jones Industrial* index of 30 large US stocks. GDP growth is reported at the beginning of each quarter for the previous quarter. To calculate matching stock returns, you'll resample the stock index to quarter start frequency using the alias QS, and aggregating using the .first() observations, as shown in the following screenshot:

```
# Import and inspect gdp_growth
gdp_growth = pd.read_csv('E:/pg/bpb/BPB-Publications/Datasets/timeseries/stock_data/gdp_growth.csv',
                         parse_dates=['date'], index_col='date')
gdp_growth.info()

# Import and inspect djia
djia = pd.read_csv('E:/pg/bpb/BPB-Publications/Datasets/timeseries/stock_data/djia.csv',
                   parse_dates=['date'], index_col='date')
djia.info()

<class 'pandas.core.frame.DataFrame'>
DatetimeIndex: 41 entries, 2007-01-01 to 2017-01-01
Data columns (total 1 columns):
gdp_growth    41 non-null float64
dtypes: float64(1)
memory usage: 656.0 bytes
<class 'pandas.core.frame.DataFrame'>
DatetimeIndex: 2610 entries, 2007-06-29 to 2017-06-29
Data columns (total 1 columns):
djia    2519 non-null float64
dtypes: float64(1)
memory usage: 40.8 KB
```

Figure 15.35: Loading gdp growth and DJI datasets

Since we have stored the data as a dataframe, let's calculate the quarterly return and plot it with respect to GDP growth, as shown in the following screenshot:

```
# Calculate djia quarterly returns
djia_quarterly = djia.resample('QS').first()
djia_quarterly_return = djia_quarterly.pct_change().mul(100)

# Concatenate, rename and plot djia_quarterly_return and gdp_growth
data = pd.concat([gdp_growth, djia_quarterly_return], axis=1)
data.columns = ['gdp', 'djia']

data.plot()
plt.show();
```

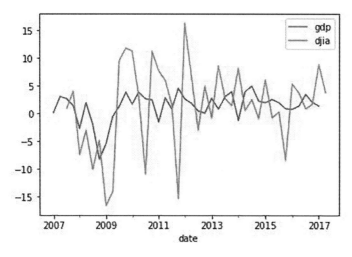

Figure 15.36: Calculating quarterly return and plotting with GDP growth

Let's explore how the monthly mean, median, and standard deviation of daily S&P500 returns have trended over the last 10 years. In this example, we will aggregate the mean, median, and standard deviation with `resample()` method:

```
# Import data
sp500 = pd.read_csv('E:/pg/bpb/BPB-Publications/Datasets/timeseries/stock_data/sp500.csv',
                    parse_dates=['date'], index_col='date')

# Calculate daily returns here
daily_returns = sp500.squeeze().pct_change()

# Resample and calculate statistics
stats = daily_returns.resample('M').agg(['mean', 'median', 'std'])

stats.plot()
plt.show()
```

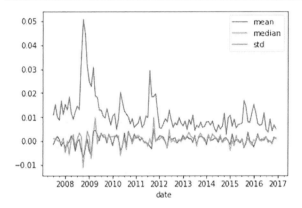

Figure 15.37: *Aggregating mean, median, and standard deviation with resample() method*

From the preceding plot, you can easily see the statistical average methods like mean as a blue line, green as standard deviation, and orange as median of daily S&P500 returns in the last 10 years.

Conclusion

In this chapter, you have learned how to manipulate and visualize time-series data. If you practice the preceding exercise in your notebook, time-series data is no more difficult for you to understand. But to know more, you need to practice more with new data. The learning from this chapter will definitely help you when you work with stock price prediction or weather prediction or sales data. In the next chapter, you will learn different time-series forecasting machine learning methods.

CHAPTER 16
Time-Series Methods

In the previous chapter, you learned the techniques of manipulating and visualizing varying types of time-series data analysis. In this chapter, you will learn about the various time-series forecasting methods using the `statsmodels` library. These statistical techniques are important to know before applying any machine learning model on time-series data. You will learn different APIs of this library to forecast time-series, by working on different examples. Having a working code example as a starting point will greatly accelerate your progress, when you apply these methods with machine learning models. You can find all the examples mentioned in this chapter in a notebook named, `Time Series Methods.ipynb`.

Structure

- What is time-series forecasting?
- Basic steps in forecasting
- Time-series forecasting techniques
- Forecast future traffic to a web page
- Conclusion

Objective

After studying this chapter, you will be familiar with the various time-series forecasting methods and apply the techniques to forecast any time-series problem.

What is time-series forecasting?

Time-series forecasting is an important area of machine learning, because there are so many prediction problems present in this world that involve a time component. Since Time-series adds an explicit order dependence between observations – time dimension, this additional dimension is both a constraint and a structure that provides a source of additional information. Making predictions is called extrapolation in the classical statistical handling of time-series data. More modern fields focus on the topic and refer to it as time-series forecasting.

Forecasting involves taking models to fit on historical data and using them to predict future observations. An important distinction in forecasting is that the future is completely unpredictable and must only be estimated from what has already happened. Some examples of time-series forecasting are as follows: forecasting the closing price of stock each day, forecasting product sales in units sold each day for a store, forecasting the number of passengers through a train station each day, forecasting unemployment for a state each quarter, forecasting the average price of petrol in a city each day, etc.

Basic steps in forecasting

Famous statisticians and econometricians, *Dr. Hyndman* and *Dr. Athanasopoulos*, have summarized 5 basic forecasting steps, which are as follows:

- **Defining the business problem**: The careful consideration of who requires the forecast and how the forecast will be used.

- **Information gathering**: The collection of historical data to analyze and model data. This also includes getting access to domain experts and gathering information that can help to best interpret the historical information, and ultimately the forecasts that will be made.

- **Preliminary exploratory analysis**: The use of simple tools, like graphing and summary statistics, to better understand the data. Review plots and summarize and note obvious temporal structures, like trends seasonality, anomalies like missing data, corruption, and outliers, and any other structures that may impact forecasting.

- **Choosing and fitting models**: Evaluate two, three, or a suite of models of varying types on the problem. Models are configured and fit to the historical data.

- **Using and evaluating a forecasting model**: The model is used to make forecasts and the performance of those forecasts is evaluated and the skill of the models estimated.

The preceding basic steps are very useful and effective, so always remember and apply the same whenever you deal with time-series data.

Time-series forecasting techniques

The `statsmodels` library has many methods for time-series forecasting. You must know some of these time-series methods/techniques, because you will not get better accuracy by only applying a machine-learning algorithm to a time-series data. The following are some common techniques, which we will cover in this chapter:

- Autoregression (AR)

- Moving Average (MA)

- Autoregressive Moving Average (ARMA)

- Autoregressive Integrated Moving Average (ARIMA)

- Seasonal Autoregressive Integrated Moving-Average (SARIMA)

- Seasonal Autoregressive Integrated Moving-Average with Exogenous Regressors (SARIMAX)

- Vector Autoregression Moving-Average (VARMA)

- Holt Winter's Exponential Smoothing (HWES)

Autoregression (AR)

Autoregression is a time-series model that uses observations from previous time steps as input to a regression equation to predict the value at the next time step. An autoregression model makes an assumption that the observations at previous time steps are useful to predict the value at the next time step. This relationship between variables is called correlation. If both variables change in the same direction (e.g., go up together or down together), it is called a positive correlation. If the variables move in opposite directions as values change (e.g., one goes up and one goes down), then it is called a negative correlation. The method is suitable for univariate time-series without trend and seasonal components. The following is an example of using Autoregression model using `statsmodels` library's API:

```
# Autoregression(AR) example
from statsmodels.tsa.ar_model import AR
from random import random
# create a sample dataset
data = [a + random() for a in range(1, 100)]
# fit model
model = AR(data)
model_fit = model.fit()
# make prediction
prediction = model_fit.predict(len(data), len(data))
prediction
```
```
array([100.6504561])
```

Figure 16.1: Example of using Autoregression model

In the preceding code cell, we fit the unconditional maximum likelihood of an AR (p) process using `statsmodels.tsa.ar_model.AR.fit()` and later we return the in-sample and out-of-sample prediction using the `predict()` method. The `predict()` method takes the first argument as the starting number of forecasting and second argument takes a number where you want to end the forecasting. In our case, the autoregression model has predicted values as 100.65 for a sample dataset.

Moving Average (MA)

This algorithm helps us to forecast new observations based on a time-series. This algorithm uses smoothing methods. The moving average algorithm is used only on the time-series that DON'T have a trend. This method is suitable for univariate time-series without trend and seasonal components. It consists of making the arithmetic mean of the last n observations contained by the time-series to forecast the next observation.

We can use the ARMA class to create an MA model and set a zeroth-order AR model. We must specify the order of the MA model in the order argument, as shown in the following screenshot:

```
# Moving Average(MA) example
from statsmodels.tsa.arima_model import ARMA
from random import random
# create a sample dataset
data = [a + random() for a in range(1, 100)]
# fit model
model = ARMA(data, order=(0, 1))
model_fit = model.fit(disp=False)
# make prediction
ma_predict = model_fit.predict(len(data), len(data))
ma_predict
```
```
array([75.32920306])
```

Figure 16.2: Order of MA model in order argument

In the preceding code cell, we have fitted the MA model by exact maximum likelihood via Kalman filter using `statsmodels.tsa.arima_model.fit()` method with `disp` as a false parameter, and later we have returned the in-sample and out-of-sample prediction using the `predict()` method. In our sample dataset example, we are getting moving average prediction as 75.33.

Autoregressive Moving Average (ARMA)

In ARMA forecasting model, both autoregression analysis and moving average methods are applied to well-behaved time-series data. ARMA assumes that the time-series is stationary and fluctuates more or less uniformly around a time-invariant mean. Non-stationary series needs to be differenced one or more times to achieve stationarity. ARMA models are considered inappropriate for impact analysis or for data that incorporates random shocks:

```
# ARMA example
from statsmodels.tsa.arima_model import ARMA
from random import random
# create a sample dataset
data = [random() for x in range(1, 100)]
# fit model
model = ARMA(data, order=(2, 1))
model_fit = model.fit(disp=False)
# make prediction
arma_pred = model_fit.predict(len(data), len(data))
arma_pred
```

```
array([0.58318755])
```

Figure 16.3: ARMA model example

In the preceding code cell, we have fitted ARIMA (p,d,q) model by exact maximum likelihood via Kalman filter using `statsmodels.tsa.arima_model.fit()` method, and later we have returned the in-sample and out-of-sample prediction using the `predict()` method. Here `disp` argument controls the frequency of the output during the iterations. The `predict()` method forecasted 0.58 as the prediction of our sample dataset.

Autoregressive Integrated Moving Average (ARIMA)

ARIMA method combines both **Autoregression (AR)** and **Moving Average (MA)** methods, as well as a differencing pre-processing step of the sequence to make the sequence stationary, called **integration (I)**. ARIMA models can represent a wide range of time-series data and are used generally in computing the probability of a future value lying between any two limits. Although this method can handle data with a trend, it does not support time-series with a seasonal component. ARIMA models are denoted with the notation ARIMA (p, d, q). These three parameters account for seasonality, trend, and noise in data.

```python
# ARIMA example
from statsmodels.tsa.arima_model import ARIMA
from random import random
# create a sample dataset
data = [x + random() for x in range(1, 100)]
# fit model
model = ARIMA(data, order=(1, 1, 1))
model_fit = model.fit(disp=False)
# make prediction
arima_pred = model_fit.predict(len(data), len(data), typ='levels')
arima_pred
```

```
array([100.57016203])
```

Figure 16.4: ARIMA model example

In the preceding code cell, we fit the ARIMA (p, d, q) model by exact maximum likelihood via Kalman filter, and then predicted it's ARIMA model in-sample and out-of-sample using `.predict()` method.

Seasonal Autoregressive Integrated Moving-Average (SARIMA)

An extension to ARIMA that supports the direct modeling of the seasonal component of the series is called SARIMA. SARIMA model combines the ARIMA model with the ability to perform the same autoregression, differencing, and moving average modeling at the seasonal level. This method is suitable for univariate time-series with the trend and/or seasonal components. The big difference between an ARIMA model and a SARIMA model is the addition of seasonal error components to the model:

```python
# SARIMA example
from statsmodels.tsa.statespace.sarimax import SARIMAX
from random import random
# create a sample dataset
data = [x + random() for x in range(1, 100)]
# fit model
model = SARIMAX(data, order=(1, 1, 1), seasonal_order=(1, 1, 1, 1))
model_fit = model.fit(disp=False)
# make prediction
sarima_pred = model_fit.predict(len(data), len(data))
sarima_pred
```

```
array([100.5407515])
```

Figure 16.5: SARIMA model

In the preceding code cell, we have fitted the model by maximum likelihood via Kalman filter, and then we have returned the fitted values using `predict()` method. Here the `SARIMAX` method has one extra argument - `seasonal_order()`, which has 4 parameters. The (p, d, q, s) order of the seasonal component of the model are for AR parameters, differences, MA parameters, and periodicity.

Here d must be an integer indicating the integration order of the process, while p and q may either be an integers indicating the AR and MA orders (so that all lags up to those orders are included) or else iterables giving specific AR and/or MA lags to include. s as an integer giving the periodicity (number of periods in season), often it is 4 for quarterly data or 12 for monthly data. The default is no seasonal effect. Next, you will see the same `SARIMA` model with an X factor.

Seasonal Autoregressive Integrated Moving-Average with Exogenous Regressors (SARIMAX)

The `SARIMAX` model is an extension of the SARIMA model that also includes the modeling of exogenous variables. Here, exogenous variables are also called covariates and can be thought of as parallel input sequences that have observations, and at the same time steps as the original series. The method is suitable for univariate time-series with the trend and/or seasonal components and exogenous variables:

```python
# SARIMAX example
from statsmodels.tsa.statespace.sarimax import SARIMAX
from random import random
# create datasets
data1 = [x + random() for x in range(1, 100)]
data2 = [x + random() for x in range(101, 200)]
# fit model
model = SARIMAX(data1, exog=data2, order=(1, 1, 1), seasonal_order=(0, 0, 0, 0))
model_fit = model.fit(disp=False)
# make prediction
exog2 = [200 + random()]
sarimax_pred = model_fit.predict(len(data1), len(data1), exog=[exog2])
sarimax_pred
```

```
array([100.09306379])
```

Figure 16.6: SARIMAX method

Consider an example of food supply chain research. During the retail stage of the **food supply chain (FSC)**, food waste and stock-outs occur mainly due to inaccurate sales forecasting, which leads to the inappropriate ordering of products. The daily demand for a fresh food product is affected by external factors, such as seasonality, price reductions, and holidays. In order to overcome this complexity and inaccuracy, while doing sales forecasting, try to consider all the possible demand influencing factors. SARIMAX model tries to account all the effects due to the demand influencing factors to forecast the daily sales of perishable foods in a retail store; it is found that the SARIMAX model improves the traditional SARIMA model.

Vector Autoregression Moving-Average (VARMA)

The VARMA method models the next step in each time-series using an ARMA model. It is the generalization of ARMA to multiply parallel time-series, e.g., multivariate time-series. The method is suitable for multivariate time-series without trend and seasonal components:

```python
# VARMA example
from statsmodels.tsa.statespace.varmax import VARMAX
from random import random
# create dataset with dependency
data = list()
for i in range(100):
    v1 = random()
    v2 = v1 + random()
    row = [v1, v2]
    data.append(row)
# fit model
model = VARMAX(data, order=(1, 1))
model_fit = model.fit(disp=False)
# make prediction
varma_pred = model_fit.forecast()
varma_pred
```

```
array([[0.58299814, 1.10249435]])
```

Figure 16.7: VARMA method

From the preceding code example, you can see that the VARMAX class in statsmodels allows estimation of VAR, VMA, and VARMA models (through the order argument), optionally with a constant term (via the trend argument). Exogenous regressors may also be included (as usual in statsmodels, by the exog argument), and in this way, a time trend may be added. Finally, the class allows measurement error (via the measurement_error argument), and allows specifying either a diagonal or unstructured innovation covariance matrix (via the error_cov_type argument).

Holt Winter's Exponential Smoothing (HWES)

The **Holt Winter's Exponential Smoothing (HWES)**, also called the **Triple Exponential Smoothing** method, models the next time step as an exponentially weighted linear function of observations at prior time steps, taking trends and seasonality into account. The method is suitable for univariate time-series with the trend and/or seasonal components:

```
# HWES example
from statsmodels.tsa.holtwinters import ExponentialSmoothing
from random import random
# create dataset
data = [x + random() for x in range(1, 100)]
# fit model
model = ExponentialSmoothing(data)
model_fit = model.fit()
# make prediction
hwes_pred = model_fit.predict(len(data), len(data))
hwes_pred
```

```
array([99.90409631])
```

Figure 16.8: HWES method

Exponential smoothing promises you the possibility of peeking into the future by building models, with which you can solve the following kind of problems - How many iPhone XR will be sold in the first 7 months? What's the demand trend for Tesla after *Elon Musk* smokes weed on a live show? Will this winter be warm?

Forecast future traffic to a web page

Now it's time to apply the learnings from this and the previous chapter to an actual time-series problem. In the following exercise, your goal is to forecast future traffic to Wikipedia pages. You can download the dataset required to form this exercise from our repository. Let's start our analysis by loading the dataset:

```
train = pd.read_csv('E:/pg/bpb/BPB-Publications/Datasets/timeseries/wiki/train_1.csv').fillna(0)
train.head()
```

	Page	2015-07-01	2015-07-02	2015-07-03	2015-07-04	2015-07-05	2015-07-06	2015-07-07	2015-07-08	2015-07-09	...	2016-12-22	2016-12-23	
0	2NE1_zh.wikipedia.org_all-access_spider	18.0	11.0	5.0	13.0	14.0	9.0	9.0	22.0	26.0	...	32.0	63.0	
1	2PM_zh.wikipedia.org_all-access_spider	11.0	14.0	15.0	18.0	11.0	13.0	22.0	11.0	10.0	...	17.0	42.0	
2	3C_zh.wikipedia.org_all-access_spider	1.0	0.0	1.0	1.0	0.0	4.0	0.0	3.0	4.0	...	3.0	1.0	
3	4minute_zh.wikipedia.org_all-access_spider	35.0	13.0	10.0	94.0	4.0	26.0	14.0	9.0	11.0	...	32.0	10.0	
4	52_Hz_I_Love_You_zh.wikipedia.org_all-access_s...	0.0	0.0	0.0	0.0	0.0	0.0	0.0	0.0	0.0	...	48.0	9.0	

5 rows × 551 columns

Figure 16.9: Loading the dataset

The training dataset has 5 rows and 551 columns. Let's first find how language affects web traffic. For this, we will use a simple regular expression to search for the language code in the Wikipedia URL. First, import the re library, and then follow this code:

```
def get_language(page):
    res = re.search('[a-z][a-z].wikipedia.org',page)
    if res:
        return res[0][0:2]
    return 'na'


train['lang'] = train.Page.map(get_language)
from collections import Counter
Counter(train.lang)
```

```
Counter({'de': 18547,
         'en': 24108,
         'es': 14069,
         'fr': 17802,
         'ja': 20431,
         'na': 17855,
         'ru': 15022,
         'zh': 17229})
```

Figure 16.10: Searching language code using regular expression

For each language, Wikipedia has different pages. To make our analysis easy, we will create dataframes to hold each language, as shown in the following screenshot:

```
lang_sets = {}
lang_sets['de'] = train[train.lang=='de'].iloc[:,0:-1]
lang_sets['en'] = train[train.lang=='en'].iloc[:,0:-1]
lang_sets['es'] = train[train.lang=='es'].iloc[:,0:-1]
lang_sets['fr'] = train[train.lang=='fr'].iloc[:,0:-1]
lang_sets['ja'] = train[train.lang=='ja'].iloc[:,0:-1]
lang_sets['na'] = train[train.lang=='na'].iloc[:,0:-1]
lang_sets['ru'] = train[train.lang=='ru'].iloc[:,0:-1]
lang_sets['zh'] = train[train.lang=='zh'].iloc[:,0:-1]

sums = {}
for key in lang_sets:
    sums[key] = lang_sets[key].iloc[:,1:].sum(axis=0) / lang_sets[key].shape[0]
```

Figure 16.11: Creating dataframes to hold each language

Let's plot all the different sets on the same plot to know how the total number of views changes over time:

```
days = [r for r in range(sums['en'].shape[0])]
fig = plt.figure(1,figsize=[10,10])
plt.ylabel('Views per Wiki Page')
plt.xlabel('Day')
plt.title('Wiki Pages in Different Languages')
labels={'en':'English','ja':'Japanese','de':'German',
        'na':'Media','fr':'French','zh':'Chinese',
        'ru':'Russian','es':'Spanish'
        }

for key in sums:
    plt.plot(days,sums[key],label = labels[key] )

plt.legend()
plt.show()
```

Figure 16.12: Plotting different sets on same plot

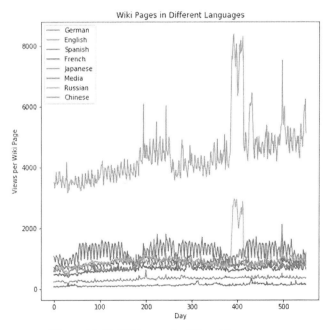

Figure 16.13: Wiki pages in different languages

From the preceding plot, you can deduce the following - English shows a much higher number of views per page. This is expected, since Wikipedia is a US-based site. The English and Russian plots show very large spikes around day 400. There's also a strange pattern in the English data around day 200. The Spanish data (see the green line) is very interesting as well. There is a clear periodic structure there, with a ~1-week fast period and what looks like a significant dip around every 6 months or so.

Since it looks like there is some periodic structure here, we will plot each of these separately, so that the scale is more visible. Along with the individual plots, we will also look at the magnitude of the **Fast Fourier Transform** (**FFT**), because Peaks in the FFT show us the strongest frequencies in the periodic signal. You can import the `fft` from the `scipy.fftpackapi`, calculate the magnitude of `fft` using `numpy`, as shown in the following screenshot:

```
from scipy.fftpack import fft
def plot_with_fft(key):

    fig = plt.figure(1,figsize=[15,5])
    plt.ylabel('Views per Page')
    plt.xlabel('Day')
    plt.title(labels[key])
    plt.plot(days,sums[key],label = labels[key] )

    fig = plt.figure(2,figsize=[15,5])
    fft_complex = fft(sums[key])
    fft_mag = [np.sqrt(np.real(x)*np.real(x)+np.imag(x)*np.imag(x)) for x in fft_complex]
    fft_xvals = [day / days[-1] for day in days]
    npts = len(fft_xvals) // 2 + 1
    fft_mag = fft_mag[:npts]
    fft_xvals = fft_xvals[:npts]

    plt.ylabel('FFT Magnitude')
    plt.xlabel(r"Frequency [days]$^{-1}$")
    plt.title('Fourier Transform')
    plt.plot(fft_xvals[1:],fft_mag[1:],label = labels[key] )
    plt.axvline(x=1./7,color='red',alpha=0.3)
    plt.axvline(x=2./7,color='red',alpha=0.3)
    plt.axvline(x=3./7,color='red',alpha=0.3)

    plt.show()
for key in sums:
    plot_with_fft(key)
```

Figure 16.14: Oce snippet for FFT magnitude

For the ease of understanding, I am only showing the German plot; rest you can see in your notebook:

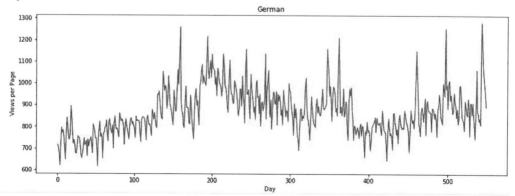

Figure 16.15: German plot

Once you see all the plots in your notebook, you will find the following insights - the Spanish data has the strongest periodic features compared to most of the other languages. For some reason, the Russian and media data do not seem to reveal any pattern. I plotted red lines, where a period of 1, 1/2, and 1/3-weeks' patterns would appear. We see that the periodic features are mainly at 1 and 1/2 weeks. This is not surprising, since browsing habits may differ on weekdays compared to weekends, leading to peaks in the FFTs at frequencies of *n/(1 week)* for integer *n*.

We've learned now that not all page views are smooth. There is some regular variation from day to day, but there are also large effects that can happen quite suddenly. Most likely, a model will not be able to predict the sudden spikes, unless it can be fed more information about what is going on in the world that day.

Now we will look at the most popular pages, which will generally be the main pages for the languages in this dataset. We will loop over the language sets using `for` loop, and then look over the pages using the key `Pages` for each language. After calculating the total, we will sort the results in the descending order. The following function will do this for us:

```python
# For each language get highest few pages
npages = 5
top_pages = {}
for key in lang_sets:
    print(key)
    sum_set = pd.DataFrame(lang_sets[key][['Page']])
    sum_set['total'] = lang_sets[key].sum(axis=1)
    sum_set = sum_set.sort_values('total',ascending=False)
    print(sum_set.head(10))
    top_pages[key] = sum_set.index[0]
    print('\n\n')
```

Figure 16.16: Most popular pages code snippet

The preceding cell will generate popular pages' list for all languages; here is an example of the German language:

```
de
                                                     Page         total
139119   Wikipedia:Hauptseite_de.wikipedia.org_all-acce...  1.603934e+09
116196   Wikipedia:Hauptseite_de.wikipedia.org_mobile-w...  1.112689e+09
67049    Wikipedia:Hauptseite_de.wikipedia.org_desktop_...  4.269924e+08
140151   Spezial:Suche_de.wikipedia.org_all-access_all-...  2.234259e+08
66736    Spezial:Suche_de.wikipedia.org_desktop_all-agents  2.196368e+08
140147   Spezial:Anmelden_de.wikipedia.org_all-access_a...  4.029181e+07
138800   Special:Search_de.wikipedia.org_all-access_all...  3.988154e+07
68104    Spezial:Anmelden_de.wikipedia.org_desktop_all-...  3.535523e+07
68511    Special:MyPage/toolserverhelferleinconfig.js_d...  3.258496e+07
```

Figure 16.17: Popular pages of German language

Let's analyze more! We have seen earlier, the the `statsmodels` package includes quite a few tools for performing time-series analysis. Here, I'll show the autocorrelation and partial autocorrelation for the most-viewed page for each language. Both methods show correlations of the signal with a delayed version of itself. At each lag, the partial autocorrelation tries to show the correlation at that lag after removing correlations at shorter lags:

```python
from scipy.fftpack import fft
def plot_with_fft(key):

    fig = plt.figure(1,figsize=[15,5])
    plt.ylabel('Views per Page')
    plt.xlabel('Day')
    plt.title(labels[key])
    plt.plot(days,sums[key],label = labels[key] )

    fig = plt.figure(2,figsize=[15,5])
    fft_complex = fft(sums[key])
    fft_mag = [np.sqrt(np.real(x)*np.real(x)+np.imag(x)*np.imag(x)) for x in fft_complex]
    fft_xvals = [day / days[-1] for day in days]
    npts = len(fft_xvals) // 2 + 1
    fft_mag = fft_mag[:npts]
    fft_xvals = fft_xvals[:npts]

    plt.ylabel('FFT Magnitude')
    plt.xlabel(r"Frequency [days]$^{-1}$")
    plt.title('Fourier Transform')
    plt.plot(fft_xvals[1:],fft_mag[1:],label = labels[key] )
    plt.axvline(x=1./7,color='red',alpha=0.3)
    plt.axvline(x=2./7,color='red',alpha=0.3)
    plt.axvline(x=3./7,color='red',alpha=0.3)

    plt.show()
for key in sums:
    plot_with_fft(key)
```

Figure 16.18: autocorrelation and partial autocorrelation

In most cases, you will see strong correlations and anticorrelations every 7 days due to weekly effects. For the partial autocorrelation, the first week seems to be the strongest, and then things start settling down:

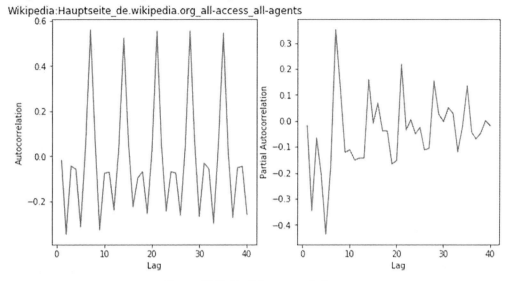

Figure 16.19: Partial autocorrelation

Let's apply one of the classical statistical forecasting methods – the ARIMA model –for a small set of pages and then we will see the insights we get from these plots:

```
cols = train.columns[1:-1]
for key in top_pages:
    data = np.array(train.loc[top_pages[key],cols],'f')
    result = None
    with warnings.catch_warnings():
        warnings.filterwarnings('ignore')
        try:
            arima = ARIMA(data,[2,1,4])
            result = arima.fit(disp=False)
        except:
            try:
                arima = ARIMA(data,[2,1,2])
                result = arima.fit(disp=False)
            except:
                print(train.loc[top_pages[key],'Page'])
                print('\tARIMA failed')
    pred = result.predict(2,599,typ='levels')
    x = [i for i in range(600)]
    i=0

    plt.plot(x[2:len(data)],data[2:] ,label='Data')
    plt.plot(x[2:],pred,label='ARIMA Model')
    plt.title(train.loc[top_pages[key],'Page'])
    plt.xlabel('Days')
    plt.ylabel('Views')
    plt.legend()
    plt.show()
```

Figure 16.20: ARIMA model applied

The preceding code will plot the data as a blue line and the `ARIMA` model will be denoted as the orange line for each language. Some of the plots will look like the following screenshots. You can see the rest of the plots in your notebook:

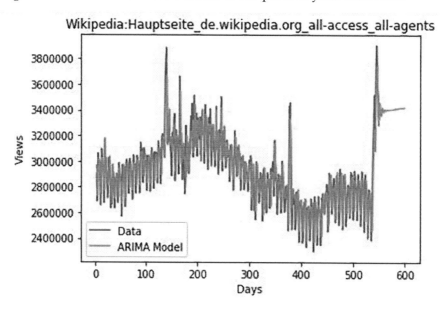

Figure 16.21: ARIMA model denoted in orange line

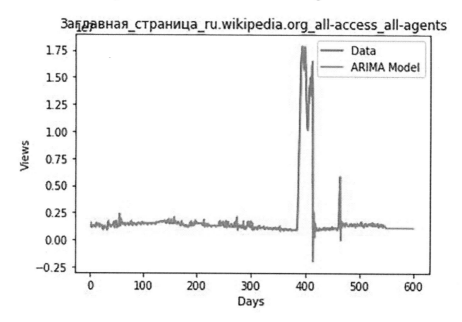

Figure 16.22: ARIMA model vs Data plot example

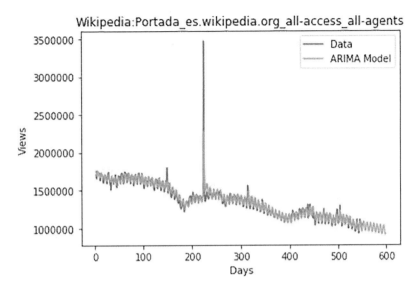

Figure 16.23: *ARIMA model vs Data plot example*

Take a good look at all the plots, and you will understand that the `ARIMA` model, in some cases, is able to predict the weekly substructure of the signal effectively. In other cases, it seems to just give a linear fit. This is potentially very useful in the weekly substructure of the signal.

What will happen when you just blindly apply the ARIMA model to the whole dataset? Try this and you will see that the results are not nearly as good as just using a basic median model.

Conclusion

The time-series method of forecasting is the most reliable, when the data represents a broad time period. Information about conditions can be extracted by measuring data at various time intervals – e.g., hourly, daily, monthly, quarterly, annually, or at any other time interval. Forecasts are the soundest when based on large numbers of observations for longer time periods to measure patterns in conditions. To get more confidence, start working on any new stock or weather dataset, and apply this chapter's learnings in forecasting. In the next chapter, you will go through various case study examples.

CHAPTER 17

Case Study-1

In the previous chapters, you have learned the basics and some advanced concepts, with the help of real-world data science problems. To begin the journey of a data scientist, as I mentioned earlier, the more you practice your learning, the more you will gain confidence. Let us work on some case studies covering the application of supervised and unsupervised machine learning techniques. These case studies will walk you through different business domains and give you a grip as a data scientist.

Predict whether or not an applicant will be able to repay a loan

Your goal: In our first study, you work for an insurance client and help them implement a machine learning model to predict the probability of whether or not an applicant will be able to repay a loan.

Your client: Your client is an international consumer finance provider with operations in 10 countries.

About dataset: The client has given his datasets having static data for all applications. One row represents one loan in their data, which you can download from our repository.

Our baseline ML models: In this example, I will apply logistic regression and random forest algorithms.

Since the objective of this competition is to use historical loan application data to predict whether or not an applicant will be able to repay a loan, this is a standard supervised classification task. Let's import all required basic libraries and read the datasets:

```python
# numpy and pandas for data manipulation
import numpy as np
import pandas as pd

# sklearn preprocessing for dealing with categorical variables
from sklearn.preprocessing import LabelEncoder

# Suppress warnings
import warnings
warnings.filterwarnings('ignore')

# matplotlib and seaborn for plotting
import matplotlib.pyplot as plt
%matplotlib inline
import seaborn as sns
```

```python
# Load and explore training data
train_df = pd.read_csv('E:/pg/bpb/BPB-Publications/Datasets/Case Studies/case_study_1/application_train.csv')
print('Training data shape: ', train_df.shape)
train_df.head()
```

Figure 17.1: Importing basic libraries and the dataset

Training data shape: (307511, 122)

	SK_ID_CURR	TARGET	NAME_CONTRACT_TYPE	CODE_GENDER	FLAG_OWN_CAR	FLAG_OWN_REALTY
0	100002	1	Cash loans	M	N	Y
1	100003	0	Cash loans	F	N	N
2	100004	0	Revolving loans	M	Y	Y
3	100006	0	Cash loans	F	N	Y
4	100007	0	Cash loans	M	N	Y

5 rows × 122 columns

Figure 17.2: Peek of the imported dataset

The training data has 307511 observations (each one a separate loan) and 122 features (variables) including the TARGET (the label we want to predict). Details related to every loan is present in a row and is identified by the feature SK_ID_CURR. The training application data comes with the TARGET indicating "0: the loan was repaid", or "1: the loan was not repaid". Similarly, we will check the testing dataset that is also provided in a separate file named `application_test.csv`:

```
# Load and explore testing data
test_df = pd.read_csv('E:/pg/bpb/BPB-Publications/Datasets/Case Studies/case_study_1/application_test.csv')
print('Testing data shape: ', test_df.shape)
test_df.head()
```

Testing data shape: (48744, 121)

	SK_ID_CURR	NAME_CONTRACT_TYPE	CODE_GENDER	FLAG_OWN_CAR	FLAG_OWN_REALTY	CNT_CHILDREN	AMT_INCOME_TOTAL
0	100001	Cash loans	F	N	Y	0	135000.0
1	100005	Cash loans	M	N	Y	0	99000.0
2	100013	Cash loans	M	Y	Y	0	202500.0
3	100028	Cash loans	F	N	Y	2	315000.0
4	100038	Cash loans	M	Y	N	1	180000.0

5 rows × 121 columns

Figure 17.3: Loading Testing dataset

In the next step, we will do **Exploratory Data Analysis (EDA)**; this is an open-ended process, where we calculate statistics and make figures to find trends, anomalies, patterns, or relationships within the data. The target is what we are asked to predict: either a 0 for the loan was repaid on time, or a 1 indicating the client had payment difficulties. We will first examine the number of loans falling into each category. Referring to the following plot, you can say that this is an imbalanced class problem. It indicates more loans were repaid on time compared to the loans that were defaulted:

```
train_df['TARGET'].value_counts()
```

```
0    282686
1     24825
Name: TARGET, dtype: int64
```

```
""" 
0 means the loan was repaid on time
1 indicating the client had payment difficulties
"""
```

```
train_df['TARGET'].astype(int).plot.hist()
```

```
<matplotlib.axes._subplots.AxesSubplot at 0x14ee2ebfc50>
```

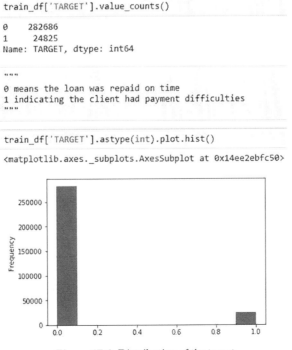

Figure 17.4: Distribution of the target

Let's examine the missing values. Here, we will look at the number and percentage of missing values in each column by writing a function. Remember, it is a coding standard to write some common functionalities in a function:

```
# check number and percentage of missing values in each column
def missing_values_table(df):
        mis_val = df.isnull().sum() # Total missing values
        mis_val_percent = 100 * df.isnull().sum() / len(df) # Percentage of missing values
        mis_val_table = pd.concat([mis_val, mis_val_percent], axis=1) # Make a table with the results
        mis_val_table_ren_columns = mis_val_table.rename(
        columns = {0 : 'Missing Values', 1 : '% of Total Values'}) # Rename the columns

        # Sort the table by percentage of missing descending
        mis_val_table_ren_columns = mis_val_table_ren_columns[
            mis_val_table_ren_columns.iloc[:,1] != 0].sort_values(
        '% of Total Values', ascending=False).round(1)

        # Print some summary information
        print ("Your selected dataframe has " + str(df.shape[1]) + " columns.\n"
            "There are " + str(mis_val_table_ren_columns.shape[0]) +
            " columns that have missing values.")

        # Return the dataframe with missing information
        return mis_val_table_ren_columns
```

Figure 17.5: Examining missing values

Now, we will apply the preceding function in training dataframe, and fill these missing values later:

```
# Missing values statistics
missing_values = missing_values_table(train_df)
missing_values.head()
```

Your selected dataframe has 122 columns.
There are 67 columns that have missing values.

	Missing Values	% of Total Values
COMMONAREA_MEDI	214865	69.9
COMMONAREA_AVG	214865	69.9
COMMONAREA_MODE	214865	69.9
NONLIVINGAPARTMENTS_MEDI	213514	69.4
NONLIVINGAPARTMENTS_MODE	213514	69.4

Figure 17.6: Missing values statistics

Let's now look at the number of unique entries in each of the object (categorical) columns:

```
# data types of each type of column
train_df.dtypes.value_counts()

float64    65
int64      41
object     16
dtype: int64
```

```
# Number of unique classes in each object column
train_df.select_dtypes('object').apply(pd.Series.nunique, axis = 0)

NAME_CONTRACT_TYPE            2
CODE_GENDER                   3
FLAG_OWN_CAR                  2
FLAG_OWN_REALTY               2
NAME_TYPE_SUITE               7
NAME_INCOME_TYPE              8
NAME_EDUCATION_TYPE           5
NAME_FAMILY_STATUS            6
NAME_HOUSING_TYPE             6
OCCUPATION_TYPE              18
WEEKDAY_APPR_PROCESS_START    7
ORGANIZATION_TYPE            58
FONDKAPREMONT_MODE            4
HOUSETYPE_MODE                3
WALLSMATERIAL_MODE            7
EMERGENCYSTATE_MODE           2
```

Figure 17.7: Checking unique entries

Let's encode these Categorical Variables or the preceding object datatype columns. We will follow the following thumb rule - if we only have two unique values for a categorical variable (such as Male/Female), then label encoding method is fine, but for more than 2 unique categories, one-hot encoding method is the safe option to handle categorical features:

```
le = LabelEncoder()
le_count = 0

for col in train_df:
    if train_df[col].dtype == 'object':
        # If 2 or fewer unique categories
        if len(list(train_df[col].unique())) <= 2:
            # Train on the training data
            le.fit(train_df[col])
            # Transform both training and testing data
            train_df[col] = le.transform(train_df[col])
            test_df[col] = le.transform(test_df[col])
            # Keep track of how many columns were label encoded
            le_count += 1

print('%d columns were label encoded.' % le_count)

3 columns were label encoded.
```

Figure 17.8: Handling categorical columns

```
# one-hot encoding of categorical variables
train_df = pd.get_dummies(train_df)
test_df = pd.get_dummies(test_df)
print('Training Features shape: ', train_df.shape)
print('Testing Features shape: ', test_df.shape)
```

```
Training Features shape:  (307511, 243)
Testing Features shape:  (48744, 239)
```

Figure 17.9: Shape of the data

One-hot encoding has created more columns in the training data because there were some categorical variables with categories not represented in the testing data. To remove the columns in the training data that are not in the testing data, we need to align the dataframes.

First, we extract the target column from the training data (because this is not in the testing data, but we need to keep this information). When we align, we must make sure to set axis = 1 to align the dataframes based on the columns and not on the rows:

```
# seperate target variable
train_labels = train_df['TARGET']
# combine the training and testing data, keep only columns present in both dataframes
train_df, test_df = train_df.align(test_df, join = 'inner', axis = 1)
# add the target back in
train_df['TARGET'] = train_labels

print('Training Features shape: ', train_df.shape)
print('Testing Features shape: ', test_df.shape)
```

```
Training Features shape:  (307511, 240)
Testing Features shape:  (48744, 239)
```

Figure 17.10: Preparing train and test data

Now the training and testing datasets have the same features which are required for machine learning. One problem we always want to lookout for before doing EDA is to find anomalies within the data. These may be due to mistyped numbers, errors in measuring equipment or that they could be valid but have extreme measurements. One way to support anomalies quantitatively is by looking at the statistics of a column using the describe method. Try using the .describe() on DAYS_EMPLOYED column and see what you find:

```
anomalous_clients = train_df[train_df['DAYS_EMPLOYED'] == 365243]
non_anomalous_clients = train_df[train_df['DAYS_EMPLOYED'] != 365243]
print('The non-anomalies default on %0.2f%% of loans' % (100 * non_anomalous_clients['TARGET'].mean()))
print('The anomalies default on %0.2f%% of loans' % (100 * anomalous_clients['TARGET'].mean()))
print('There are %d anomalous days of employment' % len(anomalous_clients))
```

```
The non-anomalies default on 8.66% of loans
The anomalies default on 5.40% of loans
There are 55374 anomalous days of employment
```

Figure 17.11: Using .describe() method

It turns out that the anomalies have a lower rate of default. Handling the anomalies depends on the exact situation, with no set rules. One of the safest approaches is just to set the anomalies to a missing value and then have them filled in (using Imputation) before machine learning.

In our case we will fill in the anomalous values with not a number (np.nan), and then create a new Boolean column indicating whether or not the value was anomalous:

```
# Create an anomalous flag column
train_df['DAYS_EMPLOYED_ANOM'] = train_df["DAYS_EMPLOYED"] == 365243

# Replace the anomalous values with nan
train_df['DAYS_EMPLOYED'].replace({365243: np.nan}, inplace = True)

train_df['DAYS_EMPLOYED'].plot.hist(title = 'Days Employment Histogram')
plt.xlabel('Days Employment')
plt.show()
```

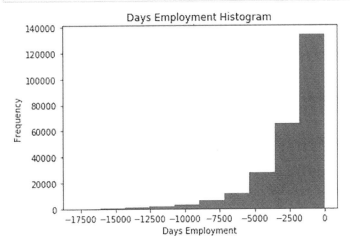

Figure 17.12: Days Employment Histogram

As an extremely important note, anything we do to the training data, we also have to do to the testing data. Repeat the preceding step in the testing dataset on your own. Now that we have dealt with the categorical variables and the outliers, we'll look for correlations between the features and the target. We can calculate the Pearson correlation coefficient between every variable and the target using the .corr dataframe method:

```
# Find correlations with the target and sort
correlations = train_df.corr()['TARGET'].sort_values()
# Display correlations
print('Most Positive Correlations:\n', correlations.tail())
print('\nMost Negative Correlations:\n', correlations.head())
```

```
Most Positive Correlations:
 REGION_RATING_CLIENT            0.058899
REGION_RATING_CLIENT_W_CITY      0.060893
DAYS_EMPLOYED                    0.074958
DAYS_BIRTH                       0.078239
TARGET                           1.000000
Name: TARGET, dtype: float64

Most Negative Correlations:
 EXT_SOURCE_3                           -0.178919
EXT_SOURCE_2                           -0.160472
EXT_SOURCE_1                           -0.155317
NAME_EDUCATION_TYPE_Higher education   -0.056593
CODE_GENDER_F                          -0.054704
Name: TARGET, dtype: float64
```

Figure 17.13: Using .corr dataframe method

Let's take a look at some of the more significant correlations: the DAYS_BIRTH is the most positive correlation (except for TARGET because the correlation of a variable with itself is always 1!). DAYS_BIRTH is the age in days of the client at the time of the loan in negative days (for whatever reason!). The correlation is positive, but the value of this feature is negative, meaning that as the client gets older, they are less likely to default on their loan (i.e., the target == 0). That's a little confusing, so we will take the absolute value of the feature and then the correlation will be negative:

```
# Find the correlation of the positive days since birth and target
train_df['DAYS_BIRTH'] = abs(train_df['DAYS_BIRTH'])
train_df['DAYS_BIRTH'].corr(train_df['TARGET'])
```

```
-0.07823930830982712
```

Figure 17.14: Finding correlation of positive days since birth and target

As the client gets older, there is a negative linear relationship with the target meaning that as clients get older, they tend to repay their loans on-time more often. Let's start looking at this variable. First, we can make a histogram of the age. We will put the X-axis in years to make the plot a little more understandable:

```
plt.hist(train_df['DAYS_BIRTH'] / 365, edgecolor = 'k', bins = 25)
plt.title('Age of Client'); plt.xlabel('Age (years)'); plt.ylabel('Count')
plt.show()
```

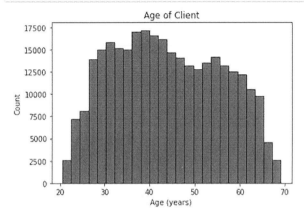

Figure 17.15: Age of client

By itself, the distribution of age does not tell us much more than that! There are no outliers (no age more than 70 years) as all the ages are reasonable. Next, we will try two simple feature construction methods for feature engineering: polynomial features and domain knowledge features. Polynomial models are a great tool for determining which input factors drive responses and in what direction. In the polynomial method, we make features that are powers of existing features as well as interaction terms between existing features, and in domain knowledge, we use our logic specific to a domain:

```
# Make a new dataframe for polynomial features
poly_features = train_df[['EXT_SOURCE_1', 'EXT_SOURCE_2', 'EXT_SOURCE_3', 'DAYS_BIRTH', 'TARGET']]
poly_features_test = test_df[['EXT_SOURCE_1', 'EXT_SOURCE_2', 'EXT_SOURCE_3', 'DAYS_BIRTH']]

# imputer for handling missing values
from sklearn.preprocessing import Imputer
imputer = Imputer(strategy = 'median')

poly_target = poly_features['TARGET']

poly_features = poly_features.drop(columns = ['TARGET'])

# Need to impute missing values
poly_features = imputer.fit_transform(poly_features)
poly_features_test = imputer.transform(poly_features_test)

from sklearn.preprocessing import PolynomialFeatures
poly_transformer = PolynomialFeatures(degree = 3)
```

Figure 17.16: New dataframe for polynomial features

```
# Train the polynomial features
poly_transformer.fit(poly_features)
# Transform the features
poly_features = poly_transformer.transform(poly_features)
poly_features_test = poly_transformer.transform(poly_features_test)
print('Polynomial Features shape: ', poly_features.shape)
```

```
Polynomial Features shape:  (307511, 35)
```

Figure 17.17: Training and transforming polynomial features

The preceding code will create a considerable number of new features. To get the names, you have to use the polynomial features `get_feature_names()` method. In this method, pass the input features' names and it will show the output as follows:

```
# get the names
poly_transformer.get_feature_names(input_features = ['EXT_SOURCE_1', 'EXT_SOURCE_2', 'EXT_SOURCE_3', 'DAYS_BIRTH'])[:15]
```

```
['1',
 'EXT_SOURCE_1',
 'EXT_SOURCE_2',
 'EXT_SOURCE_3',
 'DAYS_BIRTH',
 'EXT_SOURCE_1^2',
 'EXT_SOURCE_1 EXT_SOURCE_2',
 'EXT_SOURCE_1 EXT_SOURCE_3',
 'EXT_SOURCE_1 DAYS_BIRTH',
 'EXT_SOURCE_2^2',
 'EXT_SOURCE_2 EXT_SOURCE_3',
 'EXT_SOURCE_2 DAYS_BIRTH',
 'EXT_SOURCE_3^2',
 'EXT_SOURCE_3 DAYS_BIRTH',
 'DAYS_BIRTH^2']
```

Figure 17.18: Getting names of new features

There are 35 features with individual features raised to powers up to degree 3 and interaction terms. Now, we can see whether any of these new features are correlated with the target:

```
# Create a dataframe of the features
poly_features = pd.DataFrame(poly_features,
                        columns = poly_transformer.get_feature_names(['EXT_SOURCE_1', 'EXT_SOURCE_2',
                                                         'EXT_SOURCE_3', 'DAYS_BIRTH']))

# Add in the target
poly_features['TARGET'] = poly_target

# Find the correlations with the target
poly_corrs = poly_features.corr()['TARGET'].sort_values()

# Display most negative and most positive
print(poly_corrs.head())
print(poly_corrs.tail())
```
```
EXT_SOURCE_2 EXT_SOURCE_3                   -0.193939
EXT_SOURCE_1 EXT_SOURCE_2 EXT_SOURCE_3      -0.189605
EXT_SOURCE_2 EXT_SOURCE_3 DAYS_BIRTH        -0.181283
EXT_SOURCE_2^2 EXT_SOURCE_3                 -0.176428
EXT_SOURCE_2 EXT_SOURCE_3^2                 -0.172282
Name: TARGET, dtype: float64
DAYS_BIRTH       -0.078239
DAYS_BIRTH^2     -0.076672
DAYS_BIRTH^3     -0.074273
TARGET            1.000000
1                      NaN
Name: TARGET, dtype: float64
```

Figure 17.19: Checking correlation between target and input features

Most of the new variables have a greater (in terms of absolute magnitude) correlation with the target than the original features. When we build machine learning models, we can try with and without these features to determine if they help the model learn. We will add these features to a copy of the training and testing data and then evaluate models with and without the features because many times in machine learning, the only way to know if an approach will work is to try it out:

```
# Put test features into dataframe
poly_features_test = pd.DataFrame(poly_features_test,
                        columns = poly_transformer.get_feature_names(['EXT_SOURCE_1', 'EXT_SOURCE_2',
                                                         'EXT_SOURCE_3', 'DAYS_BIRTH']))

# Merge polynomial features into training dataframe
poly_features['SK_ID_CURR'] = train_df['SK_ID_CURR']
app_train_poly = train_df.merge(poly_features, on = 'SK_ID_CURR', how = 'left')

# Merge polnomial features into testing dataframe
poly_features_test['SK_ID_CURR'] = test_df['SK_ID_CURR']
app_test_poly = test_df.merge(poly_features_test, on = 'SK_ID_CURR', how = 'left')

# Align the dataframes
app_train_poly, app_test_poly = app_train_poly.align(app_test_poly, join = 'inner', axis = 1)

# Print out the new shapes
print('Training data with polynomial features shape: ', app_train_poly.shape)
print('Testing data with polynomial features shape:  ', app_test_poly.shape)
```
```
Training data with polynomial features shape:  (307511, 275)
Testing data with polynomial features shape:  (48744, 275)
```

Figure 17.20: Preparing data with new features

Let's do feature engineering by domain knowledge. We can make a couple of features that attempt to capture what we think may be important for telling whether a client will default on a loan. For this, you need to read about the client; for example, here you can read about the client from their website or Google, and their business on your own, and then create new features:

```
# Domain Knowledge Features
app_train_domain = train_df.copy()
app_test_domain = test_df.copy()

app_train_domain['CREDIT_INCOME_PERCENT'] = app_train_domain['AMT_CREDIT'] / app_train_domain['AMT_INCOME_TOTAL']
app_train_domain['ANNUITY_INCOME_PERCENT'] = app_train_domain['AMT_ANNUITY'] / app_train_domain['AMT_INCOME_TOTAL']
app_train_domain['CREDIT_TERM'] = app_train_domain['AMT_ANNUITY'] / app_train_domain['AMT_CREDIT']
app_train_domain['DAYS_EMPLOYED_PERCENT'] = app_train_domain['DAYS_EMPLOYED'] / app_train_domain['DAYS_BIRTH']

#repeat for test
app_test_domain['CREDIT_INCOME_PERCENT'] = app_test_domain['AMT_CREDIT'] / app_test_domain['AMT_INCOME_TOTAL']
app_test_domain['ANNUITY_INCOME_PERCENT'] = app_test_domain['AMT_ANNUITY'] / app_test_domain['AMT_INCOME_TOTAL']
app_test_domain['CREDIT_TERM'] = app_test_domain['AMT_ANNUITY'] / app_test_domain['AMT_CREDIT']
app_test_domain['DAYS_EMPLOYED_PERCENT'] = app_test_domain['DAYS_EMPLOYED'] / app_test_domain['DAYS_BIRTH']
```

Figure 17.21: Domain knowledge features

Now we will make a baseline model. In this example, I will use Logistic Regression and Random Forest model, but you must apply some new models as well. To get a baseline, we will use all features after encoding the categorical variables. We will pre-process the data by filling in the missing values (imputation) and normalizing the range of the features (feature scaling). The following code performs these pre-processing steps:

```
# get a baseline
from sklearn.preprocessing import MinMaxScaler, Imputer
# Drop the target from the training data
if 'TARGET' in train_df:
    train = train_df.drop(columns = ['TARGET'])
else:
    train = train_df.copy()
# Feature names
features = list(train.columns)
# Copy of the testing data
test = test_df.copy()
# Median imputation of missing values
imputer = Imputer(strategy = 'median')
# Scale each feature to 0-1
scaler = MinMaxScaler(feature_range = (0, 1))
# Fit on the training data
imputer.fit(train)
# Transform both training and testing data
train = imputer.transform(train)
test = imputer.transform(test_df)
# Repeat with the scaler
scaler.fit(train)
train = scaler.transform(train)
test = scaler.transform(test)
print('Training data shape: ', train.shape)
print('Testing data shape: ', test.shape)

Training data shape:  (307511, 240)
Testing data shape:  (48744, 240)
```

Figure 17.22: Code for pre-processing

Now we create the model and train the model using .fit() method, as shown in the following screenshot:

```
from sklearn.linear_model import LogisticRegression
# Make the model with the specified regularization parameter
log_reg = LogisticRegression(C = 0.0001)
# Train on the training data
log_reg.fit(train, train_labels)
```

```
LogisticRegression(C=0.0001, class_weight=None, dual=False,
          fit_intercept=True, intercept_scaling=1, max_iter=100,
          multi_class='ovr', n_jobs=1, penalty='l2', random_state=None,
          solver='liblinear', tol=0.0001, verbose=0, warm_start=False)
```

Figure 17.23: Using .fit() method

Now that the model has been trained, we can use it to make predictions, as shown in the following screenshot. We want to predict the probability of not paying a loan, so we use the model predict.proba() method. This will return m x 2 array, where m is the number of observations. The first column is the probability of the target being 0 and the second column is the probability of the target being 1 (so, for a single row, the two columns must sum to 1). We want the probability, the loan is not repaid, so we will select the second column:

```
# Make predictions
# Make sure to select the second column only
log_reg_pred = log_reg.predict_proba(test)[:, 1]
```

Figure 17.24: Making predictions

Now we will prepare our submission format in a CSV format, so that you can share it with the client. There will be only two columns: SK_ID_CURR and TARGET in CSV.

We will create a dataframe, named submit, which will have one column named as SK_ID_CURR from the test set and one column named as TARGET filled with the predictions as shown in the following screenshot:

```
# Submission dataframe
submit = test_df[['SK_ID_CURR']]
submit['TARGET'] = log_reg_pred
submit.head()
```

	SK_ID_CURR	TARGET
0	100001	0.087750
1	100005	0.163957
2	100013	0.110238
3	100028	0.076575
4	100038	0.154924

Figure 17.25: Submitting dataframe

Later we save this in a CSV file with the `.to_csv()` method of dataframes as shown in the following screenshot:

```
# Save the submission to a csv file
submit.to_csv('E:/pg/bpb/BPB-Publications/Datasets/Case Studies/case_study_1/log_reg_baseline.csv', index = False)
```

Figure 17.26: Saving in a CSV file

Now try a second model – Random Forest – on the same training data to see how that affects performance:

```
from sklearn.ensemble import RandomForestClassifier
# Make the random forest classifier
random_forest = RandomForestClassifier(n_estimators = 100, random_state = 50, verbose = 1, n_jobs = -1)
```

Figure 17.27: Random Forest Classifier model

Here, like any other model, we have initialized the Random Forest Classifier model with some parameters, like no. of estimators, random state, verbose, and no. of jobs. You can modify these parameters and try with different values:

```
# Train on the training data
random_forest.fit(train, train_labels)
# Extract feature importances
feature_importance_values = random_forest.feature_importances_
feature_importances = pd.DataFrame({'feature': features, 'importance': feature_importance_values})
# Make predictions on the test data
predictions = random_forest.predict_proba(test)[:, 1]

[Parallel(n_jobs=-1)]: Done  42 tasks       | elapsed:   32.6s
[Parallel(n_jobs=-1)]: Done 100 out of 100  | elapsed:   1.2min finished
[Parallel(n_jobs=4)]: Done  42 tasks        | elapsed:   0.3s
[Parallel(n_jobs=4)]: Done 100 out of 100   | elapsed:   0.7s finished

# Make a submission dataframe
submit = test_df[['SK_ID_CURR']]
submit['TARGET'] = predictions
# Save the submission dataframe
submit.to_csv('E:/pg/bpb/BPB-Publications/Datasets/Case Studies/case_study_1/random_forest_baseline.csv', index = False)
```

Figure 17.28: Modifying the parameters

Now we will make predictions using engineered features as shown previously. The only way to see if the previously created polynomial features and domain knowledge improved the model is to train and test a model on these features. We can then compare the submission performance to the one without these features to gauge the effectiveness of our feature engineering, as shown in the following screenshots:

```
poly_features_names = list(app_train_poly.columns)
# Impute the polynomial features
imputer = Imputer(strategy = 'median')

poly_features = imputer.fit_transform(app_train_poly)
poly_features_test = imputer.transform(app_test_poly)

# Scale the polynomial features
scaler = MinMaxScaler(feature_range = (0, 1))

poly_features = scaler.fit_transform(poly_features)
poly_features_test = scaler.transform(poly_features_test)

random_forest_poly = RandomForestClassifier(n_estimators = 100, random_state = 50, verbose = 1, n_jobs = -1)
```

Figure 17.29: Imputing and training with RFC

```
# Train on the training data
random_forest_poly.fit(poly_features, train_labels)

# Make predictions on the test data
predictions = random_forest_poly.predict_proba(poly_features_test)[:, 1]

[Parallel(n_jobs=-1)]: Done  42 tasks       | elapsed:   47.0s
[Parallel(n_jobs=-1)]: Done 100 out of 100  | elapsed:   1.8min finished
[Parallel(n_jobs=4)]: Done  42 tasks        | elapsed:   0.1s
[Parallel(n_jobs=4)]: Done 100 out of 100   | elapsed:   0.4s finished

# Make a submission dataframe
submit = test_df[['SK_ID_CURR']]
submit['TARGET'] = predictions

# Save the submission dataframe
submit.to_csv('E:/pg/bpb/BPB-Publications/Datasets/Case Studies/case_study_1/random_forest_baseline_engineered.csv',
```

Figure 17.30: Making prediction and submission

In the same way, we should also check domain features like we did using the logistic model earlier:

```
app_train_domain = app_train_domain.drop(columns = 'TARGET')
domain_features_names = list(app_train_domain.columns)
# Impute the domainnomial features
imputer = Imputer(strategy = 'median')
domain_features = imputer.fit_transform(app_train_domain)
domain_features_test = imputer.transform(app_test_domain)
# Scale the domainnomial features
scaler = MinMaxScaler(feature_range = (0, 1))
domain_features = scaler.fit_transform(domain_features)
domain_features_test = scaler.transform(domain_features_test)
random_forest_domain = RandomForestClassifier(n_estimators = 100, random_state = 50, verbose = 1, n_jobs = -1)
# Train on the training data
random_forest_domain.fit(domain_features, train_labels)
# Extract feature importances
feature_importance_values_domain = random_forest_domain.feature_importances_
feature_importances_domain = pd.DataFrame({'feature': domain_features_names, 'importance': feature_importance_values_domain})
# Make predictions on the test data
predictions = random_forest_domain.predict_proba(domain_features_test)[:, 1]
```

```
[Parallel(n_jobs=-1)]: Done   42 tasks      | elapsed:   31.8s
[Parallel(n_jobs=-1)]: Done  100 out of 100 | elapsed:  1.2min finished
[Parallel(n_jobs=4)]: Done   42 tasks      | elapsed:    0.3s
[Parallel(n_jobs=4)]: Done  100 out of 100 | elapsed:    0.7s finished
```

Figure 17.31: Checking domain features

```
# Make a submission dataframe
submit = test_df[['SK_ID_CURR']]
submit['TARGET'] = predictions
# Save the submission dataframe
submit.to_csv('E:/pg/bpb/BPB-Publications/Datasets/Case Studies/case_study_1/random_forest_baseline_domain.csv', index = False)
```

Figure 17.32: Saving submission dataframe

You can measure each model prediction by the ROC AUC metric. Calculate this for each of the preceding models and see if there is any improvement in accuracy.

Now to see which variables are the most relevant, we can look at the feature importance of the Random Forest. We may use these feature-importance as a method of dimensionality reduction in future work. So, it is important to do this step as well:

```
def plot_feature_importances(df):
    # Sort features according to importance
    df = df.sort_values('importance', ascending = False).reset_index()

    # Normalize the feature importances to add up to one
    df['importance_normalized'] = df['importance'] / df['importance'].sum()

    # Make a horizontal bar chart of feature importances
    plt.figure(figsize = (8, 4))
    ax = plt.subplot()

    # Need to reverse the index to plot most important on top
    ax.barh(list(reversed(list(df.index[:15]))),
            df['importance_normalized'].head(15),
            align = 'center', edgecolor = 'k')

    # Set the yticks and labels
    ax.set_yticks(list(reversed(list(df.index[:15]))))
    ax.set_yticklabels(df['feature'].head(15))

    # Plot Labeling
    plt.xlabel('Normalized Importance'); plt.title('Feature Importances')
    plt.show()
    return df
```

Figure 17.33: Plotting feature-importance

```
# Show the feature importances for the default features
feature_importances_sorted = plot_feature_importances(feature_importances)
```

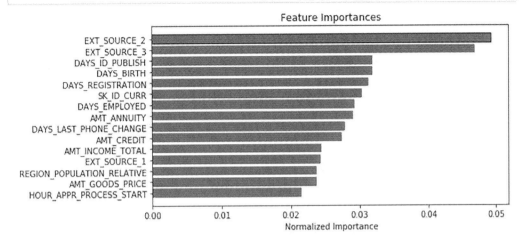

Figure 17.34: *Feature importances*

As expected, the most important features are those dealing with EXT_SOURCE and DAYS_BIRTH. We can see that there are only a handful of features with significant importance to the model, which suggests we may be able to drop many of the features without a decrease in performance (and we may even see an increase in performance.)

Conclusion

In this exercise you have made a baseline model solve an actual supervised machine learning problem. We have tried with LR and Random Forest classifiers, but other models are waiting for you to extend this base model, and see how to improve the accuracy of the model. Try to apply different models and don't forget to check the performance of your model using the ROC AUC metric! In next chapter we are going to work on another case study of spam or ham message detection.

Chapter 18

Case Study-2

Build a prediction model that will accurately classify which text messages are spam

Your goal: Build a prediction model that will accurately classify which text messages are spam.

About dataset: The SMS Spam Collection is a set of SMS-tagged messages that have been collected for SMS Spam research. It contains one set of 5,574 SMS messages in English, tagged according to being ham (legitimate) or spam. The files contain one message per line. Each line is composed of two columns: v1 contains the label (ham or spam) and v2 contains the raw text in spam.csv file.

Our ML models: Multinomial Naive Bayes and Support Vector Machines.

Let's import the required basic libraries and load the dataset in a pandas dataframe:

```
import numpy as np
import pandas as pd
import matplotlib.pyplot as plt
from collections import Counter
from sklearn import feature_extraction, model_selection, naive_bayes, metrics, svm
from IPython.display import Image
import warnings
warnings.filterwarnings("ignore")
%matplotlib inline
```

Figure 18.1: Importing required libraries

In this case study, we will use Naïve Bayes and support vector machine algorithms. In the preceding block of code, we have imported these two libraries along with some basic ones:

```
text_df = pd.read_csv('E:/pg/bpb/BPB-Publications/Datasets/Case Studies/case_study_2/spam.csv', encoding='latin-1')
text_df.head()
```

	v1	v2	Unnamed: 2	Unnamed: 3	Unnamed: 4
0	ham	Go until jurong point, crazy.. Available only ...	NaN	NaN	NaN
1	ham	Ok lar... Joking wif u oni...	NaN	NaN	NaN
2	spam	Free entry in 2 a wkly comp to win FA Cup fina...	NaN	NaN	NaN
3	ham	U dun say so early hor... U c already then say...	NaN	NaN	NaN
4	ham	Nah I don't think he goes to usf, he lives aro...	NaN	NaN	NaN

Figure 18.2: Loading the spam dataset

Although this dataset is in a clean state, before proceeding further, it is always a good practice to check the data type of the columns or missing values, which you can check using .info() and .isnull() methods. Let's check the distribution of spam vs. non-spam messages by plotting them. Since we have two categories, it is always good to plot a bar or pie chart to see the distribution. So, first we will draw the bar chart, and then we will plot a pie chart:

```
# Distribution of spam/non-spam
count_class = pd.value_counts(text_df["v1"], sort= True)
count_class.plot(kind= 'bar', color= ["green", "red"])
plt.title('Distribution of spam vs non-spam')
plt.show()
```

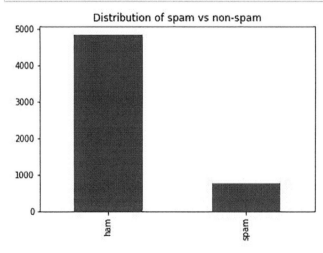

Figure 18.3: Plotting of bar graph

In the preceding screenshot, we have the same result, which in another way can be plotted as a pie chart, as shown in the following screenshot, demonstrating the result in percentage:

```
count_class.plot(kind= 'pie', autopct='%1.0f%%')
plt.title('% distribution')
plt.ylabel('')
plt.show()
```

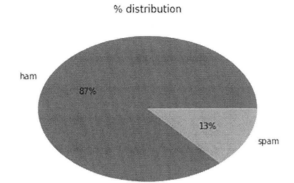

Figure 18.4: Plotting of pie chart

In the preceding chart, you can easily see that 13% of the messages are defined as spam while the rest are not spam. Next, we will see the frequencies of each word in spam and non-spam texts. For this calculation, I will use collections.Counter(), because it stores elements as dictionary keys, and their counts are stored as dictionary values:

```
# find frequencies of words in the spam and non-spam messages
ham_count = Counter(" ".join(text_df[text_df['v1']=='ham']["v2"]).split()).most_common(20)
ham_df = pd.DataFrame.from_dict(ham_count)
ham_df = ham_df.rename(columns={0: "words in non-spam", 1 : "count"})

spam_count = Counter(" ".join(text_df[text_df['v1']=='spam']["v2"]).split()).most_common(20)
spam_df = pd.DataFrame.from_dict(spam_count)
spam_df = spam_df.rename(columns={0: "words in spam", 1 : "count"})
```

Figure 18.5: Using collections.Counter()

In the preceding code cell, we are counting the frequencies of spam and ham messages using the Counter() function, and then storing each count in separate dataframes - ham_df and spam_df. Later, we are plotting the frequencies. First, we plot the most frequently appearing words in non-spam messages, as shown in the following screenshot:

```
# plot frequency of words in ham
ham_df.plot.bar(legend = False, color = 'green')
y_pos = np.arange(len(ham_df["words in non-spam"]))
plt.xticks(y_pos, ham_df["words in non-spam"])
plt.title('More frequent words in non-spam messages')
plt.xlabel('words')
plt.ylabel('number')
plt.show()
```

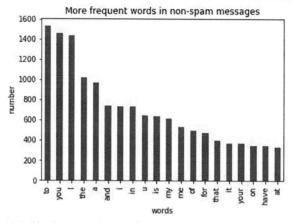

Figure 18.6: Plotting most frequently appearing words in non-spam messages

Later, we plot the most frequently appearing words in spam messages:

```
# plot frequency of words in spam
spam_df.plot.bar(legend = False, color = 'red')
y_pos = np.arange(len(spam_df["words in spam"]))
plt.xticks(y_pos, spam_df["words in spam"])
plt.title('More frequent words in spam messages')
plt.xlabel('words')
plt.ylabel('number')
plt.show()
```

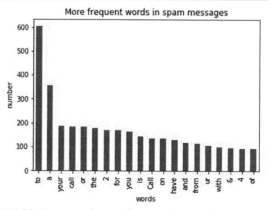

Figure 18.7: Plotting most frequently appearing words in spam messages

From the preceding plots, you can see that the majority of frequent words in both classes are stop words, such as to, a, or, and so on. Stop words are the most common words in a language that has very rare or no meaning in machine learning. It will be good to remove such words. Besides this, creating new features is also a good choice to improve model accuracy.

We'll learn how to do this in two simple steps. The `sklearn.feature_extraction` module can be used to extract features in a format supported by machine learning algorithms from datasets consisting of formats such as text. We will use `sklearn` library's `CountVectorizer` API to convert a collection of text documents to a matrix of token counts and remove stop words, as shown in the following screenshot:

```
# remove the stop words and create new features
f = feature_extraction.text.CountVectorizer(stop_words = 'english')
X = f.fit_transform(text_df["v2"])
np.shape(X)
```

```
(5572, 8404)
```

Figure 18.8: Removing stop words and creating new features

With this, we have created more than 8400 new features. Now we will start the predictive analysis. We will first map spam messages as **1** and no-spam messages as **0**. Later, we will split our data set into training set and test set:

```
text_df["v1"] = text_df["v1"].map({'spam':1,'ham':0})
X_train, X_test, y_train, y_test = model_selection.train_test_split(X, text_df['v1'], test_size=0.33, random_state=42)
print([np.shape(X_train), np.shape(X_test)])
```

```
[(3733, 8404), (1839, 8404)]
```

Figure 18.9: Splitting data into training and test set

We will train different Bayes models by changing the regularization parameter and evaluate the accuracy, recall, and precision of the model with the test set:

```
list_alpha = np.arange(1/100000, 20, 0.11)
score_train = np.zeros(len(list_alpha))
score_test = np.zeros(len(list_alpha))
recall_test = np.zeros(len(list_alpha))
precision_test= np.zeros(len(list_alpha))
count = 0
for alpha in list_alpha:
    bayes = naive_bayes.MultinomialNB(alpha=alpha)
    bayes.fit(X_train, y_train)
    score_train[count] = bayes.score(X_train, y_train)
    score_test[count]= bayes.score(X_test, y_test)
    recall_test[count] = metrics.recall_score(y_test, bayes.predict(X_test))
    precision_test[count] = metrics.precision_score(y_test, bayes.predict(X_test))
    count = count + 1
```

Figure 18.10: Training and Evaluating the performance of the model

In the preceding code cell, we are first defining parameters used in Naïve Bayes; in our case, we are using Multi Nomial Naïve Bayes algorithm. The process of training is the same as other `sklearn` API - fit the model and then make predictions. For computing the recall, we are using `metrics.recall_score()` function.

The recall is the ratio `tp / (tp + fn)` where `tp` is the number of true positives and `fn` is the number of false negatives. The recall is intuitively the ability of the classifier to find all the positive samples, so the best value is 1 and the worst value is 0.

After computing the recall, we are also computing the precision, which is the ratio of `tp / (tp + fp)` where `tp` is the number of true positives and `fp` is the number of false positives. Precision is intuitively the ability of the classifier not to label as positive, a sample that is negative.

Next, in the following code cell, we are calculating our model performance using different matrices:

```
# Let's see some learning models and their metrics
matrix = np.matrix(np.c_[list_alpha, score_train, score_test, recall_test, precision_test])
models = pd.DataFrame(data = matrix, columns =
                        ['alpha', 'Train Accuracy', 'Test Accuracy', 'Test Recall', 'Test Precision'])
models.head()
```

	alpha	Train Accuracy	Test Accuracy	Test Recall	Test Precision
0	0.00001	0.998661	0.974443	0.920635	0.895753
1	0.11001	0.997857	0.976074	0.936508	0.893939
2	0.22001	0.997857	0.977162	0.936508	0.900763
3	0.33001	0.997589	0.977162	0.936508	0.900763
4	0.44001	0.997053	0.977162	0.936508	0.900763

Figure 18.11: Calculating performance

As you can see, there are different learning models with their precisions in the preceding output cell. Now we will select the model with the best test precision, as shown in the following code cell:

```
best_index = models['Test Precision'].idxmax()
models.iloc[best_index, :]
```
```
alpha              15.730010
Train Accuracy      0.979641
Test Accuracy       0.969549
Test Recall         0.777778
Test Precision      1.000000
Name: 143, dtype: float64
```

Figure 18.12: Selecting model with best test precision

From the preceding output cell, we can see that the train and test accuracy score is almost the same, which means there is no overfitting in our model. Let's also check if there is more than one model with 100% precision:

```
models[models['Test Precision']==1].head()
```

	alpha	Train Accuracy	Test Accuracy	Test Recall	Test Precision
143	15.73001	0.979641	0.969549	0.777778	1.0
144	15.84001	0.979641	0.969549	0.777778	1.0
145	15.95001	0.979641	0.969549	0.777778	1.0
146	16.06001	0.979373	0.969549	0.777778	1.0
147	16.17001	0.979373	0.969549	0.777778	1.0

Figure 18.13: Checking other models with 100% precision

As you can see, there are more than one model having 100% precision, but there are some point differences in alpha and train accuracy score. Let's select the model which has more test accuracy:

```
best_index = models[models['Test Precision']==1]['Test Accuracy'].idxmax()
bayes = naive_bayes.MultinomialNB(alpha=list_alpha[best_index])
bayes.fit(X_train, y_train)
models.iloc[best_index, :]
```

```
alpha             15.730010
Train Accuracy     0.979641
Test Accuracy      0.969549
Test Recall        0.777778
Test Precision     1.000000
Name: 143, dtype: float64
```

Figure 18.14: Using model with more test accuracy

From the preceding output, you can easily say that the model has an alpha score of 15.730010. The model, with train accuracy 0.979641 and test accuracy 0.969549 is our best model and that is at index number 143. Let's also generate confusion Matrix for our Naïve Bayes Classifier:

```
# Confusion matrix with naive bayes classifier
m_confusion_test = metrics.confusion_matrix(y_test, bayes.predict(X_test))
pd.DataFrame(data = m_confusion_test, columns = ['Predicted 0', 'Predicted 1'],
             index = ['Actual 0', 'Actual 1'])
```

	Predicted 0	Predicted 1
Actual 0	1587	0
Actual 1	56	196

Figure 18.15: Generating confusion matrix

See the preceding confusion matrix result, and you can say that we misclassify 56 spam messages as non-spam emails, whereas we don't misclassify any non-spam message and our model has 96.95% test accuracy, which you found out just earlier. Now we will repeat the preceding steps with our second model - Support Vector Machine:

```python
# repeat same steps with Support Vector Machine
list_C = np.arange(500, 2000, 100)
score_train = np.zeros(len(list_C))
score_test = np.zeros(len(list_C))
recall_test = np.zeros(len(list_C))
precision_test= np.zeros(len(list_C))
count = 0
for C in list_C:
    svc = svm.SVC(C=C)
    svc.fit(X_train, y_train)
    score_train[count] = svc.score(X_train, y_train)
    score_test[count]= svc.score(X_test, y_test)
    recall_test[count] = metrics.recall_score(y_test, svc.predict(X_test))
    precision_test[count] = metrics.precision_score(y_test, svc.predict(X_test))
    count = count + 1
```

Figure 18.16: Using Support Vector Machine

```python
matrix = np.matrix(np.c_[list_C, score_train, score_test, recall_test, precision_test])
models = pd.DataFrame(data = matrix, columns =
            ['C', 'Train Accuracy', 'Test Accuracy', 'Test Recall', 'Test Precision'])
models.head()
```

	C	Train Accuracy	Test Accuracy	Test Recall	Test Precision
0	500.0	0.994910	0.982599	0.873016	1.0
1	600.0	0.995982	0.982599	0.873016	1.0
2	700.0	0.996785	0.982599	0.873016	1.0
3	800.0	0.997053	0.983143	0.876984	1.0
4	900.0	0.997589	0.983143	0.876984	1.0

```python
best_index = models['Test Precision'].idxmax()
models.iloc[best_index, :]
```

```
C                 500.000000
Train Accuracy      0.994910
Test Accuracy       0.982599
Test Recall         0.873016
Test Precision      1.000000
Name: 0, dtype: float64
```

Figure 18.17: Preparing dataframe with matrix data

```
models[models['Test Precision']==1].head()
```

	C	Train Accuracy	Test Accuracy	Test Recall	Test Precision
0	500.0	0.994910	0.982599	0.873016	1.0
1	600.0	0.995982	0.982599	0.873016	1.0
2	700.0	0.996785	0.982599	0.873016	1.0
3	800.0	0.997053	0.983143	0.876984	1.0
4	900.0	0.997589	0.983143	0.876984	1.0

```
best_index = models[models['Test Precision']==1]['Test Accuracy'].idxmax()
svc = svm.SVC(C=list_C[best_index])
svc.fit(X_train, y_train)
models.iloc[best_index, :]
```

```
C                  800.000000
Train Accuracy       0.997053
Test Accuracy        0.983143
Test Recall          0.876984
Test Precision       1.000000
Name: 3, dtype: float64
```

Figure 18.18: Training with SVM model

```
m_confusion_test = metrics.confusion_matrix(y_test, svc.predict(X_test))
pd.DataFrame(data = m_confusion_test, columns = ['Predicted 0', 'Predicted 1'],
             index = ['Actual 0', 'Actual 1'])
```

	Predicted 0	Predicted 1
Actual 0	1587	0
Actual 1	31	221

Figure 18.19: Confusion matrix with SVM model

In this case, we misclassify 31 spam as non-spam messages, whereas we don't misclassify any non-spam messages, indicating that the SVC model has 98.3% test accuracy, which is better than our Naïve Bayes model. That completes our goal!

Now you can classify any new text to spam or non-spam with the help of your SVM model, as shown in the following screenshot:

```
# predicting a new text using our svm model
Y = ["A loan for £950 is approved for you if you receive this SMS. 1 min verification & cash in 1 hr at www.example.co.uk
f = feature_extraction.text.CountVectorizer(stop_words = 'english')
f.fit(text_df["v2"])
X = f.transform(Y)
res=svc.predict(X)
if res==1:
    print('This text is spam')
else:
    print('This text is not a spam')
```

```
This text is spam
```

Figure 18.20: Predicting new text using SVM model

As you can see in the preceding output cell, I have added a new sentence for testing our model. Here, first we store it in a variable, as we used Y for this, then we have initialized the `CountVectorizer()` function with English stop words. Next, we have trained the model, and after the transformation of our new sentence, we are predicting the outcome, and our model has recognized this sentence as spam, which is a correct prediction.

Conclusion

If you follow this case-study, you will find that classifying any mail or message is not a tough task. Gmail, Yahoo Mail, and other email platforms are already using similar types of algorithms for such tasks. Naïve Bayes and Support Vector Machines are the two most used algorithms in spam vs. non-spam classification problems. What more you can do with this model is, try different parameters, and see what variation in accuracy you can achieve with your changes.

## CHAPTER 19

Case Study-3

Build a film recommendation engine

Your goal: Build a film recommendation engine.

About dataset: TMDB dataset contains around 5000 movies and TV series with data on the plot, cast, crew, budget, and revenues. The credit CSV (`tmdb_5000_credits.csv`) contains the movie id, title, cast, and crew details, while movie CSV file (`tmdb_5000_movies.csv`) contains the movie budget, genre, revenue, popularity, etc.

Main ML libraries: TfidfVectorizer and CountVectorizer.

About recommendation engine: A recommendation engine filters the data using different algorithms, and recommends the most relevant items to users. It first captures the past behavior of a customer, and based on that, recommends products that the users might be likely to buy. Here, we will build a movie recommendation engine based on popularity and content-based engines.

Let's load the datasets and explore them first to have a better understanding of the data:

```
credits = pd.read_csv('E:/pg/bpb/BPB-Publications/Datasets/Case Studies/case_study_3/tmdb_5000_credits.csv')
credits.info()

<class 'pandas.core.frame.DataFrame'>
RangeIndex: 4803 entries, 0 to 4802
Data columns (total 4 columns):
movie_id    4803 non-null int64
title       4803 non-null object
cast        4803 non-null object
crew        4803 non-null object
dtypes: int64(1), object(3)
memory usage: 150.2+ KB
```

Figure 19.1: Loading the datasets

```
movies = pd.read_csv('E:/pg/bpb/BPB-Publications/Datasets/Case Studies/case_study_3/tmdb_5000_movies.csv')
movies.info()

<class 'pandas.core.frame.DataFrame'>
RangeIndex: 4803 entries, 0 to 4802
Data columns (total 20 columns):
budget                  4803 non-null int64
genres                  4803 non-null object
homepage                1712 non-null object
id                      4803 non-null int64
keywords                4803 non-null object
original_language       4803 non-null object
original_title          4803 non-null object
overview                4800 non-null object
popularity              4803 non-null float64
production_companies    4803 non-null object
production_countries    4803 non-null object
release_date            4802 non-null object
revenue                 4803 non-null int64
runtime                 4801 non-null float64
spoken_languages        4803 non-null object
status                  4803 non-null object
tagline                 3959 non-null object
title                   4803 non-null object
vote_average            4803 non-null float64
vote_count              4803 non-null int64
dtypes: float64(3), int64(4), object(13)
```

Figure 19.2: Exploring the datasets

Now, before starting our analysis, first we will think about a metric that can rate or score a movie, because a movie with a 7.9 average rating and only 2 votes cannot be considered better than the movie with 7.8 as an average rating but 45 votes. In the movie's dataset, `vote_count`, `vote_average` is already present. We just have to find out the mean vote across the whole data, which can be calculated, as shown in the following screenshot:

```
# calculate mean vote
C = movies['vote_average'].mean()
C
```

6.092171559442011

Figure 19.3: Calculating the mean vote

It shows a mean rating for all the movies as approximately 6 on a scale of 10.

The next step is to determine an appropriate value for the minimum votes required to be listed in the chart. We will use the 90th percentile as our cutoff. In other words, for a movie to feature in the charts, it must have more votes than at least 90% of the movies in the list:

```
# calculate minimum votes required to be listed in the chart
m = movies['vote_count'].quantile(0.9)
m
```

1838.4000000000015

Figure 19.4: Calculating the required minimum votes

Now, we can filter out the movies that qualify for the chart:

```
# filter out the movies that qualify for the chart
q_movies = movies.copy().loc[movies['vote_count'] >= m]
q_movies.shape
```

```
(481, 23)
```

Figure 19.5: Filtering out movies qualified for the chart

We see that there are 481 movies that qualify to be on this list. Now, we need to calculate our metric for each qualified movie.

To do this, we will define a function, `weighted_rating()`. This function will calculate our metric for each qualified movie. Next, we will also define a new feature called score; the value of this feature is calculated by applying this `weighted_rating()` function to our DataFrame of qualified movies. This is our first step toward making our first basic recommender. For writing `weighted_rating()` function, you can take help from the IMDB site itself by click on the following link:

**https://help.imdb.com/article/imdb/track-movies-tv/faq-for-imdb-ratings/
G67Y87TFYYP6TWAV#**

I have represented the same formula as the following function for your ease:

```
# calculate our metric for each qualified movie
def weighted_rating(x, m=m, C=C):
    v = x['vote_count']
    R = x['vote_average']
    # Calculation based on the IMDB formula
    return (v/(v+m) * R) + (m/(m+v) * C)
```

```
# Define a new feature 'score' and calculate its value with `weighted_rating()`
q_movies['score'] = q_movies.apply(weighted_rating, axis=1)
#Sort movies based on score calculated above
q_movies = q_movies.sort_values('score', ascending=False)
#Print the top 5 movies
q_movies[['title', 'vote_count', 'vote_average', 'score']].head()
```

	title	vote_count	vote_average	score
1881	The Shawshank Redemption	8205	8.5	8.059258
662	Fight Club	9413	8.3	7.939256
65	The Dark Knight	12002	8.2	7.920020
3232	Pulp Fiction	8428	8.3	7.904645
96	Inception	13752	8.1	7.863239

Figure 19.6: metric calculation for qualified movies

Now, let's understand how to visualize five popular movies that we got from the preceding code cell:

```
# plot 5 popular movies
popular_movies = movies.sort_values('popularity', ascending=False)
plt.figure(figsize=(12,4))
plt.barh(popular_movies['title'].head(),popular_movies['popularity'].head(), align='center',
        color='yellow')
plt.gca().invert_yaxis()
plt.xlabel("Popularity")
plt.title("Popular Movies")
```

Text(0.5,1,'Popular Movies')

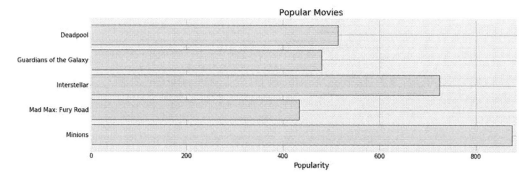

Figure 19.7: Preparing visual graph

See! It was quite easy to create our first basic popularity-based recommendation engine. But there is something to keep in mind – these popularity-based recommenders provide a general chart of recommended movies to all the users. They are not sensitive to the interests and tastes of a particular user. Now we will tackle this problem as well and we will create a more refined system – content-based recommendation engine – by including other columns like overview, cast, crew, keyword, tagline, etc., in our analysis. For this, we need to handle these texts, so that a machine learning model can understand them. We will use scikit-learn's built-in `TfIdfVectorizer` class that produces the TF-IDF matrix in a couple of lines. In this matrix, each column represents a word in the overview vocabulary (all the words that appear in at least one document), and each column represents a movie, as before. `TfIdfVectorizer` has two parts - **Term Frequency(TF)** and **Inverse Document Frequency (idf)**. TF simply tells us how many times a particular word appears in a single doc, and IDF solves the frequent and rare words in a given doc. After importing this library, we will initialize it with stop word parameter as English. This `stop_words` parameter is used to remove less-meaningful English words. Then, we will handle the missing values in the overview column, as shown in the following screenshot:

```
from sklearn.feature_extraction.text import TfidfVectorizer
tfidf = TfidfVectorizer(stop_words='english')
# handle missing values
movies['overview'] = movies['overview'].fillna('')
tfidf_matrix = tfidf.fit_transform(movies['overview'])
tfidf_matrix.shape
```

(4803, 20978)

Figure 19.8: train movies data with TF-IDF Vectorizer

With this matrix in hand, we can now compute a similarity score. We will be using the cosine similarity to calculate a numeric quantity that denotes the similarity between the two movies. We use the cosine similarity score, because it is independent of magnitude (or size) and is relatively easy and fast to calculate. Cosine similarity is a metric used to measure how similar the documents are, irrespective of their size. Since we have used the TF-IDF vectorizer, calculating the dot product will directly give us the cosine similarity score. Therefore, we will use sklearn's `linear_kernel()` instead of `cosine_similarities()`, because it is faster in executing inputs:

```
from sklearn.metrics.pairwise import linear_kernel
# compute the cosine similarity matrix
cosine_sim = linear_kernel(tfidf_matrix, tfidf_matrix)
```

Figure 19.9: Using sklearn's linear_kernel()

Now, we will define a function that takes in a movie title as an input and outputs a list of the 10 most similar movies. Firstly, for this, we need a reverse mapping of movie titles and `DataFrame` indices. In other words, we need a mechanism to identify the index of a movie in our metadata `DataFrame`, given its title:

```
# construct a reverse map of indices and movie titles
indices = pd.Series(movies.index, index=movies['title']).drop_duplicates()
```

Figure 19.10: Constructing reverse map of indices and movie titles

Next, we will define our recommendation function that will do the following steps:

- Set the index of the movie, given its title.

- Get the list of cosine similarity scores for that particular movie with all movies.

- Convert it into a list of tuples, where the first element is its position and the second is the similarity score.

- Sort the aforementioned list of tuples based on the similarity scores, that is, the second element.

- Get the top 10 elements of this list.

- Ignore the first element as it refers to self (the movie most similar to a particular movie is the movie itself).

- In the last return, the titles corresponding to the indices of the top elements.

```python
# define our recommendation function
def get_recommendations(title, cosine_sim=cosine_sim):
    idx = indices[title]
    sim_scores = list(enumerate(cosine_sim[idx]))
    sim_scores = sorted(sim_scores, key=lambda x: x[1], reverse=True)
    sim_scores = sim_scores[1:11]
    movie_indices = [i[0] for i in sim_scores]

    return movies['title'].iloc[movie_indices]
```

Figure 19.11: defining recommendation function

```python
# test our function
get_recommendations('Spectre')
```

```
1343        Never Say Never Again
4071        From Russia with Love
3162                  Thunderball
1717                   Safe Haven
11            Quantum of Solace
4339                       Dr. No
29                        Skyfall
1880                  Dance Flick
3336        Diamonds Are Forever
1743                    Octopussy
Name: title, dtype: object
```

Figure 19.12: Testing the function

That's great! Our recommendation engine has been improved.

Let's make it more mature by including the following metadata: 3 top actors, director, related genres, and movie plot keywords. From the cast, crew, and keywords features, we need to extract the three most important actors, the director and the keywords associated with that movie. Right now, our data is present in the form of *stringified* lists; we need to convert it into a safe and usable structure:

```python
# parse the stringified features into their corresponding python objects
from ast import literal_eval
features = ['cast', 'crew', 'keywords', 'genres']
for feature in features:
    movies[feature] = movies[feature].apply(literal_eval)
```

Figure 19.13: converting data into usable structure

Next, we'll write functions that will help us extract the required information from each feature:

```
# Get the director's name from the crew feature
def get_director(x):
    for i in x:
        if i['job'] == 'Director':
            return i['name']
    return np.nan
```

```
# Returns the list top 3 elements or entire list
def get_list(x):
    if isinstance(x, list):
        names = [i['name'] for i in x]
        if len(names) > 3:
            names = names[:3]
        return names
    return []
```

```
# Define new director, cast, genres and keywords features that are in a suitable form
movies['director'] = movies['crew'].apply(get_director)
features = ['cast', 'keywords', 'genres']
for feature in features:
    movies[feature] = movies[feature].apply(get_list)
```

Figure 19.14: *Writing function to extract information from features*

```
# Print the new features
movies[['title', 'cast', 'director', 'keywords', 'genres']].head()
```

	title	cast	director	keywords	genres
0	Avatar	[Sam Worthington, Zoe Saldana, Sigourney Weaver]	James Cameron	[culture clash, future, space war]	[Action, Adventure, Fantasy]
1	Pirates of the Caribbean: At World's End	[Johnny Depp, Orlando Bloom, Keira Knightley]	Gore Verbinski	[ocean, drug abuse, exotic island]	[Adventure, Fantasy, Action]
2	Spectre	[Daniel Craig, Christoph Waltz, Léa Seydoux]	Sam Mendes	[spy, based on novel, secret agent]	[Action, Adventure, Crime]
3	The Dark Knight Rises	[Christian Bale, Michael Caine, Gary Oldman]	Christopher Nolan	[dc comics, crime fighter, terrorist]	[Action, Crime, Drama]
4	John Carter	[Taylor Kitsch, Lynn Collins, Samantha Morton]	Andrew Stanton	[based on novel, mars, medallion]	[Action, Adventure, Science Fiction]

Figure 19.15: *peek of the data with new features*

The next step would be to convert the names and keyword instances into lowercase and strip all the spaces between them. This is done so that our vectorizer doesn't count the John of JohnCena and JohnCleese as the same:

```python
# Function to convert all strings to lower case and strip names of spaces
def clean_data(x):
    if isinstance(x, list):
        return [str.lower(i.replace(" ", "")) for i in x]
    else:
        if isinstance(x, str):
            return str.lower(x.replace(" ", ""))
        else:
            return ''
```

```python
# Apply clean_data function to our features.
features = ['cast', 'keywords', 'director', 'genres']
for feature in features:
    movies[feature] = movies[feature].apply(clean_data)
```

Figure 19.16: Converting names and keyword instances into lowercase and stripping spaces

We are now in a position to create our *metadata soup*, which is a string that contains all the metadata that we want to feed to our vectorizer (namely actors, director, and keywords):

```python
def create_soup(x):
    return ' '.join(x['keywords']) + ' ' + ' '.join(x['cast']) + ' ' + x['director'] + ' ' + ' '.join(x['genres'])
movies['soup'] = movies.apply(create_soup, axis=1)
```

Figure 19.17: creating meta data soup

Now, we will use sklearn's CountVectorizer() instead of TF-IDF to remove stop words and transform our newly created soup column:

```python
from sklearn.feature_extraction.text import CountVectorizer
count = CountVectorizer(stop_words='english')
count_matrix = count.fit_transform(movies['soup'])
```

```python
# compute the Cosine Similarity matrix based on the count_matrix
from sklearn.metrics.pairwise import cosine_similarity
cosine_sim2 = cosine_similarity(count_matrix, count_matrix)
```

Figure 19.18: use of Count Vectorizer and similarity check

```
# test our get_recommendations() function with our new arguement
get_recommendations('Spectre', cosine_sim2)
```

```
29                        Skyfall
11               Quantum of Solace
1084                The Glimmer Man
1234                 The Art of War
2156                     Nancy Drew
4638        Amidst the Devil's Wings
62             The Legend of Tarzan
3373        The Other Side of Heaven
4                        John Carter
72                     Suicide Squad
Name: title, dtype: object
```

Figure 19.19: testing recommendation function

Wow! You see that our recommendation engine has been successful in capturing more information due to more metadata and has given us (arguably) better recommendations. Still, there are a lot of work pending for you to improve your engine, like the language of the film was not checked; in fact, this could be important to ensure that the films recommended are in the same language as the one chosen by the user. So, add a feature in your model and see if are you getting a better result or not. This is one example of a recommendation engine that you can use as a base model. You can extend this model for different problems like product recommendation or a product category recommendation.

Conclusion

Recommendation systems are widely used in almost every e-commerce and in **over the top** (OTT) media services. For a user these systems make the experience better by helping to select the best choice over other options, as well as increase the probability of earning more revenue for a company. After completing this exercise, you have hands-on experience in building a movie recommendation engine. Now don't stop here, apply your knowledge to build a product recommendation engine or a song recommendation engine, and feel the value of a Data Scientist's work to this society.

## CHAPTER 20

Case Study-4

Predict house sales in King County, Washington State, USA, using regression

Your goal: Online property companies offer valuations of houses using machine learning techniques. This case study aims to predict house sales in King County, Washington State, USA, using regression.

About dataset: This dataset contains house sale prices for King County, which includes Seattle. It includes houses sold between May 2014 and May 2015 as described in kc_house_data.csv.

Our ML model: Linear Regression and Polynomial Regression.

Let's first read the housing data, for which I have defined an empty dataframe named evaluation. This dataframe includes **Mean Squared Error (MSE)**, R-squared, and Adjusted R-squared, which are the important metrics to compare different models. Having an R-squared value closer to one and smaller MSE means a better fit. In the following example, I will calculate these values and store them in this dataframe with my results. For this purpose, first, we will import all basic libraries along with the `sklearn` library:

```
import numpy as np
import pandas as pd
from sklearn.model_selection import train_test_split
from sklearn import linear_model
from sklearn.neighbors import KNeighborsRegressor
from sklearn.preprocessing import PolynomialFeatures
from sklearn import metrics
import matplotlib.pyplot as plt
import seaborn as sns
from mpl_toolkits.mplot3d import Axes3D
%matplotlib inline
```

```
# create evaluation metrics
evaluation = pd.DataFrame({'Model': [],
                           'Details':[],
                           'Mean Squared Error (MSE)':[],
                           'R-squared (training)':[],
                           'Adjusted R-squared (training)':[],
                           'R-squared (test)':[],
                           'Adjusted R-squared (test)':[]})
```

Figure 20.1: Importing all basic libraries

After creating our evaluation dataframe, we will load the King County dataset in a dataframe and will look into the head of this:

```
# read and explore data
df = pd.read_csv('E:/pg/bpb/BPB-Publications/Datasets/Case Studies/case_study_4/kc_house_data.csv')
df.head()
```

	id	date	price	bedrooms	bathrooms	sqft_living	sqft_lot	floors	waterfront	view	...	grade	sqft_above	sqft_basement	yr_built
0	7129300520	20141013T000000	221900.0	3	1.00	1180	5650	1.0	0	0	...	7	1180	0	1955
1	6414100192	20141209T000000	538000.0	3	2.25	2570	7242	2.0	0	0	...	7	2170	400	1951
2	5631500400	20150225T000000	180000.0	2	1.00	770	10000	1.0	0	0	...	6	770	0	1933
3	2487200875	20141209T000000	604000.0	4	3.00	1960	5000	1.0	0	0	...	7	1050	910	1965
4	1954400510	20150218T000000	510000.0	3	2.00	1680	8080	1.0	0	0	...	8	1680	0	1987

5 rows × 21 columns

Figure 20.2: peek of the housing data

Please note here, when we model a linear relationship between a response and just one explanatory variable, it is called simple linear regression. Here, I want to predict the house prices, so our response variable is the price. However, for a simple model, we also need to select a feature. When I look at the columns of the dataset, the living area (sqft) seemed the most important feature.

When we examine the correlation matrix, we may observe that the price has the highest correlation coefficient with living area (sqft), and this also supports my opinion. Thus, I decided to use the living area (sqft) as a feature, but if you want to examine the relationship between price and another feature, you may prefer that feature. We will apply this logic in our dataframe, but we will first split our dataset into 80:20 ratio, so that we can train on 80% data, and then validate our model on 20% data. Then, we will separate the target variable - price - from the training dataset, and then fit the Linear regression model on this training and target input using the `fit()` method. We will apply the same for the testing dataset. Then, we will predict the result on test data using `predict()` method. At last, we will calculate the loss of our model, using MSE metric, as shown in the following screenshot:

```
%%capture
train_data,test_data = train_test_split(df,train_size = 0.8,random_state=3)

lr = linear_model.LinearRegression()
X_train = np.array(train_data['sqft_living'], dtype=pd.Series).reshape(-1,1)
y_train = np.array(train_data['price'], dtype=pd.Series)
lr.fit(X_train,y_train)

X_test = np.array(test_data['sqft_living'], dtype=pd.Series).reshape(-1,1)
y_test = np.array(test_data['price'], dtype=pd.Series)

pred = lr.predict(X_test)
msesm = format(np.sqrt(metrics.mean_squared_error(y_test,pred)),'.3f')
rtrsm = format(lr.score(X_train, y_train),'.3f')
rtesm = format(lr.score(X_test, y_test),'.3f')

print ("Average Price for Test Data: {:.3f}".format(y_test.mean()))
print('Intercept: {}'.format(lr.intercept_))
print('Coefficient: {}'.format(lr.coef_))

r = evaluation.shape[0]
evaluation.loc[r] = ['Simple Model','-',msesm,rtrsm,'-',rtesm,'-']
evaluation
```

Figure 20.3: training and prediction on housing data

In the last three lines of the preceding code cell, we used our evaluation dataframe to calculate the metric by passing the metric scores - msesm, rtrsm, and rtesm.

You will notice in the following output that we are getting mean squared error or regression loss as 254289.149 for our simple model:

```
Average Price for Test Data: 539744.130
Intercept: -47235.81130290043
Coefficient: [282.2468152]

C:\Users\prateek1.gupta\AppData\Local\Continuum\anaconda3\lib\site-packages\sklearn\model_selection\_split.py:2026: FutureWarni
ng: From version 0.21, test_size will always complement train_size unless both are specified.
  FutureWarning)
```

	Adjusted R-squared (test)	Adjusted R-squared (training)	Details	Mean Squared Error (MSE)	Model	R-squared (test)	R-squared (training)
0	Simple Model		-	254289.149		0.492	-	0.496	-
1	Simple Model		-	254289.149		0.492	-	0.496	-
2	Simple Model		-	254289.149		0.492	-	0.496	-

Figure 20.4: Average price for test data

Because we have just two dimensions at the simple regression, it is easy to draw it. The below chart determines the result of the simple regression. It does not look like a perfect fit but when we work with real-world datasets, having a perfect fit is not easy:

```
plt.figure(figsize=(6.5,5))
plt.scatter(X_test,y_test,color='darkgreen',label="Data", alpha=.1)
plt.plot(X_test,lr.predict(X_test),color="red",label="Predicted Regression Line")
plt.xlabel("Living Space (sqft)", fontsize=15)
plt.ylabel("Price ($)", fontsize=15)
plt.xticks(fontsize=13)
plt.yticks(fontsize=13)
plt.legend()

plt.gca().spines['right'].set_visible(False)
plt.gca().spines['top'].set_visible(False)
```

Figure 20.5: plot the house price vs space

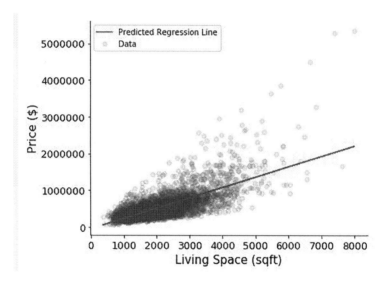

Figure 20.6: Predicted regression line data

In the preceding case, we have used a simple linear regression and found a poor fit, because data looks scattered around the line. To improve this model, I am planning to add more features. However, in this case we should be careful about the overfit, which can be detected by the high difference between the training and test evaluation metrics. When we have more than one feature in linear regression, it is defined as multiple regression. Then, it is time to check the correlation matrix before fitting a multiple regression.

Having too many features in a model is not always a good thing, because it might cause overfit and worse results when we want to predict values for a new dataset.

Thus, if a feature does not improve your model a lot, not adding it may be a better choice.

Another important thing is a correlation; if there is a very high correlation between two features, keeping both of them is not a good idea (most of the time). For instance, `sqt_above` and `sqt_living` columns in the datasets are highly correlated. This can be estimated when you look at the definitions of the dataset.

Just to be sure, you can double-check this by looking at the correlation matrix, which we will draw next. However, this does not mean that you must remove one of the highly correlated features, for instance, bathrooms and `sqrt_living`. They are highly correlated, but I do not think that the relation between them is the same as the relation between `sqt_living` and `sqt_above`. Let's draw a correlation matrix with all these features:

```
features = ['price','bedrooms','bathrooms','sqft_living','sqft_lot','floors',
            'waterfront','view','condition','grade','sqft_above','sqft_basement',
            'yr_built','yr_renovated','zipcode','sqft_living15','sqft_lot15']

mask = np.zeros_like(df[features].corr(), dtype=np.bool)
mask[np.triu_indices_from(mask)] = True

f, ax = plt.subplots(figsize=(16, 12))
plt.title('Pearson Correlation Matrix',fontsize=25)

sns.heatmap(df[features].corr(),linewidths=0.25,vmax=1.0,square=True,cmap="BuGn_r",
            linecolor='w',annot=True,mask=mask,cbar_kws={"shrink": .75});
```

Figure 20.7: Correlation matrix

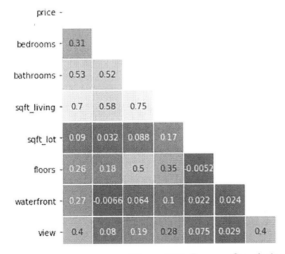

Figure 20.8: Pearson Correlation Matrix

After looking into the correlation matrix, we can examine the features and reach some useful analytical conclusions. Furthermore, plotting charts and examining the data before applying a model is a very good practice, because we may detect some possible outliers or decide to do some normalizations. This is not a must, but getting to know the data using visualization is always good.

Now, to determine bedrooms, floors, or bathrooms/bedrooms vs. price comparison, I preferred boxplot, because we have numerical data and they are not continuous as 1,2,... bedrooms, 2.5, 3,... floors (probably 0.5 stands for the penthouse):

```
f, axes = plt.subplots(1, 2,figsize=(15,5))
sns.boxplot(x=train_data['bedrooms'],y=train_data['price'], ax=axes[0])
sns.boxplot(x=train_data['floors'],y=train_data['price'], ax=axes[1])
axes[0].set(xlabel='Bedrooms', ylabel='Price')
axes[1].yaxis.set_label_position("right")
axes[1].yaxis.tick_right()
axes[1].set(xlabel='Floors', ylabel='Price')

f, axe = plt.subplots(1, 1,figsize=(12.18,5))
sns.boxplot(x=train_data['bathrooms'],y=train_data['price'], ax=axe)
axe.set(xlabel='Bathrooms / Bedrooms', ylabel='Price');
```

Figure 20.9: creating box plot

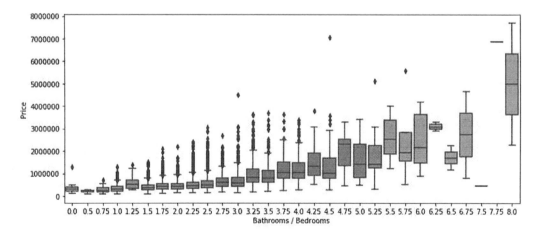

Figure 20.10: Graphical representation of bathrooms and bedrooms

Let's create a complex model manually to find out if we get a better regression loss or not. For this purpose, we will include six features of the dataset for predicting the outcome, and then we will repeat the same steps as we have done earlier:

```
features1 = ['bedrooms','bathrooms','sqft_living','sqft_lot','floors','zipcode']
complex_model_1 = linear_model.LinearRegression()
complex_model_1.fit(train_data[features1],train_data['price'])

print('Intercept: {}'.format(complex_model_1.intercept_))
print('Coefficients: {}'.format(complex_model_1.coef_))

pred1 = complex_model_1.predict(test_data[features1])
msecm1 = format(np.sqrt(metrics.mean_squared_error(y_test,pred1)),'.3f')
rtrcm1 = format(complex_model_1.score(train_data[features1],train_data['price']),'.3f')
artrcm1 = format(adjustedR2(complex_model_1.score(train_data[features1],train_data['price']),train_data.shape[0],len(features1)),
rtecm1 = format(complex_model_1.score(test_data[features1],test_data['price']),'.3f')
artecm1 = format(adjustedR2(complex_model_1.score(test_data[features1],test_data['price']),test_data.shape[0],len(features1)),'.3

r = evaluation.shape[0]
evaluation.loc[r] = ['Complex Model-1','-',msecm1,rtrcm1,artrcm1,rtecm1,artecm1]
evaluation.sort_values(by = 'R-squared (test)', ascending=False)
```

Figure 20.11: creating a complex model

```
Intercept: -57221293.13485877
Coefficients: [-5.68950279e+04  1.13310062e+04  3.18389287e+02 -2.90807628e-01
 -5.79609821e+03  5.84022824e+02]
```

	Adjusted R-squared (test)	Adjusted R-squared (training)	Details	Mean Squared Error (MSE)	Model	R-squared (test)	R-squared (training)
3	Complex Model-1		-	248514.011	0.514	0.519	0.518
0	Simple Model		-	254289.149	0.492	-	0.496	-
1	Simple Model		-	254289.149	0.492	-	0.496	-
2	Simple Model		-	254289.149	0.492	-	0.496	-

Figure 20.12: prediction on complex data

From the preceding output, you can say that the uurfirst complex model decreased the MSE to 248514.011, which means we can add additional features to our model and again plot boxplots for further examination, as shown in the following screenshot:

```
f, axes = plt.subplots(1, 2,figsize=(15,5))
sns.boxplot(x=train_data['waterfront'],y=train_data['price'], ax=axes[0])
sns.boxplot(x=train_data['view'],y=train_data['price'], ax=axes[1])
axes[0].set(xlabel='Waterfront', ylabel='Price')
axes[1].yaxis.set_label_position("right")
axes[1].yaxis.tick_right()
axes[1].set(xlabel='View', ylabel='Price')

f, axe = plt.subplots(1, 1,figsize=(12.18,5))
sns.boxplot(x=train_data['grade'],y=train_data['price'], ax=axe)
axe.set(xlabel='Grade', ylabel='Price');
```

Figure 20.13: plot the box plot

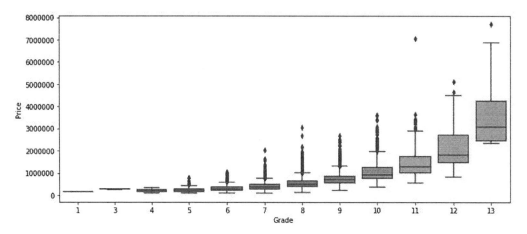

Figure 20.14: box plot of house price vs grade

Let's add some more features and repeat the same steps:

```
features2 = ['bedrooms','bathrooms','sqft_living','sqft_lot','floors','waterfront','view',
             'grade','yr_built','zipcode']
complex_model_2 = linear_model.LinearRegression()
complex_model_2.fit(train_data[features2],train_data['price'])

print('Intercept: {}'.format(complex_model_2.intercept_))
print('Coefficients: {}'.format(complex_model_2.coef_))

pred2 = complex_model_2.predict(test_data[features2])
msecm2 = format(np.sqrt(metrics.mean_squared_error(y_test,pred2)),'.3f')
rtrcm2 = format(complex_model_2.score(train_data[features2],train_data['price']),'.3f')
artrcm2 = format(adjustedR2(complex_model_2.score(train_data[features2],train_data['price']),train_data.shape[0],len(features2)),'
rtecm2 = format(complex_model_2.score(test_data[features2],test_data['price']),'.3f')
artecm2 = format(adjustedR2(complex_model_2.score(test_data[features2],test_data['price']),test_data.shape[0],len(features2)),'.3

r = evaluation.shape[0]
evaluation.loc[r] = ['Complex Model-2','-',msecm2,rtrcm2,artrcm2,rtecm2,artecm2]
evaluation.sort_values(by = 'R-squared (test)', ascending=False)
```

Figure 20.15: adding more features and making prediction

```
Intercept: 13559209.611222725
Coefficients: [-3.80981692e+04  5.03031727e+04  1.71370475e+02 -2.68019419e-01
   2.21944912e+04  5.53865017e+05  4.70338164e+04  1.23642184e+05
  -3.88306990e+03 -6.82180496e+01]
```

		Details	Mean Squared Error (MSE)	Model	R-squared (test)	R-squared (training)
Adjusted R-squared (test)	Adjusted R-squared (training)					
4	Complex Model-2	-	210486.689	0.651	0.650	0.655	0.654
3	Complex Model-1	-	248514.011	0.514	0.514	0.519	0.518
0	Simple Model	-	254289.149	0.492	-	0.496	-
1	Simple Model	-	254289.149	0.492	-	0.496	-
2	Simple Model	-	254289.149	0.492	-	0.496	-

Figure 20.16: result of the prediction on more data

From the preceding result, you can see that adding more features in our complex model 2 is decreasing the regression log, i.e., in our case, it is now 210486.689. Always remember, for the linear models, the main idea is to fit a straight line to our data. However, if the data has a quadratic distribution, this time choosing a quadratic function and applying a polynomial transformation, may give us better results. Let's see how we can choose a quadratic function and apply the polynomial transformation in the following screenshot:

```
polyfeat = PolynomialFeatures(degree=2)
X_trainpoly = polyfeat.fit_transform(train_data[features2])
X_testpoly = polyfeat.fit_transform(test_data[features2])
poly = linear_model.LinearRegression().fit(X_trainpoly, train_data['price'])

predp = poly.predict(X_testpoly)
msepoly1 = format(np.sqrt(metrics.mean_squared_error(test_data['price'],pred)),'.3f')
rtrpoly1 = format(poly.score(X_trainpoly,train_data['price']),'.3f')
rtepoly1 = format(poly.score(X_testpoly,test_data['price']),'.3f')

polyfeat = PolynomialFeatures(degree=3)
X_trainpoly = polyfeat.fit_transform(train_data[features2])
X_testpoly = polyfeat.fit_transform(test_data[features2])
poly = linear_model.LinearRegression().fit(X_trainpoly, train_data['price'])

predp = poly.predict(X_testpoly)
msepoly2 = format(np.sqrt(metrics.mean_squared_error(test_data['price'],pred)),'.3f')
rtrpoly2 = format(poly.score(X_trainpoly,train_data['price']),'.3f')
rtepoly2 = format(poly.score(X_testpoly,test_data['price']),'.3f')

r = evaluation.shape[0]
evaluation.loc[r] = ['Polynomial Regression','degree=2',msepoly1,rtrpoly1,'-',rtepoly1,'-']
evaluation.loc[r+1] = ['Polynomial Regression','degree=3',msepoly2,rtrpoly2,'-',rtepoly2,'-']
evaluation.sort_values(by = 'R-squared (test)', ascending=False)
```

Figure 20.17: Applying polynomial transformation

In the preceding code cell, we have first initialized the Polynomial Features with degree 2 for generating polynomial and interaction features. Then we have fit and transformed these features using fit_transform() method, and then we have trained our linear regression model using the fit() method as we did earlier.

Next, we repeat the same step but for degree 3. After this, you can calculate each degree's regression log and score, and then apply our evaluation dataframe to it, just as we did earlier.

You will get the following result after executing the preceding steps:

	Adjusted R-squared (test)	Adjusted R-squared (training)	Details	Mean Squared Error (MSE)	Model	R-squared (test)	R-squared (training)
6	Polynomial Regression	degree=3	254289.149	0.749	-	0.723	-
5	Polynomial Regression	degree=2	254289.149	0.730	-	0.716	-
4	Complex Model-2	-	210486.689	0.651	0.650	0.655	0.654
3	Complex Model-1	-	248514.011	0.514	0.514	0.519	0.518
0	Simple Model	-	254289.149	0.492	-	0.496	-
1	Simple Model	-	254289.149	0.492	-	0.496	-
2	Simple Model	-	254289.149	0.492	-	0.496	-

Figure 20.18: comparison of all predictions

When we look at the preceding evaluation table, MSE values are confusing to select the best model, because many models have the same MSE value. For removing this confusion, we must see the R-squared (test) values also. An R-squared value, closer to 100%, denotes a good correlation; so, in our case it seems our 3rd-degree Polynomial Regression model is the best model for our problem having a 74.9% R-squared value. That completes our goal!

Always start with a simple model, and then increase its complexity by adding its features and check different evaluation metric scores. Although it is a time-consuming process, it is one of the best ways to get a stable and highly accurate model.

Try to add some new features, check the evaluation metric, and see if you are getting a more valid score or not.

Conclusion

Congratulations! You have built a very good model to predict house sales. Such types of models are very helpful for sales, and they can help the sales representatives to focus on important features of a property to sell. Now you have hands-on experience in dealing with sales-related problems. So, go on and apply this knowledge to predict store sales or product sales, and see how you can help the company with your data-driven skills.

## CHAPTER 21

Python Virtual Environment

After completing the last 20 chapters of this book, you are quite ready to transform your title from an *Aspiring Data Scientist* to a *Data Scientist*. In the real-world, when you will work with a company, you will often find yourself in a new project from time to time. To share my experience with you, I had worked on three different projects in a single year, and each project had different Python environments: one was using Python 2.7, the second was on Python 3.6, and third was on Python 3.7. Uninstalling a version and then reinstalling the required version in your machine with a project to project is a tedious task. Also, it is not a good practice. Not only do we have to do this step for Python, we also need to do this for various libraries that we have installed. In the first bonus chapter of this book, you will learn about the Python virtual environment to solve this environment change issue. Along with this, you will also learn some of the best practices while working on your first Data Science project.

Structure

- What is a Python virtual environment?
- How to create and activate a virtual environment?
- How to open Jupyter notebook with this new environment?
- How to set up an activated virtual environment in PyCharm IDE?

- What is the `requirements.txt` file?

- What is `README.md` file?

- Upload your project in GitHub

Objective

The main objective of this chapter is to teach you some best practices while working on a project. In the real world, you use your Jupyter notebook for your analysis. Still, you will share your final analysis in the form of a project consisting of Python file/files, txt files organized in several folders. After completing this chapter, you will be quite familiar with such best practices.

What is a Python virtual environment?

If you open the Anaconda Prompt, you will see the following text is showing at the start of the prompt - (base) just as in the following screenshot:

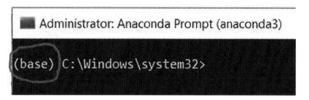

Figure 21.1: Anaconda prompt

As the name says, it is the default base environment of your Python and other libraries installed. Instead of using this base environment, from now onwards, you will use an isolated Python environment, known as the Python virtual environment. The benefit of using this environment is that every new project has its own Python version and other dependent Python libraries. You don't need to uninstall and reinstall Python with every new project. The beauty of using a Python virtual environment is that there are no limits to its number. You can create as many environments as you want.

How to create and activate a virtual environment?

Since we are using Anaconda from the beginning of this book, we will use conda to create and activate a virtual environment in our machine. To create a Python virtual environment, open Anaconda Prompt with admin rights and use the following command: `conda create --name <Virtual_ENV_NAME> python=<Version>`

Please replace <Virtual_ENV_NAME> with any name and <Version> with your specific Python version. If you want to check the Python version installed in your machine, just run python -version in the same Anaconda prompt. Following is a screenshot of my Anaconda Prompt:

```
(base) C:\Windows\system32>conda create --name new_py_virtual python=3.7.3
```

Figure 21.2: new_py_virtual Anaconda prompt

In the preceding example, I have given my virtual environment name as new_py_ virtual, and my Python version is 3.7.3. Once you run this command, the prompt will take a few seconds, and it will collect all required packages for creating your new Python virtual environment:

```
Administrator: Anaconda Prompt (anaconda3) - conda  create --name new_py_virtual python=3.7.3                          —

(base) C:\Windows\system32>conda create --name new_py_virtual python=3.7.3
Collecting package metadata (current_repodata.json): done
Solving environment: failed with repodata from current_repodata.json, will retry with next repodata source.
Collecting package metadata (repodata.json): done
Solving environment: done

## Package Plan ##

  environment location: C:\Users\prateek.g\AppData\Local\Continuum\anaconda3\envs\new_py_virtual

  added / updated specs:
    - python=3.7.3


The following NEW packages will be INSTALLED:

  ca-certificates    pkgs/main/win-64::ca-certificates-2019.11.27-0
  certifi            pkgs/main/win-64::certifi-2019.11.28-py37_0
  openssl            pkgs/main/win-64::openssl-1.1.1d-he774522_3
  pip                pkgs/main/win-64::pip-19.3.1-py37_0
  python             pkgs/main/win-64::python-3.7.3-h8c8aaf0_1
  setuptools         pkgs/main/win-64::setuptools-44.0.0-py37_0
  sqlite             pkgs/main/win-64::sqlite-3.30.1-he774522_0
  vc                 pkgs/main/win-64::vc-14.1-h0510ff6_4
  vs2015_runtime     pkgs/main/win-64::vs2015_runtime-14.16.27012-hf0eaf9b_1
  wheel              pkgs/main/win-64::wheel-0.33.6-py37_0
  wincertstore       pkgs/main/win-64::wincertstore-0.2-py37_0


Proceed ([y]/n)?
```

Figure 21.3: New Python virtual environment

When asked, press y and enter. It will install the required packages, and your new Python virtual environment will be created:

```
Proceed ([y]/n)? y

Preparing transaction: done
Verifying transaction: done
Executing transaction: done
#
# To activate this environment, use
#
#     $ conda activate new_py_virtual
#
# To deactivate an active environment, use
#
#     $ conda deactivate


(base) C:\Windows\system32>
```

Figure 21.4: Installing required packages

Once the new environment is created, we need to activate it. You can activate it by running the following command: `conda activate <Virtual_ENV_NAME>`. The same command you can also see in your Anaconda Prompt console:

```
(base) C:\Windows\system32>conda activate new_py_virtual

(new_py_virtual) C:\Windows\system32>
```

Figure 21.5: Activating the new enviornment

Notice the starting line of your console. In my example, the (base) environment is changed to (`new_py_virtual`). In the same way, you will see your environment name. This means you have successfully created and activated the environment. Now you can install any Python package using command `pip install <package_name>` in this newly created virtual environment. Once you finish your work, you can close this console, and when you want to start your work again, you just need to open Anaconda Prompt, run the following command `conda activate <Virtual_ENV_NAME>`. That's it. Your previous environment is ready for reuse. If you want to create another Python virtual environment, open a different Anaconda Prompt, and repeat the previously mentioned steps with your required Python version and with a different environment name.

How to open Jupyter notebook with this new environment?

Once you create your new Python virtual environment and install all required Python packages, the next step is to open your Jupyter notebook with this environment. The step is straightforward. You just need to use the `jupyter notebook` command in the same Anaconda Prompt. Before using that command, you will first create a new directory, and from there, you will open your Jupyter notebook. It is our first good practice to create a directory structure for our project. For this first step, create a new folder in your local disk and copy its path. For example, I have created a new folder named as `example_notebook` in the following path `E:\prateekg\docs\BPB\Bonus\` and copied the path till the newly created folder. In my case, the full path is `E:\prateekg\docs\BPB\Bonus\` example. Now in the same Anaconda Prompt, go to the path you have copied and run the following command: `jupyter notebook --notebook-dir <path_till_new_folder>`.

My Anaconda Prompt screen looks like the following screenshot:

Figure 21.6: Opening a Jupyter Notebook

Once you press *Enter*, a new browser window will open showing your notebook folder. In my case, it looks like the following screenshot:

Figure 21.7: Browser window

In the same way, you can also open any existing notebook. You just need to give its path to the command `jupyter notebook --notebook-dir`. For creating a new Jupyter notebook, just click on **New** dropdown, select **Python 3,** and it will open a new notebook in a new tab.

How to set an activated virtual environment in PyCharm IDE?

Till now, you have learned the setup of the Python virtual environment with your notebook. Next step is to learn how to do the same with PyCharm IDE. Once you set this up, you can directly run your Python files in PyCharm console. Since in the real-world project, you will most probably use PyCharm IDE, I will show you how to complete this setup. If you have not installed PyCharm IDE in your machine, please follow *Chapter 4: Package, Function and Loop* of this book, where I have already described this. Open PyCharm, go to **File** and click on the **Open** link. Paste the path of your newly created folder. Make sure that after pasting the path, your folder should be selected automatically. If not, then manually select the folder. The screen will look like the following screenshot:

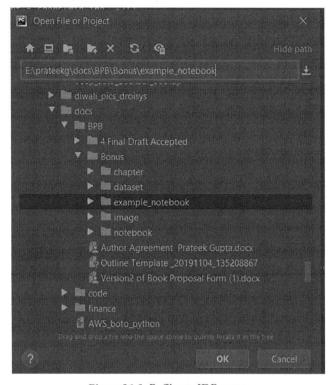

Figure 21.8: PyCharm IDE screen

Click on **OK** button, PyCharm will be opened and it will start the indexing of your imported project. The project will look like the following screenshot in PyCharm:

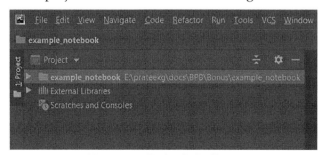

Figure 21.9: Project in PyCharm

Now, we will setup our virtual environment with this project. For this purpose, press *Ctrl+Alt+s* keys or choose **File** | **Settings** (for Windows and Linux or PyCharm) | **Preferences** for macOS. Then select **Project <project name>** | **Project Interpreter**. It will open the following pop-up in your screen:

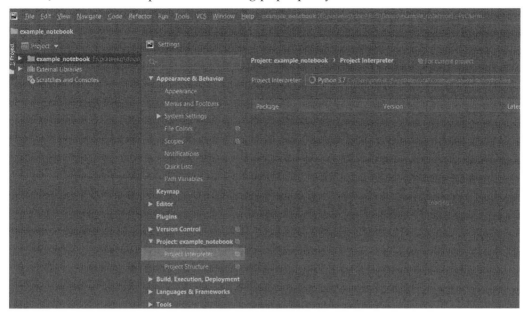

Figure 21.10: *Project Interpreter in PyCharm*

Once you select the **Project Interpreter** option, on the right-hand side, you will see a drop-down under the name **Project Interpreter**. Click on that drop-down and select **Show All...** option. Now select the option having your newly created environment name, if it exists, or click on **+** icon to manually search it. In my case, I clicked on **+** icon, and a new pop up appeared. From there, select **Conda Environment** as shown on the left menu and then select **Existing Environment**. Next, from the dropdown next to this option, select the option having your newly created virtual environment name and click on Ok buttons till you come in the main PyCharm window:

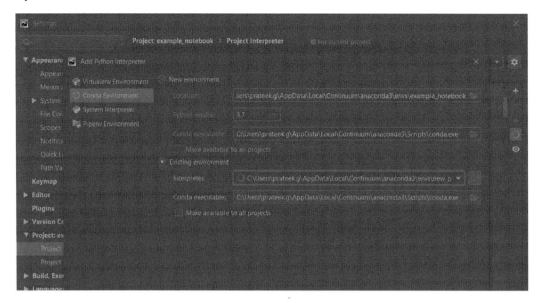

Figure 21.11: Virtual environment Settings

Once you click on all **OK** buttons, PyCharm will start the indexing of your project. You can see this process in the bottom right-most corner of your PyCharm IDE. It looks like the following screenshot:

Figure 21.12: Indexing in PyCharm

Wait for this indexing to complete. Once it's done, your project is configured with this virtual environment. When you open PyCharm IDE next time, you don't need to do this step again. PyCharm will automatically use this virtual environment with this project.

What is requirements.txt file?

Till now, we have created our project directory and imported it in PyCharm IDE with a virtual environment. The next step is to make a `requirements.txt` file in our project. `requirements.txt` file is a simple text file containing your installed Python libraries with its version as key-value pairs. This file is required to setup your project quickly in any new environment. Any new user can read this file and simply run this instead of installing packages one by one. To create this file, we will use the `pip freeze` command. Open a new Anaconda Prompt, activate your newly created Python virtual environment, and go to the path of your project directory. In my case, it looks like the following screenshot:

▪ Administrator: Anaconda Prompt (anaconda3)

```
(base) C:\Windows\system32>activate new_py_virtual

(new_py_virtual) C:\Windows\system32>cd E:\prateekg\docs\BPB\Bonus\example_notebook

(new_py_virtual) C:\Windows\system32>e:

(new_py_virtual) E:\prateekg\docs\BPB\Bonus\example_notebook>
```

Figure 21.13: Path of the project directory

Now run the following command: `pip freeze > requirements.txt`. This command will save all your Python libraries in a newly created `.txt` file. Once you run the preceding command, go to your project folder, where you will find your `requirements.txt` file. The same you can also see in PyCharm IDE. For my project, it looks like the following in PyCharm:

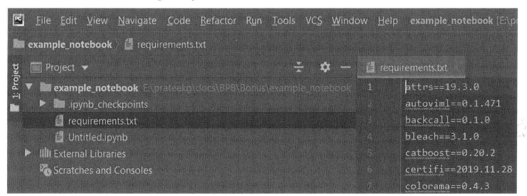

Figure 21.14: requirements.txt file view

If you see `requirements.txt` file, as shown in the preceding screenshot, it means you have successfully created it. Now anyone can install all required libraries of your project in his/her machine by just running the following command: `pip install -r requirements.txt`.

What is README.md file?

The next best practice to use in your project is to have a `README.md` file. This file contains information about your project in such a way that a new user can understand the goal of your project, how to setup, and be able to run the code. Since this is the first file that any new user searches in a project, it should be good enough to understand. You can create a simple text file and change its extension to `.md` from

.txt for creating this file. Here, the extension .md means markdown. It's a mark-up language for text formatting. You can edit this file in any text editor. For creating this file in PyCharm, right-click on your project, go to **New**, and select **File** option:

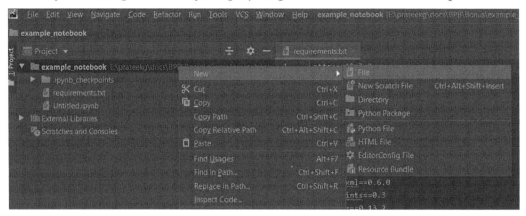

Figure 21.15: Creating readme.md file

Enter the name as README.md and click on the **OK** button. This file is created in your project directory. The next step is to fill this file as per your project. Here, I am sharing a snippet of this file, in which you can use a template for your project and can easily edit as per your need.

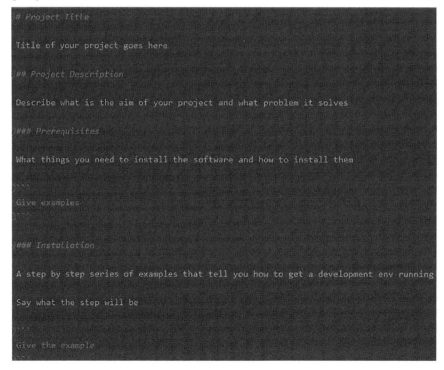

Figure 21.16: README.md file preview

You can find the complete project structure in our shared repository. In the next few chapter, you will add on new files in this project structure, and in the end, you will have a complete project structure.

Upload your project in GitHub

Once your project is ready, you will need to share it with other team members, so that they can use it. For sharing, copy-pasting the code and shaing via mail or pen-drive, is a very bad practice, and often restricted in an organization. For this purpose, you should know how to use GitHub. GitHub is a Git repository hosting service, and it provides a web-based interface. To use this, you need to register yourself in GitHub first. Open the following link in the browser: **https://github.com/** and click on **Sign up** link for registration. Once you are successfully registered, the next step is to create a repository there. After logging into GitHub, you will see the new button on the right side of the **Repositories**:

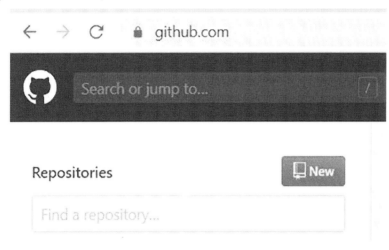

Figure 21.17: *Repository in GitHub*

Click on **New** button. A new screen will be opened and you will be asked to enter the repository name. Fill the name field and click on `Create repository` button:

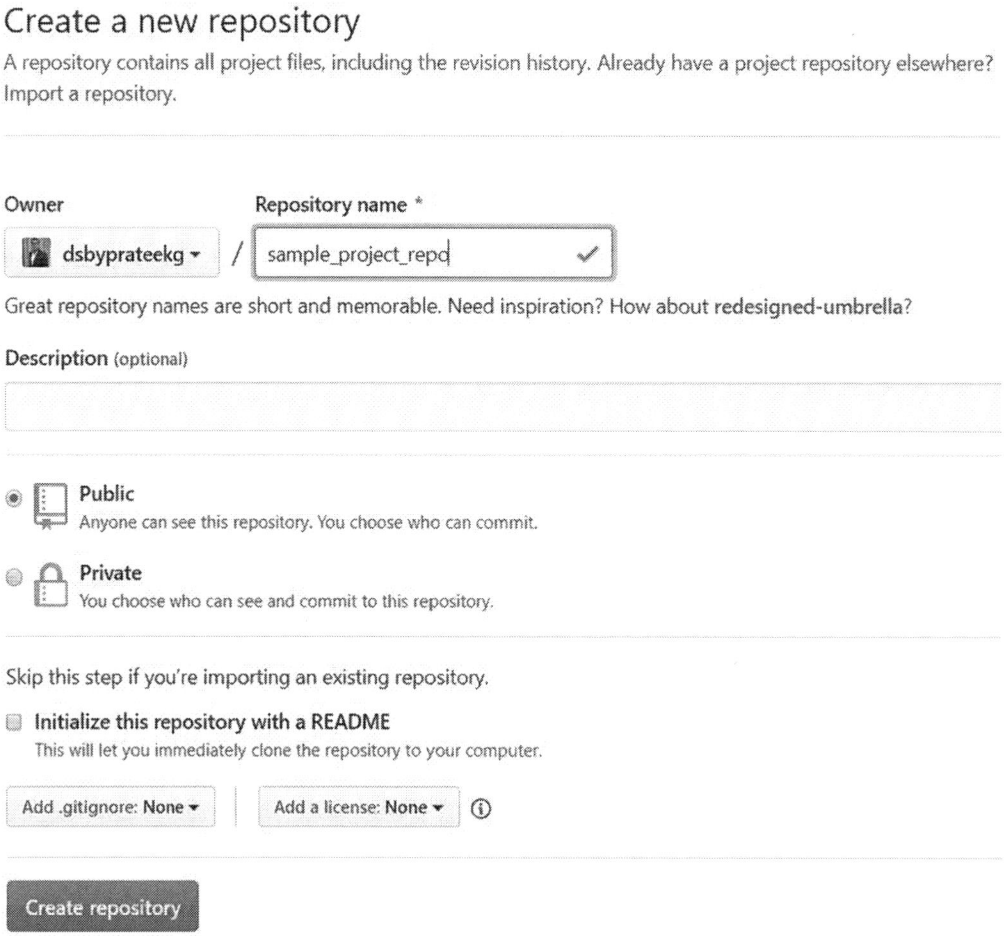

Create a new repository

A repository contains all project files, including the revision history. Already have a project repository elsewhere? Import a repository.

Owner   Repository name *

  dsbyprateekg ▾ / sample_project_repo   ✓

Great repository names are short and memorable. Need inspiration? How about **redesigned-umbrella**?

Description (optional)

◉ 📘 **Public**
  Anyone can see this repository. You choose who can commit.

◯ 🔒 **Private**
  You choose who can see and commit to this repository.

Skip this step if you're importing an existing repository.

☐ **Initialize this repository with a README**
  This will let you immediately clone the repository to your computer.

Add .gitignore: None ▾ | Add a license: None ▾ ⓘ

Create repository

Figure 21.18: Creating new repository

Once you click on `Create repository`, a new screen will be opened, asking you to upload existing code in the repository. For this, we will use the command-line option. For the command-line option, we will use the Git Bash. You can download the Git Bash from the following link: **https://gitforwindows.org/**.

Once you download and install the Git Bash, just type Git Bash from search option in your windows machine and click on Git Bash. It will open a command-line console. Now, copy your newly created project directory path and paste the following: cd `E:/prateekg/docs/BPB/Bonus/example_notebook`. Don't forget to replace '\' with '/' before running the command. It looks like the following screenshot:

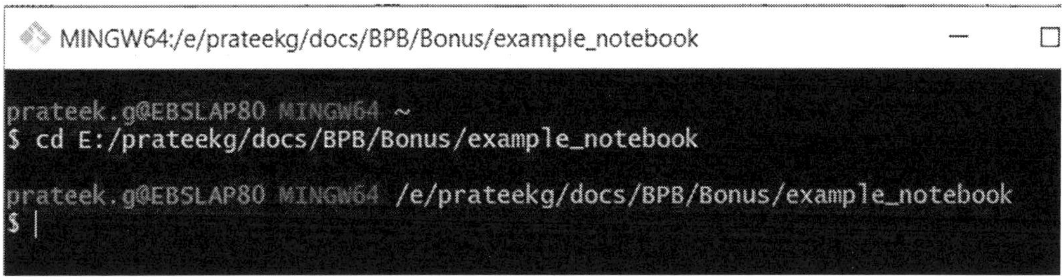

Figure 21.19: GitBash command window

Next, you just need to run the following commands one-by-one:

```
git init
git add <your_file_to_add>
git commit -m <"commit_message">
git remote add origin <your_repo_git_link>
git push -u origin master
```

For example, when I run command `git` in it, my repository is initialized:

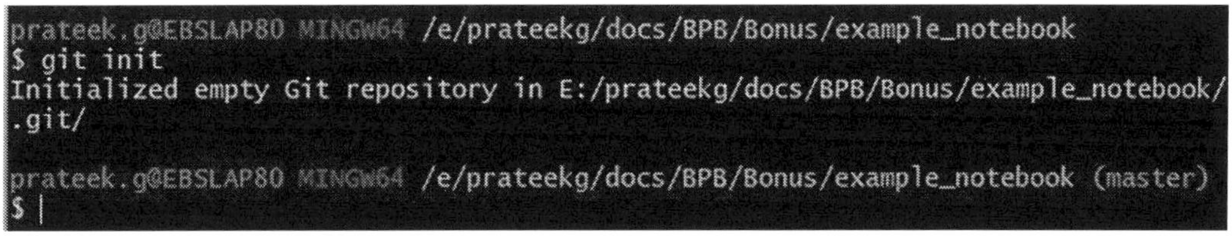

Figure 21.20: initializing the repo in GitBash

Next, the second command will add my files to the repository. If you want to add all files at once, you just need to give a dot(.) instead of the file name. I recommend adding files one by one to avoid any error:

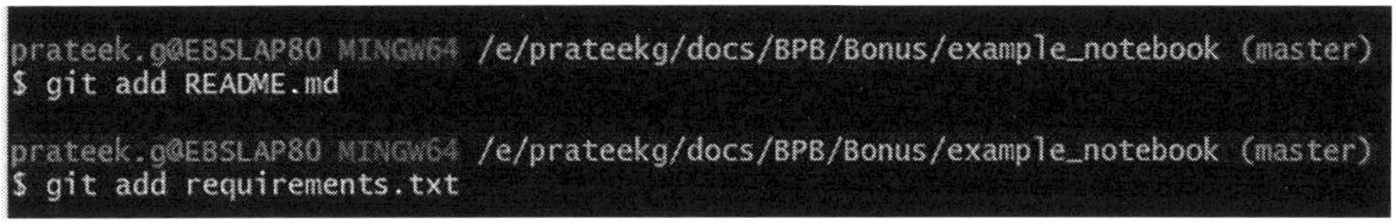

Figure 21.21: Adding files

After adding files, we need to commit these files with a message using the third command:

```
prateek.g@EBSLAP80 MINGW64 /e/prateekg/docs/BPB/Bonus/example_notebook (master)
$ git commit -m "first commit"
[master (root-commit) 2c1bd30] first commit
 Committer: Prateek Gupta <prateek.g@droisys.local>
Your name and email address were configured automatically based
on your username and hostname. Please check that they are accurate.
You can suppress this message by setting them explicitly. Run the
following command and follow the instructions in your editor to edit
your configuration file:

    git config --global --edit

After doing this, you may fix the identity used for this commit with:

    git commit --amend --reset-author

 2 files changed, 113 insertions(+)
 create mode 100644 README.md
 create mode 100644 requirements.txt
```

Figure 21.22: Committing files

After committing the files, we need to push our local repository to the remote repository using the fourth command:

```
prateek.g@EBSLAP80 MINGW64 /e/prateekg/docs/BPB/Bonus/example_notebook (master)
$ git remote add origin https://github.com/dsbyprateekg/sample_project_repo.git
```

Figure 21.23: Pushing local repository to remote repository

As the last step, we just need to push local changes to our GitHub repository using the fifth command:

```
prateek.g@EBSLAP80 MINGW64 /e/prateekg/docs/BPB/Bonus/example_notebook (master)
$ git push -u origin master
Enumerating objects: 4, done.
Counting objects: 100% (4/4), done.
Delta compression using up to 12 threads
Compressing objects: 100% (4/4), done.
Writing objects: 100% (4/4), 1.24 KiB | 1.24 MiB/s, done.
Total 4 (delta 0), reused 0 (delta 0)
To https://github.com/dsbyprateekg/sample_project_repo.git
 * [new branch]      master -> master
Branch 'master' set up to track remote branch 'master' from 'origin'.
```

Figure 21.24: Pushing local changes to GitHub repository

That's it! Now, when you refresh your GitHub profile, you will see your added files, `README.md` and `requirements.txt`, as shown in the following screenshot:

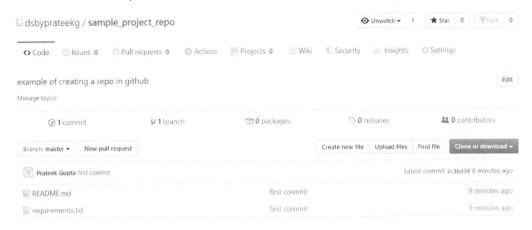

Figure 21.25: Files added

Conclusion

In this chapter, you have learned some of the best practices that you will use in any organization. Python virtual environment gives you the ability and freedom to install a specific version of packages. On the other hand, `requirements.txt` file makes your project easy to install in any other system, and from `README.md` file, any new user can understand your work easily. You also learned how to use GitHub. Follow the steps mentioned in this chapter, or download the project from our repository, import it in PyCharm, and use this as a template for any of your projects. In the next chapter, you will learn about a new gradient boosting algorithm – CatBoost.

## CHAPTER 22

Introduction to An Advanced Algorithm - CatBoost

In *Chapter 13: Supervised Machine Learning* and *Chapter 14: Unsupervised Machine Learning*, you have learned how to solve supervised and unsupervised machine learning problems using Python's `scikit-learn` library. One essential step in using the `scikit-learn` library is to handle categorical data before modeling. What technique we use for converting the categorical data into numerical form affects the model performance directly. Leaving certain features means making your prediction weak. So it is an important step and requires strong knowledge of your dataset. What if this step can be automated? What if instead of focusing on this conversion, you can give your attention to training? Sounds interesting! In this chapter, you will learn one of the advanced algorithm - CatBoost, which will automate this conversion for you.

Structure

- What is a Gradient Boosting algorithm?
- Introduction to CatBoost
- Install CatBoost in Python Virtual Environment
- How to solve a classification problem with CatBoost?
- Push your notebook in your GitHub repository

Objective

Data Science is an emerging field. The frequency of new algorithm coming in this field is very rapid. Every new algorithm comes in the market with improved features, and they outperform older algorithms. As a Data Scientist, we need to update ourselves daily, and we should try to use them in our work. Following the same thought, in this chapter, you will learn about gradient boosting and CatBoost algorithms. Also, you will learn how to use CatBoost in solving a real dataset problem.

What is a Gradient Boosting algorithm?

Gradient boosting is an efficient algorithm for converting weak learners into better learners. Here, a weak learner is also known as a weak hypothesis. Adaptive Boosting, also known as AdaBoost, was the first boosting algorithm. The three essential elements used by a gradient boosting algorithm are loss function, weak learner, and additive model. You have used different loss functions in classification, and regression problems, for example, mean squared error and logarithmic loss. So, as per the type of problem, gradient boosting algorithm uses the loss function. For choosing the weak learner, gradient boosting chooses decision trees. Here, trees are constructed with best split points, and subsequent models are added to correct the errors in predictions. Please note here that trees are added one at a time, and existing trees are not changed in this algorithm. While adding the trees, this algorithm makes sure to minimize the loss. Examples of gradient boosting algorithms are CatBoost, XGBoost, and LightGBM. These algorithms have achieved the state-of-the-art results in a variety of practical tasks. Our focus in this chapter will be on CatBoost.

Introduction to CatBoost

CatBoost, developed by *Yandex* researchers and engineers in 2017, is a high performance open source library for gradient boosting on decision trees. With default parameters, CatBoost gives excellent results, and it works very fast on large datasets using GPU. It reduces overfitting while constructing a model, and it can handle certain features automatically. CatBoost can be used to solve both classification and regression problems. The most attractive feature of CatBoost is to handle certain features. Here, certain feature is a feature having a discrete set of values that are not necessarily comparable with each other, for example, city name. We generally convert these features into numerical form before the training. CatBoost handles categorical features during the training time and we don't need to convert them into numerical form. You will learn about its parameters later in this chapter.

Install CatBoost in Python virtual environment

In the previous chapter, you created a virtual environment using conda command. We will use the same environment from now onwards. You can again use that environment. For this open Anaconda Prompt with admin rights, activate the environment by just running the following command: `conda activate <Virtual_ENV_NAME>`. Your base location will be changed to your virtual environment name. Now, install the CatBoost using the following command: `pip install catboost`:

```
■ Administrator: Anaconda Prompt (anaconda3)

(base) C:\Windows\system32>activate new_py_virtual

(new_py_virtual) C:\Windows\system32>pip install catboost
```

Figure 22.1: Installing CatBoost

CatBoost has some inbuilt visualization capability. For using this capability, you need to run the following command as well: `pip install ipywidgets`, and then you need to activate the notebook widget by running the following command: `jupyter nbextension enable --py widgetsnbextension`:

```
(new_py_virtual) C:\Windows\system32>jupyter nbextension enable --py widgetsnbextension
Enabling notebook extension jupyter-js-widgets/extension...
      - Validating: ok
```

Figure 22.2: Enabling catboost widgets

Once you see the ok message in the console, it means you have successfully installed the CatBoost. While installing, if you get any `Module Not found` Error, then please install that library using `pip install` command and then proceed to the next step.

How to solve a classification problem with CatBoost?

Once you complete the previous step, you are ready to use CatBoost. Let's open our notebook in our activated virtual environment, as we did in the previous chapter:

```
(new_py_virtual) C:\Windows\system32>jupyter notebook --notebook-dir E:\prateekg\docs\BPB\Bonus\example_notebook
```

Figure 22.3: Open notebook

Once the notebook is opened in the browser, create a new notebook there and give it a name. Now to understand how to use CatBoost, we must use a dataset. Infact, to understand CatBoost's categorical feature handling capability, we need a dataset that has more certain features; also that dataset should be a real-world dataset. We don't need to go anywhere to download such a dataset. CatBoost provides inbuilt datasets processing with some real-world datasets, including UCI Adult Data Set, Kaggle Amazon Employee Access Data Set, Kaggle Titanic Data Set, etc.; you can load these datasets from `catboost.datasets` directly. For our first example of this chapter, we will use the Titanic Data Set. You can find this dataset description from the following link: **https://www.kaggle.com/c/titanic/data**. Let's load this dataset along with NumPy, as shown in the following screenshot:

```
# load titanic dataset and numpy library
from catboost.datasets import titanic
import numpy as np
```

Figure 22.4: Loading Titanic Data set

After running the preceding cell, the Titanic dataset will be imported. After importing the dataset, the next step is to load the training and testing dataset. For this, we just need to fetch the `titanic()` function. Let's fetch both datasets and check the shape of the loaded datasets:

```
# read training and test dataset
train_df, test_df = titanic()
# print datasets shape
train_df.shape, test_df.shape

((891, 12), (418, 11))
```

Figure 22.5: Checking shape of datasets

So, we have 891 samples in the training dataset and 418 samples in the testing dataset. Let's check the top five data of the training dataset using dataframe's `head()` function:

```
# check training dataset top 5 content
train_df.head()
```

	PassengerId	Survived	Pclass	Name	Sex	Age	SibSp	Parch	Ticket	Fare	Cabin	Embarked
0	1	0	3	Braund, Mr. Owen Harris	male	22.0	1	0	A/5 21171	7.2500	NaN	S
1	2	1	1	Cumings, Mrs. John Bradley (Florence Briggs Th...	female	38.0	1	0	PC 17599	71.2833	C85	C
2	3	1	3	Heikkinen, Miss. Laina	female	26.0	0	0	STON/O2. 3101282	7.9250	NaN	S
3	4	1	1	Futrelle, Mrs. Jacques Heath (Lily May Peel)	female	35.0	1	0	113803	53.1000	C123	S
4	5	0	3	Allen, Mr. William Henry	male	35.0	0	0	373450	8.0500	NaN	S

Figure 22.6: Using head() function

Here, the `Survived` column is our target variable, which we need to predict for testing dataset. 1 (yes) means a person had survived, and 0 (no) means the person has not survived. Next, we will check the data type of the columns:

```
# check data types
train_df.dtypes

PassengerId        int64
Survived           int64
Pclass             int64
Name              object
Sex               object
Age              float64
SibSp              int64
Parch              int64
Ticket            object
Fare             float64
Cabin             object
Embarked          object
dtype: object
```

Figure 22.7: Checking datatype of columns

As you can see, there are many categorical columns in this dataset, which is indeed needed here! But before applying CatBoost, we must check the missing values and then fix them. Let's check the missing values first:

```
# check missing values
train_df.isnull().sum()

PassengerId          0
Survived             0
Pclass               0
Name                 0
Sex                  0
Age                177
SibSp                0
Parch                0
Ticket               0
Fare                 0
Cabin              687
Embarked             2
dtype: int64
```

Figure 22.8: Checking missing values

From the preceding output cell, we can see that the Age column has 177, Cabin column has 687, and the Embarked column has two missing values in our training dataset. Check for yourself, the missing values in the testing dataset, as well! Now we will fix each missing value one-by-one. Let's fill the Age column's missing values with it's median:

```
# fill missing values in Age column with median
train_df['Age'] = train_df['Age'].fillna((train_df['Age'].median()))
test_df['Age'] = test_df['Age'].fillna((test_df['Age'].median()))
```

Figure 22.9: Fixing missing values

Next, we will fill the Embarked column's missing values with the most frequent one:

```
# fill missing values in Embarked column with the most frequent one
train_df.Embarked.fillna('S', inplace=True)
test_df.Embarked.fillna('S', inplace=True)
```

Figure 22.10: Filling missing values in Embarked column

Now, the last remaining column with missing values is Cabin, and it is in very high number. Instead of removing this column, let's fill this column's missing values with any random string:

```
# Replace missing values with "U0" in Cabin column in both dataset
train_df['Cabin'][train_df.Cabin.isnull()] = 'U0'
test_df['Cabin'][test_df.Cabin.isnull()] = 'U0'
```

Figure 22.11: Replacing missing values in Cabin column

Have you checked the missing values in the testing dataset? If yes, you will see there is an extra column with missing values - Fare. Let's handle this column's missing values also:

```
# fill missing value in Fare column with median
test_df['Fare'] = test_df['Fare'].fillna((test_df['Fare'].median()))
```

Figure 22.12: Handling missing values in Fare column

Now, if you check the missing values in both dataset again, you will find all missing values are filled. In the next step, we will separate the target column from our training dataset:

```
# Now our train and test dataset have no missing values
# Let's seperate target variable from training dataset
X = train_df.drop('Survived', axis=1)
y = train_df.Survived
```

Figure 22.13: Separating target column from training dataset

Next, we will split the training dataset into training and validation dataset to avoid overfitting:

```
# split our training dataset into train and validate datasets
from sklearn.model_selection import train_test_split

X_train, X_validation, y_train, y_validation = train_test_split(X, y, train_size=0.75, random_state=123)

X_test = test_df
```

Figure 22.14: Splitting training dataset

Until now, all steps that we have followed here, you have already seen in *Chapter 13* and *Chapter 14* of this book. There is nothing new. Now, we can move to our main goal - how to use CatBoost? For this, let's import CatBoost and other required libraries and then create CatBoost classifier model, as shown in the following screenshot:

```
# import CatBoost and required libraries
from catboost import CatBoostClassifier, Pool, cv
from sklearn.metrics import accuracy_score
```

```
# create a simple CatBoost model
model = CatBoostClassifier(eval_metric='Accuracy', use_best_model=True, random_seed=42)
```

Figure 22.15: Importing CatBoost

In the preceding input cells, we have first imported the `CatBoostClassifier`, since our problem is a classification `ml` problem. If you are working on the regression `ml` problem, then you need to use `CatBoostRegressor`. Next, we have imported `Pool`. `Pool` class is used for data processing in `CatBoost`. We pass our features data into the `Pool` constructor. The `cv` is used for doing cross-validation. You will see the exact use of these in further steps. While initializing our classifier, we have enabled `use_best_model` parameter for saving the best model:

Next, we will make a list of certain features. Here, I am making this list with all columns having `object` data type. You can update the list as per your understanding of the categorical features. Then I will pass this list in the model training step, as shown in the following screenshot:

```
string_features = ['Name', 'Sex', 'Ticket', 'Cabin', 'Embarked']
```

```
# start training of the model
model.fit(X_train, y_train, cat_features = string_features, eval_set=(X_validation, y_validation), plot=True)
```

Figure 22.16: Training of the model

Here, for model training, we are using `mode.fit()` function, which you already know. Along with parameters like - input training `dataset(X_train)`, and target `variable(y_train)`, here, we are passing our categorical features list in `cat_ features` parameter. This is the parameter that will take care of all heavy lifting with certain features. For validation purposes, we have used `eval_set` parameter with our validation dataset, and also enabled another interesting parameter - plot. The plot feature will plot metric values, custom loss values, and time data during training. Once you run the preceding cell, model training will start, and during the training, you will see a running plot in the Jupyter notebook output cell until the training ends. In the end, you will see the number of boosting steps with the best accuracy on validation dataset, as shown in the following screenshot:

```
bestTest = 0.8744394619
bestIteration = 165

Shrink model to first 166 iterations.

: <catboost.core.CatBoostClassifier at 0x1e479c26b00>
```

Figure 22.17: Best iteration and accuracy

See, without handling certain features on your own, you have got 87% validation accuracy. Sounds great, right! Let's cross-validate our model by doing some cross-validation also. For this, we will use 5-fold cross-validation with `Pool` constructor, as shown in the following screenshot:

```
#for the data is not so big, we use the cross-validation(cv) for the model, to find how
#good the model is ,I just use the 5-fold cv
cv_params = model.get_params()
cv_params.update({
    'loss_function': 'Logloss'
})
cv_data = cv(Pool(X,y,cat_features=string_features),cv_params,fold_count=5,plot=True)
```

Figure 22.18: Using 5-fold cross-validation with Pool constructor

Here, we are using logarithmic loss as our loss function and five-fold for cross-validation. You can change the value of `fold_count` from 5 to 10, or it's default value three and see the effect on your own. Once you run the preceding cell, you will again see the plot during the cross-validation. You can click anywhere on this plot and it will show you some interesting points in zoom:

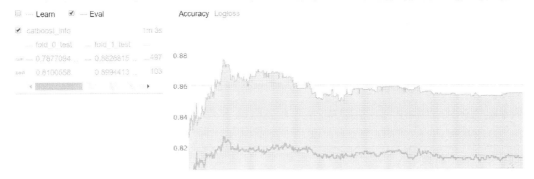

Figure 22.19: Plot of CV during training

Once the cross-validation is done, you will see the training and validation accuracy, as shown in the following screenshot:

```
994:    learn: 0.9826047    test: 0.8114030 best: 0.8260354 (103)    total: 2m 17s    remaining: 688ms
995:    learn: 0.9826047    test: 0.8114030 best: 0.8260354 (103)    total: 2m 17s    remaining: 551ms
996:    learn: 0.9826047    test: 0.8125330 best: 0.8260354 (103)    total: 2m 17s    remaining: 413ms
997:    learn: 0.9826047    test: 0.8125330 best: 0.8260354 (103)    total: 2m 17s    remaining: 276ms
998:    learn: 0.9826047    test: 0.8114030 best: 0.8260354 (103)    total: 2m 17s    remaining: 138ms
999:    learn: 0.9826047    test: 0.8114030 best: 0.8260354 (103)    total: 2m 17s    remaining: 0us
```

Figure 22.20: Training and validation accuracy

You can also print the best `cv` accuracy, as shown in the following screenshot:

```
# print best result
print('Best validation accuracy score: {:.2f}±{:.2f} on step {}'.format(
    np.max(cv_data['test-Accuracy-mean']),
    cv_data['test-Accuracy-std'][np.argmax(cv_data['test-Accuracy-mean'])],
    np.argmax(cv_data['test-Accuracy-mean'])
))
```

Figure 22.21: Printing best cv accuracy

The output of the preceding cell is shown in the following screenshot:

```
Best validation accuracy score: 0.83±0.05 on step 103
```

Figure 22.22: Best accuracy result

Let's print the precise validation score as well:

```
# validate accuracy
print('Precise validation accuracy score: {}'.format(np.max(cv_data['test-Accuracy-mean'])))
```

```
Precise validation accuracy score: 0.8383838383838383
```

Figure 22.23: *Printing precise validation score*

We are getting 83% accuracy with `CatBoost`. It's amazing right? Try the same dataset and use some other classification algorithms, which you have learnt earlier and see if you can match this accuracy. Next, you can make prediction on some data with this model. For making prediction, you just need to call `model.predict(X_test)`. In the next step, you can save this model, and then reload the saved model for your further use, as shown in the following screenshot:

```
# save our model
model.save_model('catboost_titanic_model.dump')
```

```
# load saved model
model.load_model('catboost_titanic_model.dump')
```

```
<catboost.core.CatBoostClassifier at 0x1e479c26b00>
```

Figure 22.24: *Reloading saved model*

Since this dataset is from Kaggle, it requires final submission in specific CSV format having `PassengerId` and `Survived` columns only. Let's make prediction on test data and save them in Kaggle required format:

```
# make the kaggle submission file
import pandas as pd
submission = pd.DataFrame()
submission['PassengerId'] = X_test['PassengerId']
submission['Survived'] = model.predict(X_test)
```

```
submission.to_csv('titanic_submission.csv', index=False)
```

Figure 22.25: *Making Kaggle submission file*

Push your notebook in your GitHub repository

In the previous chapter, you uploaded your project structure in your GitHub repository. Since you have solved anml problem in this chapter, it's time to push your changes to your repository. If you have successfully ended this chapter, then you will have a notebook, your saved model in `.dump` format, and your final submission file.

You will push all these into your GitHub repository. Before committing, it's better to make a new folder inside your project directory `catboost_example` and paste all required files there. Now, open GitBash and go to your project directory/path and run git commands, which you ran in the previous chapter one-by-one. Following are some screenshots of my terminal with output for the same:

◈ MINGW64:/e/prateekg/docs/BPB/Bonus/example_notebook

```
prateek.g@EBSLAP80 MINGW64 ~
$ cd E:/prateekg/docs/BPB/Bonus/example_notebook

prateek.g@EBSLAP80 MINGW64 /e/prateekg/docs/BPB/Bonus/example_notebook (master)
$ git init
Reinitialized existing Git repository in E:/prateekg/docs/BPB/Bonus/example_note
book/.git/

prateek.g@EBSLAP80 MINGW64 /e/prateekg/docs/BPB/Bonus/example_notebook (master)
$ git add catboost_example
warning: LF will be replaced by CRLF in catboost_example/Solving_a_classificatio
n_ml_problem_using_CatBoost.ipynb.
The file will have its original line endings in your working directory
```

Figure 22.26: Initialize and add changes to the Repo

```
prateek.g@EBSLAP80 MINGW64 /e/prateekg/docs/BPB/Bonus/example_notebook (master)
$ git commit -m "first commit"
[master 95f8769] first commit
 Committer: Prateek Gupta <prateek.g@droisys.local>
Your name and email address were configured automatically based
on your username and hostname. Please check that they are accurate.
You can suppress this message by setting them explicitly. Run the
following command and follow the instructions in your editor to edit
your configuration file:

    git config --global --edit

After doing this, you may fix the identity used for this commit with:

    git commit --amend --reset-author

 3 files changed, 7556 insertions(+)
 create mode 100644 catboost_example/Solving_a_classification_ml_problem_using_C
atBoost.ipynb
 create mode 100644 catboost_example/catboost_titanic_model.dump
 create mode 100644 catboost_example/titanic_submission.csv

prateek.g@EBSLAP80 MINGW64 /e/prateekg/docs/BPB/Bonus/example_notebook (master)
$ git push -u origin master
Enumerating objects: 7, done.
Counting objects: 100% (7/7), done.
Delta compression using up to 12 threads
Compressing objects: 100% (6/6), done.
Writing objects: 100% (6/6), 581.16 KiB | 8.18 MiB/s, done.
Total 6 (delta 0), reused 0 (delta 0)
To https://github.com/dsbyprateekg/sample_project_repo.git
   2c1bd30..95f8769  master -> master
Branch 'master' set up to track remote branch 'master' from 'origin'.
```

Figure 22.27: Pushing changes to the Repo

Once you refresh your GitHub repository page, you will see `catboost_example` folder with added files in your repository as I see in my repository:

Figure 22.28: CatBoost example folder with added files

Conclusion

In this chapter, you learnt an advanced gradient boosting algorithm, which, as of now, is being widely used in solving classification machine learning problems due to its higher speed and accuracy. You can find more details of CatBoost from their official link as well: **https://catboost.ai/docs/concepts/python-reference_parameters-list.html.** All the steps mentioned in this chapter are present as a Jupyter notebook `Solving_a_classification_ml_problem_using_CatBoost.ipynb` in our repository. I have also added an advanced notebook named as `performance_prediction_catboost_prateekg.ipynb`, which will guide you to use the best of the CatBoost to achieve the number one rank in a `hackethon`. Go ahead and download the notebook and see yourself in the first rank of that `hackethon`. In the next final chapter of this book, you will find a question-answer series related to the learning of all chapters, which will help you in your interview preparation as well.

CHAPTER 23

Revision of All Chapters' Learning

If you have completed all previous chapters of this book, you have gained all the essential skills of a Data Scientist that any company expects from a fresher. You have learned the required theory plus code implementation by working on real-world datasets. In this chapter, you will revise 51 must-know data science questions and their answers. These questions-answers will help you in your coming interviews since these basic questions are a must-know for cracking any Data Science interview. Although Data Science is a vast field, the starting point of any of your interviews will be these questions. So, let's start your revision.

1. **What do you understand by Data in Data Science?**

   Data is the plural form of datum, which means a single piece of information. Structured data, unstructured data, and semi-structured data are the three types of data we see on a daily basis. SQL data or tabular data is the example of structure data, images/audio/video/email, etc., are examples of unstructured data, and data in CSV/XML/JSON, etc., are known as semi-structured data.

2. **Explain Data in terms of Statistics?**

   In statistics, most of the data fall into the following two categories: Numerical data and Categorical data. Numerical data is also known as **Quantitative** data. **Numerical** data is further divided into the following two categories:

Discrete data and Continuous data. **Discrete** data have distinct and separate values. We can only count the discrete data, but we cannot measure it. For example, the number of heads count in 12 flips of a coin is discrete data. **Continuous** data can be measured but not counted, for example, the weight of a person. Categorical data represents characteristics, for example, a person's gender. We can represent them in number, but they don't have any meaning. Categorical data is also divided into the following two categories: **Nominal** and **Ordinal**. Nominal data represents discrete units and has no order, for example, language you speak. Ordinal data represents discrete units, but with an order, for example, your educational background.

3. **What essential tools with Python do you use for your Data Science work?**

Anaconda. It is an industry-standard for open source data science. We don't need to install Python separately if Anaconda is installed. It provides Jupyter notebook, which we use for our data science work. Besides Anaconda, we use PyCharm IDE for coding and GitHub repository for code pushing into the repository.

4. **What do you understand by machine learning (ML)?**

Machine learning is the science of getting computers or machines to act without being explicitly programmed. Machine learning helps computers to learn from past data and act accordingly for the new unseen data.

5. **What are the different types of machine learning (ML)?**

Based on the various data problem, machine learning (ML) is divided into the following three main types: **Supervised**, **Unsupervised**, and **Reinforcement** learning. In supervised ML, we have the past/previous data of a problem having input examples with the target variable. To solve such problems, this learning uses a model to learn the mapping between input and target. A model is fit on training data and then used to predict test data having input examples only. Unsupervised ML operates only on input data without the target variable. It works without any guidance. In reinforcement ML, an agent operates in an environment and learns from the feedback; for example, teaching a computer to play a game.

6. **What are the main types of supervised ML problems?**

Classification and **Regression** are the two types of supervised ML problems. In classification, we predict a class label, for example, predicting if a mail is a spam or ham. In regression, we predict a numerical value, for example, predicting house prices of an area.

7. **What algorithms do you use for solving a classification ML problem?**

    Logistic Regression, Decision Tree, K Nearest Neighbors, Linear Discriminant Analysis, Naive Bayes, Support Vector Machine, Random Forest, CatBoost, XGBoost, etc.

8. **What algorithms do you use for solving a regression ML problem?**

    Linear Regression, Decision Tree, K Nearest Neighbors, Support Vector Machine, Random Forest, CatBoost, XGBoost, etc.

9. **What are the main types of unsupervised ML problems?**

    Clustering and **Association** are the two main types of unsupervised ML problems. Clustering involves finding groups in data, for example, grouping online customers by their purchasing behaviors. The association involves finding rules that describe more significant portions of data, for example, person who purchased product A also tend to purchase product B.

10. **What are some popular unsupervised ML algorithms?**

    K-Means Clustering, Hierarchical Clustering, Principal component analysis, etc.

11. **What are parametric and non-parametric machine learning algorithms?**

    Any algorithm that makes strong assumptions about the form of the mapping or target function is called a parametric algorithm, and those who do not make strong assumptions about the mapping or target function are known as non-parametric ML algorithms. Linear Regression and Linear Discriminant Analysis are two examples of parametric algorithms. Decision Trees, Naïve Bayes, and Support Vector Machines are three examples of non-parametric ML algorithms.

12. **What is mapping function?**

    The mapping function, also known as the target function is a function that a supervised ML algorithm aims to approximate.

13. **What is Bias in machine learning (ML)?**

    Bias is the simplifying assumptions made by a model in machine learning (ML) to make the mapping/target function more comfortable to learn. Generally, parametric algorithms are high bias in nature.

14. **What is the Variance in machine learning (ML)?**

    Variance is the amount that the estimate of the target function will change if different training data was used. Generally, non-parametric algorithms are high variance in nature.

15. **What is the Bias-Variance trade-off?**

Any supervised machine learning algorithm aims to achieve low bias and low variance. As we know, parametric algorithms often have a high bias, but a low variance and non-parametric algorithms have high variance but low bias. Therefore, there is often a battle to balance out bias and variance in machine learning. This tension is known as the Bias-Variance trade-off. While solving an ML problem, we try to make a balance between bias and variance.

16. **What is overfitting and underfitting in ML?**

Overfitting and underfitting are the two leading causes of poor performance in machine learning. Overfitting means learning the training data so well but performing very poorly on new unseen data. Underfitting means neither learning the training data properly nor working properly in new unseen data. Overfitting is the most common problem in machine learning.

17. **How can you limit overfitting while solving an ML problem?**

We can limit overfitting by applying the following two essential techniques: **Use k-fold cross-validation** and **Hold back a validation dataset**. The benefit of using **k-fold cross-validation** technique is that it allows us to train and test our model k-times on different subsets of training data and build up an estimate of the performance of a machine learning model on unseen data. A **validation** dataset is simply a subset of our training data that we hold back from our machine learning algorithms until the very end of our project and then compare the training and validation dataset accuracy. Both techniques assure our model is generalized very well.

18. **Explain some common statistical summary you use in your analysis?**

1) **Mean**: Mean is the average of the numbers in a list or a dataset's column.

2) **Mode**: Mode is the most common number in a dataset or a list.

3) **Median**: Median is the middle of the set of numbers.

4) **Standard Deviation**: It is the average spread of the points from the mean value.

19. **What is a Linear Regression?**

Linear Regression is a statistical and machine learning model that assumes a linear relationship between the input variable (x) and the single output variable (y). When there are multiple input variables, it is known as multiple linear regression. The representation equation of a simple linear regression model is $y = c + m * x$ where c is the **intercept**, also known as **bias coefficient** and *m* is slope of the line. Learning a linear regression model means estimating the values of the coefficients used in the representation. So, the goal is to find the best estimates for the coefficients to minimize the errors in predicting *y* from *x*. We use linear regression to solve supervised (regression) ML problems. In Python, we use `scikit-learn.linear_model.LinearRegression` class to use this algorithm.

20. **What are the key assumptions of linear regression?**

To make best use of linear regression model, we must structure our data according to the following assumptions:

1) Linear regression assumes that the relationship between our input and output is linear.

2) Linear regression assumes that our input and output variables are not noisy.

3) Linear regression assumes that our input variables are not highly correlated.

4)   Linear regression assumes that our input and output variables have a Gaussian distribution.

5) Linear regression assumes that our input variables are in same scale.

21. **What is the most common method to calculate the values of the coefficients in linear regression model?**

Ordinary Least Squares: When we have more than one input, we can use Ordinary Least Squares to estimate the values of the coefficients. In Ordinary Least Squares method, for a given regression line through the data, we calculate the distance from each data point to the regression line, square it, and sum all of the squared errors together. This is the quantity that ordinary least squares seek to minimize.

22. **What are the two regularization methods for linear regression?**

Regularization methods are extensions of the training of the linear model. These methods not only minimize the sum of the squared error of the model on the training data using Ordinary Least Squares, they also reduce the complexity of the model. Two regularization methods for linear regression are as follows:

1) **Lasso Regression**: It is also called *L1 regularization* where Ordinary Least Squares method is modified to also minimize the absolute sum of the coefficients.

2) **Ridge Regression**: It is also called *L2 regularization* where Ordinary Least Squares method is modified to also minimize the squared absolute sum of the coefficients.

23. **What is Logistic Regression?**

Logistic Regression is a statistical and machine learning model, which is used to solve supervised (classification) ML problems. In fact, logistic regression is made for solving binary (two-class) classification problems, but it can be used for solving multi-class problem also. Logistic regression uses logistic or sigmoid function to model the probability of the default class. Logistic function is an S-shaped curve that can take any real number and map it between *0* and *1*. The equation of this function is *1 / (1 + e ^ -value)* where e is the base of natural logarithms and value is the actual numerical value we want to transform. Since logistic regression predicts the probabilities, the probability prediction is transformed into 0 or 1 by the logistic function. If the probability is greater than 0.5, we can take the output as a prediction for the default class (class 0), otherwise the prediction is for the other class (class 1). The coefficients of the logistic regression algorithm must be estimated from our training data. This is done using maximum-likelihood estimation. In Python, we use `sklearn.linear_model.LogisticRegression` class to use this algorithm.

24. **What are logistic regression assumptions?**

The assumptions made by logistic regression about the distribution and relationships in our data are much the same as the assumptions made in linear regression:

1) Logistic regression assumes a linear relationship between the input variables and the output.

2) Logistic Regression predicts the output in binary form.

3) Logistic regression assumes no error (outliers) in the output variable.

4) Logistic Regression assumes that our input variables are not highly correlated.

5) Logistic Regression assumes that input variables are in the same scale.

25. **What is Linear Discriminant Analysis?**

Logistic regression is a classification algorithm, traditionally limited to solve only two-class classification problems, and it can become unstable when the classes are well separated. If we have more than two classes, then the **Linear Discriminant Analysis (LDA)** addresses these points, and is the go-to linear method for multiclass classification problems. LDA assumes that our data is Gaussian (each variable is shaped like a bell curve when plotted) and each attribute has the same variance (values of each variable vary around the mean by the same amount on average). With these assumptions, the LDA model estimates the mean and variance from our data for each class. We use `sklearn.discriminant_analysis.LinearDiscriminantAnalysis` class to use this algorithm in Python.

26. **What are Decision Trees?**

Decision Trees are also known as **Classification and Regression Trees (CART)**, because this algorithm can be used to solve both types of supervised ML problems. The representation for the CART model is a binary tree, where each node represents a single input variable (x) and a split point on that variable, assuming the variable is numeric. The leaf nodes of the tree contain an output variable (y), which is used to make a prediction. CART uses a greedy approach to divide the input space where all the values are lined up, and different split points are tried and tested using a cost function. The split with the lowest cost is selected. A split point is a single value of a single attribute. All input variables and all possible split points are evaluated, and the very best split point is chosen each time. For classification ML problems, the Gini index function is used, which indicates how pure the leaf nodes are. For regression problems, the cost function, that is minimized to choose spit points, is the sum squared error.

27. **What is Naive Bayes?**

Naive Bayes is a classification algorithm for solving both binary and multiclass classification problems. It is called Naive Bayes because the calculation of the probabilities for each hypothesis is simplified to make their calculation tractable. Instead of calculating the values of each attribute value, they are assumed to be conditionally independent, given the target value. This assumption is extreme but works very well in real-world data. Training with this algorithm is high-speed, since no coefficients are needed to be fitted by optimization procedures, and only the probability of each class, and the probability of each class given different input (x) values, need to be calculated. We use `sklearn.naive_bayes` class to use this algorithm.

28. **What is hypothesis?**

A hypothesis is a function that best describes the target in our supervised machine learning problems. We can say that it is a guess that requires some evaluation. The hypothesis, that an algorithm would come up with, depends upon our data and also depends upon the restrictions and biases that we have imposed on our data. In statistics, we conduct some hypothetical tests on our data to draw some conclusion. A reasonable hypothesis is testable; it can be either true or false. These tests are conducted based on some assumptions, which lead us to the following two terms: **Null Hypothesis (H0)** and **Alternate Hypothesis (H1)**. H0 is the default assumption and suggests no effect, while H1 suggests some effect. H1 is the violation of the test's assumption. H1 means that the evidence suggests that the H0 can be rejected.

29. **What is k-Nearest Neighbors algorithm?**

K-Nearest Neighbors (**KNN**) algorithm is used to solve both classification and regression ML problems. KNN stores the entire dataset for modeling; so, it makes a prediction using the training dataset directly. Predictions are made for a new data point by searching through the entire training set for the k's most similar instances and then summarizing the output variable for those k instances. For regression, this might be the mean output variable; in classification, this might be the mode (or most common) class value. To determine which of the k instances in the training dataset are most similar to a new input, a distance measure is used. For real-valued input variables, the most popular distance measure is Euclidean distance. Euclidean distance is calculated as the square root of the sum of the squared differences between a point x and point y across all input attributes. Other popular distance measures are Hamming distance, Manhattan distance, etc. Euclidean is a good distance measure to use if the input variables are similar in type (e.g., all measured widths and heights). Manhattan distance is an excellent measure to use if the input variables are not similar in type (such as age, gender, height, etc.). We use `sklearn.neighbors` class to use this algorithm in Python.

30. **What is Support Vector Machines?**

Support Vector Machines or SVM algorithm is used to solve both classification and regression ML problems. According to this algorithm, the numeric input variables (x) in our data form an n-dimensional space. For example, if we had three input variables, this would form a three-dimensional space. A hyperplane is a line that splits these input variable spaces. In SVM, a hyperplane is selected to best separate the points in the input variable space by their class - either class 0 or class 1. The distance between the line and the closest data points is referred to as the margin. The best or optimal line that can separate the two classes is the line that has the largest margin. This is called the **Maximal-Margin hyperplane**. The margin is calculated as the perpendicular distance from the line to only the closest points. These points are called the support vectors. Since real data is messy, we cannot separate them perfectly with a hyperplane. To solve this problem, a soft margin classifier is introduced. In practice, SVM algorithm is implemented using a kernel. This kernel can be linear, polynomial, or radial, based on our data problem. SVM assumes that our inputs are numeric, so if we have categorical inputs, we may need to convert them to binary dummy variables. We use `sklearn.svm` class to use this algorithm in Python.

31. **What is Random Forest?**

Random Forest is a type of ensemble machine learning algorithm called **Bootstrap Aggregation or bagging**. The bootstrap is a powerful statistical method for estimating a quantity from a data sample and an ensemble method is a technique that combines the predictions from multiple machine learning algorithms together to make more accurate predictions than any individual model. Bootstrap Aggregation is a general procedure that can be used to reduce the variance for those algorithms that have high variance, like decision trees (CART). Decision trees are very sensitive to data; they train on, and so if training data is changed, the resulting decision tree can be quite different. Random Forest algorithm handles this drawback by learning subtress in such a way that resulting predictions from all of the subtrees have less correlation. In other words we can say that a random forest is a meta estimator that fits a number of decision tree classifiers on various sub-samples of the dataset and uses averaging to improve the predictive accuracy. We use `sklearn.ensemble` class to use `RandomForestClassifier()` or `RandomForestRegressor()` in Python.

32. **What is Boosting?**

Boosting is an ensemble technique that attempts to create a strong classifier from a number of weak classifiers. This is done by building a model from the training data, then creating a second model that attempts to correct the errors from the first model. Models are added until the training set is predicted perfectly or a maximum number of models are added. CatBoost is an example of boosting technique.

33. **What performance metrics do you use for evaluating a classification ML problem?**

Classification Accuracy, Log Loss, Area under ROC Curve, Confusion Matrix, Classification Report.

34. **Explain Classification Accuracy?**

Classification Accuracy is the most common evaluation metric for classification problems. It is the number of correct predictions made as a ratio of all predictions made. We can use `accuracy_score()` function from `sklearn.metrics` class or `classification_report()` function from `sklearn.metrics` class to calculate accuracy.

35. **Explain Log Loss?**

Log loss is a performance metric for evaluating the predictions of probabilities of membership to a given class. Smaller log loss is better and a value of 0 represents a perfect log loss. We can use `log_loss()` function from `sklearn.metrics` class to calculate log loss.

36. **What is Area Under ROC Curve?**

    Area Under ROC Curve (or **ROC AUC**) is a performance metric for evaluating binary classification problems mainly. An ROC Curve is a plot of the true positive rate and the false positive rate for a given set of probability predictions at different thresholds. These different thresholds are used to map the probabilities to class labels. The area under the curve is then the approximate integral under the ROC Curve. We can use `roc_auc_score()` function from `sklearn.metrics` class to use this metric.

37. **What is Confusion Matrix?**

    The confusion matrix is a presentation table of the accuracy of a model with two or more classes. The table presents predictions on the x-axis and accuracy outcomes on the y-axis. The cells of the table are the number of predictions made by a machine learning algorithm. The confusion matrix shows the ways in which our classification model is confused when it makes predictions.

38. **What is a Classification Report?**

    Python's `scikit-learn` library provides a convenience report, when working on classification problems to give us a quick idea of the accuracy of a model using a number of measures. The `classification_report()` function from `sklearn.metrics` class displays the precision, recall, f1-score, and support for each class.

39. **What are some common metrics for evaluating a regression ML problem?**

    Mean Absolute Error, Mean Squared Error, R^2.

40. **Explain Mean Absolute Error?**

    Mean Absolute Error (**MAE**) is the average of the absolute differences between predictions and actual values. It gives an idea of how wrong the predictions were. We can sue `mean_absolute_error()` function from `sklearn.metrics` class to use this metric. The best value of MAE is 0.0.

41. **Explain Mean Squared Error?**

    Mean Squared Error (**MSE**) is similar to the mean absolute error. It provides a gross idea of the magnitude of the error. Best value of MSE is 0.0 and we can use `mean_squared_error()` function from `sklearn.metrics` class to calculate this metric.

42. **Explain R^2?**

    R^2 (R Squared) metric provides an indication of the goodness of fitting of a set of predictions to the actual values. This measure is also called the coefficient of determination. Best possible score of RMSE is 1.0 and it can be negative. A perfect model would get score of 0.0. We can sue `r2_score()` function form `sklearn.metrics` class to compute this metric.

43. **Is accuracy a right metric for every classification ML problem?**

No, accuracy metric can be misleading if we have an unequal number of observations in each class or if we have more than two classes in our dataset. We must calculate confusion matrix, which can give us a better idea of what our classification model is getting right and what types of errors it is making. Besides this, Precision, Recall, and f1-score from classification report can give us correct performance measurement.

44. **How do you calculate confusion matrix?**

For calculating a confusion matrix, first we need a test or validation dataset with expected outcome values, then we make a prediction for each row in our test dataset. At last, from the expected outcomes and predictions count, we see the following two points: the number of correct predictions for each class and the number of incorrect predictions for each class, organized by the class that was predicted. These numbers are organized in a table or in a matrix, where each row of the matrix corresponds to a predicted class and each column of the matrix corresponds to an actual class. The counts of correct and incorrect classification are then filled into the matrix. The total number of correct predictions for a class go into the expected row for that class value, and the predicted column for that class value. In the same way, the total number of incorrect predictions for a class go into the expected row for that class value and the predicted column for that class value. In Python, from `sklearn.metrics` class, we import `confusion_matrix()` function to calculate this matrix.

45. **Explain classification report values?**

From `sklearn.metrics` class, we use `classification_report()` function to calculate the report. This report displays the precision, recall, f1-score and support for each class. Precision is the number of positive predictions divided by the total number of positive class values predicted. It is also called the **Positive Predictive Value** (**PPV**). Precision can be thought of as a measure of a classifier's exactness. Recall is the number of positive predictions divided by the number of positive class values in the test data. It is also called Sensitivity or the True Positive Rate. Recall can be thought of as a measure of a classifier's completeness. F1-Score conveys the balance between the precision and the recall. If we are looking to select a model based on a balance between precision and recall, the F1-Score is our choice. Formulas of these three metrics are as follows:

- **F1_Score** = 2 * ((Precision * Recall) / (Precision + Recall))
- **Precision** = True Positives / (True Positives + False Positives)
- **Recall** = True Positives / (True Positives + False Negatives)

46. **What do you mean by Rescaling? What techniques have you used for rescaling?**

Data rescaling is an important part of data preparation before applying machine learning algorithms. Most of the machine learning algorithms work very well, if data is on same scale and give worst results if we avoid this. Converting features in same scale is known as rescaling. Normalization is a technique for rescaling. Normalization refers to rescaling real valued numeric attributes into the range 0 and 1. We can use `sklean.preprocessing` class for rescaling and `normalize()` function is used for this purpose. Other than this function, we can also use `MinMaxScaler` class from `sklean.preprocessing` for rescaling.

47. **What is Standardization?**

Standardization refers to shifting the distribution of each attribute to have a mean of zero and a standard deviation of one. It is a useful technique to transform attributes with a Gaussian distribution and differing means and standard deviations to a standard Gaussian distribution with a mean of 0 and a standard deviation of 1. We can use `StandardScaler` class from `sklean.preprocessing` for standardization.

48. **How do you improve your machine learning model result?**

For improving our machine learning model result, we use `scikit-learn.model_selection` class's Grid Search CV or Randomized Search CV method. Grid Search CV method builds and evaluates a model for each combination of algorithm parameters specified in a grid. Randomized Search CV method samples algorithm parameters from a random distribution for a fixed number of iterations, then a model is constructed and evaluated for each combination of parameters chosen.

49. **What cycle do you follow while working on a predictive modeling data science problem?**

I follow the following 5 cycle while solving my predictive modeling data science problem: define the problem, prepare the data, spot-check different algorithms, improve the model, save and deploy the model.

50. **What is data leakage in ML?**

Data leakage is a problem in machine learning while developing a predictive model. Data leakage is when information from outside the training dataset is used to create the model. It is a serious problem for the following reason: creating overly optimistic models that are practically useless and cannot be used in production. To overcome this problem, we should always use cross validation and hold back validation dataset. If possible, we should use both techniques. As a good practice, we must perform data preparation steps (feature selection, outlier removal, encoding, feature scaling, etc.) within cross validation folds.

51. **How do you select the best features from your dataset?**

    If we have a lot of input features and we want to use only important features to our model, then we can use the feature selection technique. One common feature selection technique from scikit-learn's library is: **Recursive Feature Elimination (RFE)**. It works by recursively removing attributes and building a model on those attributes that remain. It uses the model accuracy to identify which attributes contribute the most to predict the target attribute. Some algorithms, like Random Forest and CatBoost have inbuilt feature importance methods - `feature_importances_` and `eval_features()` respectively.

Conclusion

You have come a long way in a short amount of time. You have developed the important and valuable skillset of being able to solve different machine learning problems. This is just the beginning of your journey. Data Science is very broad and you need to practice daily and make a habit of reading about new algorithms/ techniques coming in this field. To master the data science, your next step is to get familiar with various real world problems and their solutions. For this, I recommend you to join **https://www.kaggle.com/**, participate in any past challenge there, apply your learning to solve that challenge without seeing the solutions, and in the end, compare your approach with a winner approach. In this way, you will gain practical knowledge of solving a business problem with Data Science. You can follow BPB Publications's catalog and also my GitHub profile: **https://github.com/ dsbyprateekg**. I want to take a moment and sincerely thank you for letting me help you start your journey with Data Science. I hope you keep learning and have fun as you continue to master Data Science.

Index

Made in the USA
Middletown, DE
14 July 2022